# WHAT DOCTORS EAT

TIPS, RECIPES, and the ULTIMATE EATING
PLAN for LASTING WEIGHT LOSS
and PERFECT HEALTH

# WHAT DOCTORS EAT

TASNEEM BHATIA, MD,
and the Editors of *Prevention*®

RODALE.

# Contents

# Acknowledgments

First, we would like to thank all of the health experts who shared their insights, wisdom, and favorite dishes with us. They were generous with their knowledge and their time and this book literally would not exist without them.

Heather Zhou, RD, put in many long hours and a lot of heart into the development of The Doctors' Diet. Her attention to detail ensured that this plan is healthy and satisfying—and that it would deliver results! Heather, thanks for your dedication, flexibility, and terrific ideas.

Angela Giannopoulos was instrumental to this book on so many levels. Thank you a hundred times over, Angela, for your organizational skills, your great attitude, and your willingness to do whatever necessary, whenever necessary.

Marilyn Hauptly, Chris Krogermeier, Sara Cox, and Debbie McHugh kept the trains running on time even when they threatened to derail! Your patience and guidance were very much appreciated. Alexandra Sacher's help was invaluable. Gratitude to JoAnn Brader and Michelle Stanten. Amy King, and George Karabotsos—thank you for making this book look good. And thanks to editor Trisha Calvo for pulling it all together.

# CHAPTER 1

# What Do Doctors Know About Nutrition? Plenty!

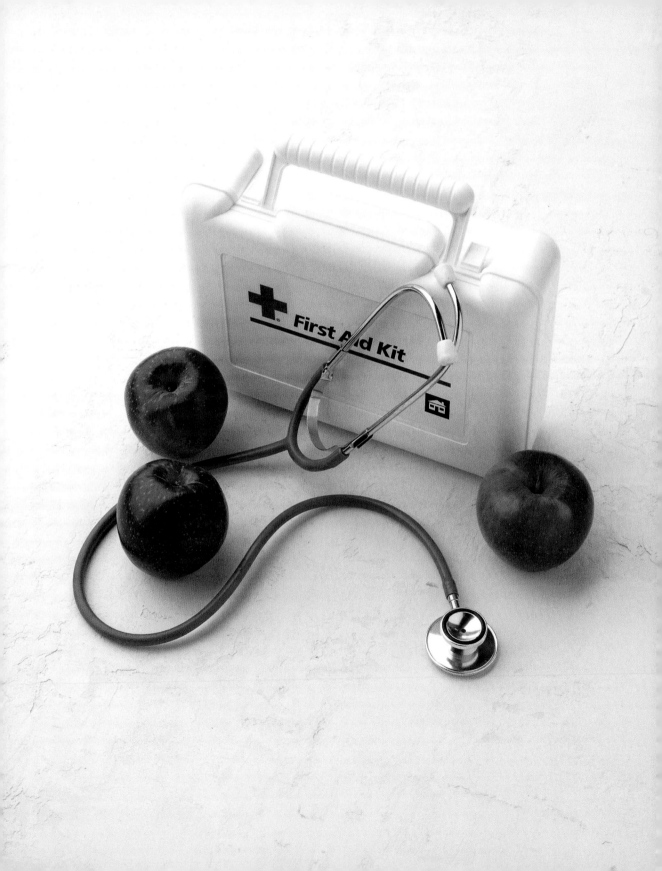

IKE COPS WHO EAT DOUGHNUTS, THE DOCTOR WHO IS OVER-
weight, out of shape, and clueless about nutrition is etched in our collective
consciousness. We've all heard that in 4 years of medical school, students
get just a few paltry weeks of nutrition training. Fast-food chains have
sprouted up on the premises of many hospitals, and you'll find plenty of white coats
among the customers. Writers for shows like *ER* and *Grey's Anatomy* build scenes
around TV docs quickly scarfing down burgers, fries, pizza, candy bars, or chips, or
unwinding with several cocktails in a bar after a long, stressful shift—and sometimes both in the same episode! Given all this, why would anyone want to know
what doctors eat?

Because more and more doctors no longer fit that made-for-TV stereotype. In
many medical centers, private practices, medical schools, teaching hospitals, and
research labs across the country, there are doctors, exercise physiologists, psychol-
ogists, scientists, and dietitians who believe in the power of food and use their
knowledge of nutrition to keep themselves, their families, and their patients
healthy. I'm one of them, and in this book you'll meet more than 60 other health-
care professionals who also practice what they preach. While some of us have

always had a certain level of nutritional awareness, others are recent converts, convinced by the overwhelming body of evidence that's been accumulating over the past several years. Some immersed themselves in the topic as their own health declined. Certainly all of us have had patients who got better simply by changing their diets and moving their bodies.

Just like everyone else, doctors lead busy, full lives in a world where food—mostly the kind we shouldn't be eating too often—is everywhere and technology makes being sedentary very easy. So we know that making the right choices can sometimes be tough. But when you're familiar with the research, you're compelled to act. Without a doubt, eating right and having other healthy habits—like exercising regularly, managing stress, and avoiding toxins such as cigarette smoke and pesticides—are proven ways to prevent heart disease, diabetes, cancer, and a plethora of other serious illnesses. Some evidence even shows that diet, alone or as part of an overall healthy lifestyle, can halt the progression of or even *reverse* the course of some conditions. According to the results of a study published in the journal *Preventive Medicine,* people who followed just one of three habits—either eating a healthy diet, exercising, or avoiding smoking—were 40 percent less likely to die early than those who had no healthy behaviors. Those who scored a trifecta? They cut their odds by *82 percent.*

Even for doctors, though, it can be tempting to think, "I'm healthy now, so I don't have to worry about diet and exercise too much. I'll make some changes when life and work settle down." What the health pros featured in this book have come to realize is that being nutritionally savvy—and acting on what they know—has immediate benefits. It gives them the energy to take care of their families, their patients, and themselves on a daily basis. If they eat the wrong foods, skip exercise, or push themselves too hard, they pay the price: fatigue, excess weight, bad skin, blue mood, and frequent colds. And you don't need to own a stethoscope for that to apply to you: It's true no matter who you are, where you live, or what you do.

## THE "REAL" FOOD FACTOR

My path to nutritional awareness came after frustration with my own health and a lot of tears. As a medical student, my understanding of nutrition was limited. I was swayed by the "fat-free" craze of the 1980s, so I loaded up on the carbs. (Pasta and white rice? Healthy! Eat as much as you want. Nuts and avocados? Fatty! Avoid them at all costs.) I exercised aggressively and didn't concern myself with calories, protein, or healthy fats. Honestly, I didn't even know that I needed to worry about those things.

I followed the same type of diet throughout my residency, patting myself on the back when I had a green salad with fat-free dressing for lunch or popcorn for dinner.

I knew to stay away from junk food and fried food, so I thought I was a healthy eater. Night shifts, day shifts, weekend shifts, family demands—I was on a crazy stress roller coaster, but I continued to try to sustain myself on low-calorie, low-fat foods.

Fast-forward a few years, to when the "payback" began. At the age of 28, I battled weight gain, acne, and hormonal irregularities. My hair, which was once my crowning glory, started coming out in chunks. I actually had bald patches! I spent a lot of the money I was finally earning visiting other doctors, aestheticians, and personal trainers, only to find they offered no real solution to my problems.

It was around that time that I became interested in traditional Chinese and ayurvedic medicine, and this led to one of those personal "aha" moments. These modes of healing place great importance on nutrition, and it quickly occurred to me that my high-sugar, low-protein, and *very* low-fat diet was making me sick. One thing led to another, and I immersed myself in nutrition research. I learned about the benefits of omega-3 fatty acids, the importance of olive oil, and the roles insulin production and inflammation play in disease and how the right foods could control both. I bumped up my protein intake, cut back on refined carbs, and welcomed nuts, avocados, olive oil, and, yes, even cheese and butter back into my life. I learned to cook, rather than relying on popcorn and takeout. I rediscovered the pleasures of food and found out that you don't have to deprive yourself to eat healthfully.

Within a few weeks of changing my diet, I had more energy. I lost weight and my skin cleared up. Within 2 years, my hair was just as lush as it used to be. So much for the doctors I saw who shook their heads and said, "If you don't take this medication, you'll be bald in a few years." Turns out, all I needed was to eat smarter.

I was motivated to heal myself, and I did. Then I wanted to share what I had learned with my patients. My experience led me to go back for more training and become an integrative physician. I studied under Andrew Weil, MD—the pioneering Western medical doctor who was among the first to embrace holistic health. (He's

## RESEARCH REPORT

**FROM THE LAB OF: J. Carson Smith, PhD,** department of kinesiology at the University of Maryland School of Public Health

**AN EXERCISE BONUS** A brisk walk can lift your spirits, but this study shows that it may also make you more resilient to stress. This study measured anxiety levels in people either before and after a 30-minute workout or before and after 30 minutes of rest. Both activities were equally soothing. But when the participants were tested again after being shown a series of images designed to increase anxiety, the researchers noted a difference. Those who had rested felt as anxious as they did at the start of the experiment, while the exercisers stayed calm.

one of the doctors featured in this book; see page 253.) Today, I'm the medical director of my own holistic health practice in Atlanta. And as it happens, by emphasizing the role food plays in disease prevention and as part of the cure, I've come back to my profession's roots.

## FOOD AS MEDICINE

Doctors and nutrition have a long and complicated history. In 470 BC, Hippocrates, the founder of modern medicine, famously said, "Let food be thy medicine and medicine be thy food." While he believed that there was a rational cause for illness, his treatments focused on diet, rest, and fresh air.

Ayurvedic and traditional Chinese medicine, systems that date back thousands of years, also base their healing principles on food. "He that takes medicine and neglects diet wastes the skills of the physician," according to an old Chinese proverb. In Chinese medicine, all areas of a person's life are believed to have an impact on his or her health, and nutrition is an important part of the healing process. Diets are tailored to individual illnesses and constitutions. There were no pharmaceuticals,

## RESEARCH REPORT

**FROM THE LAB OF: Axel Steiger,** senior psychiatrist at the Max Planck Institute of Psychiatry

## A PICTURE'S WORTH A THOUSAND CALORIES

Why is it that when you walk by the pizzeria or bakery and peek into the store window you're suddenly hungry—even if you just ate? This study uncovered the science behind this phenomenon. When people were shown enticing images of food, their levels of the appetite-inducing hormone ghrelin spiked. This is the first study to prove that the production of ghrelin can be controlled by external factors. You don't have to cancel your subscription to your favorite food magazine, but if your mouth starts to water over an image of a frosted three-layer cake, ask yourself, "Am I truly hungry?" before you head for the kitchen.

high-tech procedures, or medical "specialists" in ancient times. Even though these are available today, ayurveda and traditional Chinese medicine are still the primary forms of health care for millions of people around the world.

Medicine and nutrition took diverging paths with the onset of the Industrial Revolution, when the pursuit of science and understanding of disease became the goal. Where illness had once been considered a mind-body imbalance that could be altered by changing one's lifestyle or using a plant-based remedy, people now turned to laboratories, scientific experiments, and operating rooms as the primary sources of medical knowledge. This shift led to many great advances—vaccinations, pasteurization, and antibiotics among them. Surgical techniques progressed, and the concept of anesthesia evolved. In the process, though, nutrition lost its place as the centerpiece of healing. You learned about procedures, diagnostics, surgeries, medications, and illnesses in medical school; you didn't hear much about diet, lifestyle, and wellness. It wasn't until 1985, when the National Academy of Sciences recommended that medical schools reintroduce nutrition curricula, that we began to come full circle. We aren't quite there yet. Currently, approximately two-thirds of US medical schools integrate nutrition into their curricula, but the focus on nutrition is still minimal.

The irony is that the majority of chronic diseases in the United States are preventable. Our most common causes of disability and death are the same diseases that cost us the most to treat, both as individuals and as a society: heart disease, cancer, stroke, diabetes, and arthritis. In many cases, these diseases are the result of our most concerning epidemic: obesity. According to the Centers for Disease Control and Prevention (CDC), one out of every three adults is obese, as is approximately one in five children between the ages of 6 and 19. As doctors, we're trained to look for the science behind this epidemic, but many of us are realizing that the cause is not a scientific mystery: It's the aggregate result of poor nutrition, diminished physical activity, and stressed lifestyles.

This is the breed of doctors and other health-care professionals we interviewed for this book: Those who pursue diet, exercise, and lifestyle factors when treating

---

## RESEARCH REPORT

**FROM THE LAB OF: Lisa Powell, PhD,** Health Policy Center of the Institute for Health Research and Policy at the University of Illinois at Chicago

## HELP YOUR KIDS EAT HEALTHIER Eating out increases a

child's calorie intake—even if the restaurant isn't of the fast food variety. When young children dined at full-service restaurants, they took in 160 extra calories a day; when they had fast food, the calorie count increased by 126. Teens ate 267 and 310 additional calories, respectively. All of the kids drank more soda and got more saturated fat and sugar when they dined out compared to dining at home. The solution to this unpalatable problem? Eat in more often; the easy recipes in this book will help.

their patients, rather than only prescribing the latest miracle pill. They are not providers who are on the fringe of medicine but include many of the best and brightest medical minds in our country. We can divide the body into heart, lung, skin, or brain, but no matter what our specialty, nutrition plays an integral role in healing our patients. I've seen how powerful it can be in my own practice. High cholesterol declines faster with dietary changes than it does with medications. Some women who struggle with infertility and endure multiple rounds of expensive IVF treatments find themselves pregnant after making a dietary change. Autoimmune disorders can slowly go into remission when a patient improves his or her diet. I know my colleagues have similar stories and that they, too, have discovered the difference nutrition and lifestyle can make to their own well-being.

To share their collective wisdom, we asked these medical professionals what they do in their own lives to stay lean and healthy, and what they recommend to their patients to do the same. We asked them what they've learned from their patients. We asked them what kinds of exercise they do, how they manage stress, and even what their favorite healthy dishes are (and why). They gave us an incredible collection of tips, insights, and healthy recipes.

As we pored over their answers, we were amazed by all of the useful tricks and tips they had for blending a healthy lifestyle with the demands of a modern, busy life. You'll find advice and recipes for favorite healthy dishes in each doctor's individual profile in Chapter 6 (starting on page 123).

What struck us even more than the usefulness of their advice, though, was how remarkably consistent the underlying diet tenets were. Although their backgrounds are diverse, fundamentally, they adhere to the same eating styles: a semi-vegetarian diet—heavy on fruits, vegetables, whole grains, healthy fats, and seafood and light on meat, sugar, and refined carbs. This kind of diet controls two of the biggest contributors to disease: insulin imbalance and inflammation. (You'll read more about these risk factors in Chapter 2.) The way these health pros approached exercise was surprisingly similar as well: Get the maximum results in the minimum amount of time, and make exercise as convenient as possible, so you won't find reasons to avoid it.

We pooled their collective wisdom and combined it with the latest scientific research to develop a 30-day diet that will not only help you lose weight but also seriously reduce your risk for developing the leading chronic diseases. Doctors know a diet that helps you drop pounds but neglects proper nutrition and health is, frankly, a waste of time. Even if you do lose weight, an unbalanced plan can make you feel so lethargic and cranky that you won't be able to adhere to it for long. Strict diets that completely eliminate foods or food groups (except those designed for people who need to avoid gluten or other foods due to food sensitivities or allergies) are neither practical nor beneficial for your body, brain, or mood. Who wants to "sacrifice" one of the greatest pleasures in life—food? Who wants to be thin on the outside but feel lousy and be decidedly unhealthy on the inside? Not the health experts in this book—and, as it turns out, not the average American.

A recent Mintel survey found that consumers are moving away from "minus" messages, like "low-fat" and "weight maintenance," and are more attracted to lifestyles and products that focus on the positive. People are learning to focus on the benefits that foods provide and on being healthy, rather than just on being skinny. In other words, it's all about what you gain, not what you give up.

The people in these pages are health-care providers, yes, but they're also people who have discovered that there is a way to eat, a methodology, a science, that builds energy, stimulates minds, maintains weight, and fights disease. They are the busy professionals who don't reach for fast food out of desperation, but instead pack their own lunches and cook their own meals. They eat with health in mind—while never forgetting that food is meant to be pleasurable—and are capable of getting as excited about a perfectly ripe peach or fresh stalk of asparagus as some people do about chocolate cake. They are moms and dads, Little League coaches, and volunteers, and they need their diets and workouts to be simple and not require a huge time investment. And they want *you* to get as much out of what they've learned as they do.

Welcome to *What Doctors Eat!*

# CHAPTER 2

# How Food Can Save Your Life

'D UNDERSTAND IF THE FIRST THOUGHT YOU HAD WHEN YOU READ the title of this chapter was: "Well, duh! We need to eat to survive—that's how food saves your life." That's true, of course. Even a subpar diet can provide enough carbohydrates, protein, fat, and nutrients to keep your body functioning. What you want, though, is a diet that will keep your body *thriving*. Eat the right balance of foods and you will have more energy, keep your weight under control, and help prevent or postpone the development of cancer, heart disease, diabetes, osteoporosis, and Alzheimer's—diseases that both cut lives short and, for many, result in years of living with pain and disability. Surgery, drugs, and other treatments can keep many people alive for a long time. But your diet and other lifestyle habits are often what determine whether you'll feel well enough to enjoy those years.

At the start of the 20th century, the top three causes of death were pneumonia, tuberculosis, and diarrhea. The discovery of penicillin and other medicines, as well as improved hygiene, greatly reduced the number of cases of these illnesses, and today they account for far fewer deaths. If at the same time that we were eradicating communicable diseases, we ate the same way and continued to move as much as our great grandparents' generation did, there's a very good chance that our life

RESEARCH REPORT

FROM THE LAB OF: **Hidde P. van der Ploeg, PhD**, Sydney School of Public Health, University of Sydney

## STAND UP FOR YOUR HEALTH

Even if you work out faithfully every day, you still need to pay attention to how much you move during the time you aren't breaking a sweat. In this study of people age 45 and over, those who sat for 11 or more hours a day were 40 percent more likely to die during a 3-year period than those who sat less than 4 hours a day—even when vigorous exercise was taken into account. Sitting 8 hours bumped up the risk by 15 percent. Standing while talking on the phone or watching your kid play soccer are good ways to start spending less time in your chair.

expectancy and the quality of our lives would be phenomenal today. But that's not what happened. Instead, as the threat of those illnesses was being knocked out, our diets changed significantly: We now eat far more sugar, meat, refined carbs, and total calories than we did even 50 years ago. And we are far more sedentary; most of us sit for hours a day—in the car, at our desks, on the couch at home. And study after study has linked these differences to our increasing rates of heart disease, cancer, and stroke—the top three causes of death and disability today.

## THE PLEASURE PRINCIPLE

So what is the "right" balance of foods? Before I answer that question, let me tell you what it's not. Several years ago, a friend decided that she'd kick off her plan to "finally get fit and healthy" with a weeklong stay at a spa. She ate a diet developed for her by the spa's nutritionist, and she took many exercise classes while she was there. When she came home, I asked her how she liked it. "I enjoyed the classes," she said. "And I could eat like that for the rest of my life—if I only had 6 months to live!" The plan was 1,200 calories a day (far too little, given the amount of exercise she was doing), and dinner practically every night was broiled chicken or fish, a green vegetable, and a whole grain—but with no seasoning, oil, or anything else to excite her taste buds.

My friend's experience, unfortunately, reflects what many of us think a healthy diet has to be: boring, tasteless, and punishing. To lose weight, you have to subsist on broiled chicken, steamed broccoli, brown rice, piles of undressed greens, carrot and celery sticks, and melba toast. And, thanks to advertising, it seems that the only fun, enjoyable foods are breaded and deep-fried whole onions, cheese fries, preservative-filled sponge cakes with "creamy filling," and chili dogs. The truth is, "healthy and delicious" and "fun and nutritious" are not mutually exclusive. You can stay slim and protect your health while still really enjoying what you're eating.

In fact, the healthiest way to eat is truly the most pleasurable way to eat. Flavor boosters like nuts and olive oil aren't just tasty—they also contain healthy fats that control inflammation and help you absorb nutrients from other foods, plus antioxidants that fight cell damage. Spices and fresh or dried herbs aren't just flavorful afterthoughts; they contain disease-fighting phytochemicals. The compounds that give fruits and vegetables the bright colors that make them so appealing are the same ones responsible for many of their health benefits. And the fiber that makes whole grains so satisfyingly chewy also keeps your system running smoothly, fills you up, and fights heart disease and cancer.

## THE AMERICAN DIET: NOT A PRETTY PICTURE

The typical American diet is neither healthy nor satisfying, and I would make a case that it's not really pleasurable, either. On average, men take in 2,656 calories and women take in 1,811 calories every day—an increase of 200 to 300 calories compared to the early 1970s.

Our diets are filled with sugar, white-flour products, and animal protein. Each person eats an average of 22 teaspoons of added sugar a day (352 calories' worth).

This is a truly alarming figure when you realize that the most you should consume each day is 6 teaspoons if you are a woman and 9 if you are a man. Our per capita meat and poultry consumption is 276 pounds a year—or three-quarters of a pound per day. As a result, we don't have much room for the good stuff. We're supposed to get 25 to 30 grams of fiber every day, but most of us reach just 15 grams. Only 11 percent of the grains and grain products we eat are whole grains. We eat half the fruit and vegetable servings we should, and the majority of the vegetables we do eat are starchy and relatively high in calories. Even then, we aren't making the best choices: Instead of roasted potatoes and corn on the cob, more than one-third of our starchy vegetable intake is in the form of french fries and potato chips. We average a measly 1.73 servings of dark green vegetables and 0.35 serving of orange vegetables *a week*.

A diet centered on animal fat, starch, and sugar may be palatable, but it's not tasty or satisfying. There are no flavors that make you sit up and take notice, so you eat without really paying attention—and that causes you to eat more. Plus, this sort of diet causes blood sugar spikes and crashes that lead to fatigue and overall mental dullness. What's pleasurable about that?

## The Health Ramifications

Eating this way can upset your body's normal functioning and lead to two abnormalities that are very likely at the root of obesity, cancer, heart disease, diabetes, and other illnesses: excess insulin and excess inflammation.

INSULIN. Any source of carbohydrate—from amaranth to applesauce, spaghetti to soda—is broken down and converted to glucose, which is what we measure when we test blood sugar levels. This simple sugar is the energy source for every cell in your body, but in order to use it, you need insulin, a hormone produced by your pancreas. Insulin works like a key: It unlocks your cells so glucose can enter. Ideally, blood sugar rises gradually, insulin is produced at a steady rate, glucose is

# RESEARCH REPORT

**FROM THE LAB OF: Alicja Wolk, DrMedSci**, division of nutritional epidemiology, Institute of Environmental Medicine, Karolinska Institute, Sweden

## VEG OUT FOR YOUR HEART

Maybe you pop a multivitamin every day for "extra insurance," but your heart would feel more secure if you added an extra serving or two of fruits and vegetables. While pills can contain several antioxidants (such as vitamin C and beta-carotene) that help control inflammation and protect cells against damage, they simply don't supply the thousands of antioxidants present in produce. Dr. Wolk and her colleagues followed more than 1,000 women for 10 years to see how their total antioxidant intake affected their odds of having a heart attack. Those who ate an average of seven servings of fruits and veggies a day had a 20 percent lower risk than women who ate an average of $2\frac{1}{2}$ servings. What's clear from this study is that antioxidants don't do their work in isolation, they have a synergistic effect, so you need a variety of them in your diet.

absorbed by the cells, blood sugar declines gradually, and the pancreas stops making insulin until your next meal. However, foods that are digested quickly cause spikes in blood sugar, and your body responds with a flood of insulin. If this happens continually, your body can become resistant to insulin and you need to produce even more of it to normalize your blood sugar level. Eventually your pancreas cannot keep up with the demand and you develop diabetes. Excess insulin also forces your body to use glucose for energy all the time, which inhibits fat burning. Since your body's ability to store glucose is limited, you get hungrier more often (a signal that you need to replenish your store), which causes you to eat more. Needless to say, this makes weight loss extremely difficult.

INFLAMMATION. Inflammation is a normal part of a healthy immune system response; it helps to both heal injuries and kill germs. But low-grade chronic inflammation is at the root of almost every chronic disease we currently battle, including heart disease, diabetes, cancer, and autoimmune diseases. For example, when "bad" LDL cholesterol injures artery walls by burrowing into them, it sets off a massive, prolonged immune-system counterattack that leads to heart attacks and strokes and contributes to high blood pressure. Consuming refined carbohydrates, eating too many calories at once, and a high intake of certain types of fat—namely animal fat; trans fats; and corn, safflower, sunflower, and sesame oils (found in a lot of processed foods)—trigger inflammation in your body. So do abnormal insulin production and carrying too much weight on your frame. Fat cells churn out pro-inflammatory proteins called cytokines, and the more fat cells you have, the more of those proteins your body can create.

## CHANGE YOUR DIET, CHANGE YOUR LIFE

Our health pros design their own diets to keep these two factors in check, and the way they do so is remarkably consistent. Although personal tastes differ, the brain doctor, the cardiologist, the oncologist, the obstetrician, the registered dietitian, and the exercise physiologist all follow the principles of a blend of three eating styles: Mediterranean, low-glycemic-index, and semi-vegetarian diets. (The Doctors' Diet in Chapter 5 was inspired by our experts' consensus and gives you a detailed dietary prescription.) Individually, these dietary approaches have been shown to be the most effective for disease prevention and weight control. Together, they may be even more powerful.

### The Mediterranean Connection

The people who live in Spain, southern France, Italy, and Greece love to eat, yet they are some of the healthiest, longest-lived people in the world. The first research to prove this was the landmark Seven Countries Study that started in 1958 and continued for more than 50 years. It looked at the connections between diet and lifestyle and heart disease and stroke in men living in Italy, France, the United States, the former Yugoslavia, Greece, Japan, and the Netherlands. One of the main findings was that a traditional Mediterranean diet—lots of fruit, green vegetables, grains, cheese, olive oil, beans, red wine, and yogurt, with some fish, poultry, and eggs—significantly reduced the odds of heart disease compared with the diets of the other countries. Since then, studies have shown that a Mediterranean way of eating reduces the odds of dying from any cause by 9 percent, from heart disease and stroke by 9 percent, and from cancer by 6 percent. In a research analysis, scientists at the Harvard School of Public Health concluded that a Mediterranean diet could prevent 90 percent of cases of type 2 diabetes, 80 percent of cases of heart disease, and 70 percent of strokes. There's also evidence that this style of diet protects against Alzheimer's disease, Parkinson's disease, depression, rheumatoid arthritis, and infertility.

From a nutrient perspective, the Mediterranean diet is high in healthy mono-unsaturated and omega-3 fats, fiber, antioxidants, and phytochemicals. It is low in saturated fat, animal protein, refined carbs, and sugar. These factors work together

## RESEARCH REPORT

**FROM THE LAB OF: Yessenia Tantamango, MD,** Loma Linda University

## FOUR FOODS THAT FIGHT COLON CANCER In a

study of nearly 3,000 people, those who regularly ate beans, cooked green vegetables, brown rice, and dried fruit significantly cut their risk of colon polyps, thereby lowering the odds for colon cancer. And you don't have to stuff yourself with these foods to get the benefits, either. Three servings of beans and dried fruit a week reduced the risk by 33 and 26 percent, respectively. One serving of cooked green veggies a day led to a 24 percent drop. Just one serving a week of brown rice cut risk by a whopping 40 percent.

synergistically to reduce inflammation, insulin resistance, and body fat. Researchers at the University of Naples determined that people who followed a Mediterranean diet without any emphasis on controlling calories weighed an average of
4 pounds less than those who ate a Western diet. When calories were limited, the
difference in weight was $8\frac{1}{2}$ pounds.

You can embrace a Mediterranean style of eating without moving to the Amalfi
Coast or a Greek island—or even without using a drizzle of olive oil. (Although from
a flavor perspective, I wouldn't recommend this!) A meal of vegetable soup, salmon,
and brown rice pilaf with carrots and peas is just as Mediterranean nutitionally as
minestrone and *linguine con le vongole* (linguine with clams). The idea is to focus on
the overall pattern, not the specific foods.

## Low Glycemic Index, Decoded

A food's glycemic index (GI) is a measure of how quickly carbohydrate foods are
digested and converted to glucose. Foods that have little or no carbohydrate, like
meat or nuts, do not have a GI value. The scale ranges from zero to 100; a food that
ranks 55 or less is low GI, while one that's 70 or more is high GI. (Pure glucose
scores 100.) High-GI foods are digested quickly and cause a rush of glucose into
your bloodstream, prompting a large release of insulin. Low-GI foods are broken
down slowly, keeping your blood sugar stable. Constant fluctuations in GI lead to
erratic insulin metabolism, causing inflammation.

A high-GI diet increases your chances of developing a wide variety of diseases. In an analysis of 37 studies, Australian researchers calculated that a high-
GI diet boosted the risk of diabetes by 40 percent, gallbladder disease by
26 percent, heart disease by 25 percent, and breast cancer by 8 percent, when
compared to a low-GI diet.

Factors that influence a food's GI include the amount and type of fiber in the
food, the amount and type of total carbohydrate, and the amount of protein or fat.

Eating a high-GI food in combination with low-GI ones at the same meal helps blunt the rise in glucose. Another important component is the particle size of the food. This means that ground whole wheat (like the flour used in whole wheat bread) has

---

**TAKE THE SLOW CARB ROUTE** Choosing foods with a low-glycemic index or combining high-GI foods with low-GI foods in the same meal can help keep insulin and inflammation under control. Here's where some common foods rank.

| | |
|---|---|
| Potatoes, mashed | 83 |
| White rice, long grain | 76 |
| Watermelon | 72 |
| Bread, whole wheat | 71 |
| Cantaloupe | 70 |
| Potato, baked with skin | 69 |
| Rice, brown | 66 |
| Orange juice | 57 |
| Quinoa | 53 |
| Spaghetti, regular | 50 |
| Oatmeal | 50 |
| Orange | 47 |
| Bulgur | 46 |
| Spaghetti, whole wheat | 42 |
| Apples | 40 |
| Strawberries | 40 |
| Lentils | 37 |
| Black beans | 30 |
| Grapefruit | 25 |
| Kidney beans | 19 |

**Source:** The International GI Database. University of Sydney. glycemicindex.com

a higher GI than bulgur (cracked wheat), instant oats have a higher GI than rolled (old-fashioned) oats, and applesauce has a higher GI than whole apples. As a rule of thumb, the closer a food is to its natural state, the lower its GI.

## The Pros of Being a Part-Time Vegetarian

Some of our experts are vegetarians. Some eat dairy, eggs, and often fish, but not meat or poultry. Others are vegan and eat no animal products at all. Any of these styles of eating can be healthy, but they aren't necessarily guaranteed to be. (I know vegetarians who don't like vegetables!) Combine a diet based mostly on plant foods with enough healthy fats and low-GI foods, though, and you have a perfect recipe for health.

The Doctors' Diet is not a vegetarian diet, but it's close to one. The advantage of including the occasional small (4- to 6-ounce) serving of meat or poultry in your diet is that it makes it easier to get the protein you need to build and sustain lean muscle mass. At the same time, though, cutting back is beneficial. One of the most comprehensive studies to date, published in the *Archives of Internal Medicine*, tracked more than 37,000 adults and found that simply eating one vegetarian meal a day could lower your risk of dying from cancer or heart disease by as much as 20 percent. Most people find that having the option of eating a little meat makes a diet more palatable, and if you eliminate animal products completely, it's tough to get enough omega-3s, vitamin B$_{12}$, vitamin D, calcium, and iron without relying on supplements. The Doctors' Diet is both satisfying and nutrient rich, making it easy to stick with for life.

When it comes to beef, pork, and poultry, many of our experts stress that they opt for organic or grass-fed and finished varieties. Not only do these meats tend to come from farms where the animals are treated humanely, the farms themselves are better for the environment than industrial farms, and the meat that comes from these animals is healthier than the alternative. Organic, grass-fed and finished beef contains 60 percent more omega-3s, 200 percent more vitamin E, and two to three

---

## RESEARCH REPORT

**FROM THE LAB OF: Bing Lu, MD, Dr.Ph,** Brigham and Women's Hospital

### HOW SODA HURTS YOUR BODY
No one would ever consider soft drinks health food, but the ways they can damage your health just keeps growing. This preliminary study found a connection between soda drinking and osteoarthritis in men. All of the participants had arthritis at the start of the study. Researchers determined their soft drink consumption, the severity of their joint damage, and their weight at the start of the study and once a year for 4 years. The results: drinking five or more sodas a week was associated with a worsening of arthritis. And although excess weight stresses joints, surprisingly the men who showed the greatest progression of disease were those who were *not* obese, indicating that it's the ingredients in the soda, not the calories, that are responsible.

times more conjugated linoleic acids (CLA), all of which help ward off heart disease, cancer, and diabetes. As an added bonus, certified-organic cows are raised without added hormones or routine antibiotics, and the grass or grain they eat cannot contain pesticides, chemical fertilizers, or genetically modified organisms. These meats are pricey, but because you'll be eating less of them on this diet, you'll probably save money in the end.

The one type of meat you should cut out completely, if you can, is processed meat—that includes most deli meats, bacon, and hot dogs. The combination of sodium, saturated fat, and preservatives (called nitrates) they contain raise your risk of heart disease and cancer. A BLT, pastrami sandwich, or hot dog at the ballpark a few times a year is fine, but don't make processed meat regular weekly fare.

<hr>

When you combine these three dietary approaches—Mediterranean, low-glycemic-index, and semi-vegetarian—you are probably as close to a perfect diet as you can get without calibrating every milligram of fiber, protein, fat, vitamins, and minerals that goes into your mouth. In fact, even if you did that, chances are you'd be missing the X factor that makes these eating styles so extraordinarily good for you. When scientists try to break down foods into their individual parts to discover the "magic bullet" at their center, the results are often disappointing. Study after study shows that the "magic" derives from the combination of foods that work synergistically in the body in ways we understand—and in ways that are yet to be discovered.

# CHAPTER 3

# Foods That Heal

F YOU WERE A CONTESTANT ON *JEOPARDY!* AND THE CLUE WAS "Doctors' favorite food," based on the info we got from the experts in this book, your answer should be, "What is wild salmon?" When you consider its disease-fighting, brain-boosting potential, it's not a surprise. What we did find interesting, though, were the other foods that were mentioned again and again. (Coffee? Dark chocolate? Aren't they supposed to be *bad* for you?) Andrew Weil, MD, one of our experts, says, "Don't fixate on superfoods. There are so many great foods, you don't want to limit yourself." We couldn't agree more! Yet some foods do pack a bigger nutritional punch than others. From blueberries and dark chocolate to kale and salmon, here are 18 of our experts' favorite foods and the compelling reasons to work them into *your* diet.

# APPLES

**PROTECT AGAINST:**
HEART DISEASE, HIGH CHOLESTEROL, OBESITY, AND STROKE

**KEY NUTRIENTS:**
ANTIOXIDANTS AND SOLUBLE FIBER

POOR APPLES. Their ubiquity leads us to pass right by them in the produce aisle on our way to something sexier and "better" for us, like mangosteen or pluots.

Well it's time to increase your apple IQ. Not only are apples among the most portable, inexpensive, and truly varied fruits (with 7,500 different kinds, there's an apple for every taste preference, from sweet to tart), they're also true health power-houses. Their fiber content makes apples super-satisfying. In one study, people who crunched on one 15 minutes before a meal ate 15 percent fewer calories at the meal. That translated to a 60-calorie deficit, once you factor in the calories in the apple. That may not sound like a lot, but if you did it once a day, you'd lose 6 pounds over the course of a year almost effortlessly.

About one-third of the fiber in apples is soluble, which is the type that helps to lower cholesterol. You need 3 to 5 grams of soluble fiber a day to get that effect; a medium apple has 2 grams. And apples keep your cardiovascular system ticking along in another way, too: They're rich in the antioxidant flavonoid quercetin and polyphenol compounds that have anti-inflammatory properties. A Dutch study found that having one medium apple a day can reduce your stroke risk by about 43 percent.

Apples looking a little better to you now?

# ASPARAGUS

**PROTECTS AGAINST:**
BLOATING, CANCER, DIGESTIVE UPSET, AND OBESITY

**KEY NUTRIENTS:**
FOLATE, GLUTATHIONE, INULIN, AND SAPONINS

THE NEXT time you're serving veggies and dip, consider swapping out the celery sticks for asparagus spears. When it comes to nutrient density, this elegant vegetable is hard to beat. For a measly 28 calories, seven large spears provide 72 percent of your daily vitamin K—a nutrient required for blood clotting and bone health. You also get 3 grams of fiber, 20 percent of your daily vitamin A in the form of cancer-fighting carotenoids, 18 percent of your folate, 17 percent of your iron, and some vitamin $B_6$ and vitamin E.

And that's not all! Asparagus is a good source of three compounds that are hard to find in many foods: inulin, glutathione, and saponins. Inulin is a type of fiber that has prebiotic properties. That means it serves as fuel for the healthy bacteria in your intestinal system, a characteristic that is probably responsible for asparagus's reputation as a folk remedy for digestive woes. Asparagus is considered a leading anti-inflammatory food in part due to its high concentration of glutathione, which some scientists consider to be the most powerful antioxidant. This compound strengthens your immune system's infection-fighting capabilities and also helps correct the cell damage that is often a first step in the development of cancer. Saponins are phytochemicals that may help lower cholesterol and reduce cancer risk.

While there are no studies to prove it, asparagus is said to have a diuretic effect and may help ease bloating. Those properties, combined with its high-fiber and low-calorie count, mean that asparagus is a good food to have in your diet if you're trying to lose weight. Some people also claim that asparagus alleviates hangovers. One small study found that asparagus extract enhanced the liver's ability to process alcohol and protected liver cells from the damage that alcohol can cause—but that was in test tubes. So go ahead and stick an asparagus spear in your Bloody Mary, if you like. Just don't expect it to protect you from a pounding head if you indulge in one too many.

---

# AVOCADOS

**PROTECT AGAINST:**
CANCER, DIABETES, HEART DISEASE, MACULAR DEGENERATION, AND OBESITY

**KEY NUTRIENTS:**
BETA-CAROTENE, FIBER, FOLATE, LUTEIN, MONOUNSATURATED FAT, PHYTOSTEROLS, POTASSIUM, AND ZEAXANTHIN

EVER NOTICE that when you have guacamole as an appetizer you barely have room for your tacos? That's because avocados are packed with a potent combination of fiber and healthy fats—there are 8 grams and 18 grams, respectively, in $\frac{1}{2}$ cup of guac! Including the creamy green fruit (yes, avocados are a fruit) with your meal can keep you feeling full. A study at Loma Linda University in California showed that people who had half an avocado produced more leptin—the fullness hormone—for up to 3 hours after they ate.

Two-thirds of the fat in avocados is monounsaturated, which helps lower insulin levels and facilitate weight loss. What's more, a mono-rich diet helps you lose belly fat specifically.

Monounsaturated fats provide a variety of other health benefits: They reduce inflammation, cholesterol, triglycerides, and blood sugar, and they ward off age-related memory decline. Monos even help keep skin plump and smooth by replenishing the protective layer of moisture-trapping fatty acids that surrounds skin cells.

Avocados are also the richest fruit source of phytosterols, compounds that alter the way your body processes cholesterol and may help lower LDL (or "bad") cholesterol levels. Avocados are also packed with the B vitamin folate, which is important for heart health and for protecting against birth defects, as well as carotenoids such as beta-carotene, lutein, and zeaxanthin. These antioxidants help promote eye health and protect against cancer and heart disease. What's more, avocados help you absorb more of these antioxidants from any other foods you eat at the same time. In a study from Ohio State University, researchers served men and women lettuce, carrot, and spinach salads. When the salad contained avocado, the participants absorbed 8.3 times the alpha-carotene, 13.6 times the beta-carotene, and 4.3 times the lutein they did when they ate an avocado-free salad.

With so many benefits, there has to be a catch, right? Well yes, but it's a small one: The high fat content of avocados means they're also high in calories compared with other fruits and vegetables. Just one half of a medium-size avocado has 114 calories. So watch your portion sizes and have your guac with crudités, instead of chips.

# BEANS

**PROTECT AGAINST:**
DIABETES, HEART DISEASE, AND OBESITY

**KEY NUTRIENTS:**
ANTIOXIDANTS, FOLATE, POTASSIUM, PROTEIN, AND SOLUBLE FIBER

WE ALL know the old adage about beans, but they *are* indeed good for your heart—and the rest of your body, too. They're the chameleons of the food world, able to play a variety of nutritional roles. Beans can count as a protein, a "good" carb, and even a vegetable serving.

One of their most powerful properties is soluble fiber. Beans contain more of this compound than almost any other food. Soluble fiber absorbs water in your digestive tract, which means it leaves your stomach slowly, having a beneficial effect on your weight (because you feel fuller longer) and your blood sugar levels. In a report from the National Health and Nutrition Examination Survey, scientists found that people who ate beans were 23 percent less likely to have large waists than those who never ate beans. And researchers from the University of Toronto found that people with type 2 diabetes who ate mostly low-glycemic-index foods such as nuts and beans improved their blood sugar levels and were at lower risk for heart disease than people who ate mostly whole grain breads, cereals, and brown rice.

Soluble fiber also interferes with the absorption of dietary cholesterol, so it can lower your blood cholesterol levels. Researchers at Arizona State University Polytechnic in Mesa found that adding $\frac{1}{2}$ cup of beans to soup reduces cholesterol levels by up to 8 percent.

Black beans, red kidney beans, and other dark-colored beans are as high or higher in antioxidants as colorful fruits and vegetables. But that doesn't mean that paler beans have no value. For instance, white beans give you 100 milligrams of calcium per $\frac{1}{2}$ cup—a respectable amount! And lentils are one of the best sources of the B vitamin folate, which is so important in lowering the risk of birth defects and also plays a role in heart and brain health.

The rest of that childhood chant—the line that rhymes with heart—is, unfortunately, also true. Beans contain complex sugars called oligosaccharides that can't be digested. They are fermented by the good bacteria in your gut, producing gas and bloating. But you can both reduce beans' oligosaccharides and make your body more resistant to them. Soaking beans overnight and then cooking them in fresh water or rinsing canned beans can help remove the sugars. (Rinsing canned beans also removes about 40 percent of their sodium, so it's a good idea whether you suffer from bean-related bloat or not.) Drink lots of water when you eat beans (or any other high-fiber food), and start with small portions so your digestive system adjusts. That way, you get the health benefits without the unpleasant consequences.

# BERRIES

**PROTECT AGAINST:**
CANCER, DIABETES, HEART DISEASE, MEMORY LOSS, AND OBESITY

**KEY NUTRIENTS:**
ANTHOCYANINS, ANTIOXIDANTS, FIBER, AND VITAMIN C

IT'S AMAZING what eating just a handful of berries can do for your health. In a study involving 200,000 men and women, those who ate 1 cup of blueberries a week had a 23 percent lower risk of developing diabetes. Having $\frac{1}{2}$ cup of blueberries or 1 cup of strawberries a week protected the brains of elderly women (with an average age of 74) from age-related memory decline. Harvard researchers estimated that the berry eaters delayed their cognitive decline by as much as $2\frac{1}{2}$ years.

The "magic" ingredients in berries responsible for these benefits appear to be anthocyanins—red and blue pigments that are powerful antioxidants. These compounds have also been linked to a lower risk of a variety of cancers. On top of that, each berry type comes with its own nutritional bonus: Blueberries have the highest concentration of anthocyanins. Raspberries have the most fiber—at 8 grams per cup, ounce for ounce more than any other fruit. One cup of strawberries has more vitamin C than you need in a day. Cranberries have five times the antioxidant power of broccoli, plus they're a natural probiotic, which means they'll enhance good bacteria levels and protect you from foodborne illnesses. Blackberries help lower cholesterol and blood pressure, and they can play a key role in keeping diabetes, heart disease, and cancer at bay. And berries have some of the lowest calorie counts of all fruits, ranging from 53 per cup for strawberries to 84 per cup for blueberries.

Although berries are delicate and their season is short, you can freeze fresh berries for up to a year, or you can buy packaged frozen ones. Just be sure to check the labels as some brands come loaded with sugar. Cranberries in their natural state are so tart that cranberry products are often terribly oversweetened. You're better off buying fresh cranberries and making your own relish or sauce, adding as little sugar as possible. Or you can combine cranberries with sweet fruits (such as oranges, pears, or apples) and avoid added sugar altogether.

# BROCCOLI

**PROTECTS AGAINST:**
CANCER AND HEART DISEASE

**KEY NUTRIENTS:**
FIBER, FOLATE, SULFORAPHANE, AND VITAMIN C

MALIGNED BY a president and millions of picky eaters, broccoli has a reputation for being a bitter-tasting vegetable with an unpleasant odor. But that's not broccoli's fault—blame the chef! Too often broccoli is overcooked, which turns it an unappetizing, drab green, makes it mushy, and concentrates the sulfur compounds that are responsible for some of its strong flavor. If you've been a broccoli-hater, you owe it to your health to give it another try. Along with other members of the cruciferous family, like cabbage, cauliflower, brussels sprouts, broccoli rabe, bok choy, and turnips, broccoli is a true nutrition all-star.

Let's start with the basics: A cup of broccoli gives you a hefty dose of calcium, manganese, potassium, phosphorus, magnesium, iron, fiber, folate, and vitamins C and K. It also has 3 grams of protein. Broccoli's cancer-fighting compounds include carotenoids and especially sulforaphane. Japanese researchers found that women with breast cancer who ate a lot of broccoli and other cruciferous vegetables cut their risk of a recurrence by 35 percent and their chances of dying from the disease by 62 percent in a 3-year period. Other studies have shown that men at risk for prostate cancer who ate about a pound of broccoli a week experienced more gene changes linked to a reduced chance of developing cancer, and that cruciferous vegetables even cut the odds of lung cancer in smokers by 20 to 55 percent. (But don't use that as an excuse to smoke!)

The saddest thing about overcooking broccoli is that it destroys many of the nutrients. To get the benefits of broccoli and learn to love it, blanch it in boiling water for a few minutes, or steam it until it turns bright green. That's when you know it's tender enough to eat, but still crunchy enough to enjoy. Serving broccoli with whole grains or nuts helps to soften the bitterness, as does pairing it with sweeter vegetables like red peppers, carrots, or caramelized onions. Stir-frying broccoli with garlic does the trick, too. If all else fails, try broccolini, which has a similar nutritional profile but a milder, peppery flavor.

# COFFEE

**PROTECTS AGAINST:**
CANCER, DIABETES, PARKINSON'S DISEASE, AND STROKE

**KEY NUTRIENTS:**
BORON, CAFFEINE, CHROMIUM, AND POLYPHENOLS

WHETHER WE get it from a specialty shop, a good old-fashioned diner, or a pot in the kitchen, Americans love coffee. We drink an average of 3 cups per person each day. Although we savor that warm comfort, soothing aroma, and caffeine hit, most of us at one time or another have wondered: How bad is this for me? Relax. Coffee, in fact, has many perks.

Swedish researchers found that women who drink 5 cups a day are 57 percent less likely to get an aggressive form of breast cancer than those who don't drink coffee. And according to another study, just 1 cup a day protects against liver cancer.

But the powers of this magical brew don't stop there. Drinking more than one daily cup of coffee is associated with a 22 to 25 percent lower risk of stroke, according to a study in the journal *Stroke*. Harvard researchers found that coffee lowers your odds of developing type 2 diabetes by 29 to 54 percent. And having 1 to 3 cups a day cuts your risk of Parkinson's disease, enhances short-term memory, and helps prevent dementia.

Most of the disease-fighting benefits of coffee don't come courtesy of caffeine, but are due to its polyphenol antioxidants. Coffee is right up there with fruit as a source of these compounds, and because of our high intake, it's the number one source of antioxidants in the American diet.

That doesn't mean, though, that caffeine has no value. While too much can leave you jittery and interfere with sleep, it does keep you alert. (Many a doctor doing an extra hospital shift can attest to this!) It also improves endurance. In one study, recreational runners improved their 5-K times by 1 percent after drinking a cup of high-test coffee. A study in the journal *Physiology and Behavior* showed that caffeine boosts metabolism by about 16 percent. And people who drank caffeinated coffee had a lower risk of basal cell carcinoma, the most common type of skin cancer, according to a study in *Cancer Research*. (Decaf was not protective.) A word to the wise: Take your java black or with a little milk or cream. Gourmet coffee drinks can contain more calories and sugar than a can of soda.

# DARK CHOCOLATE

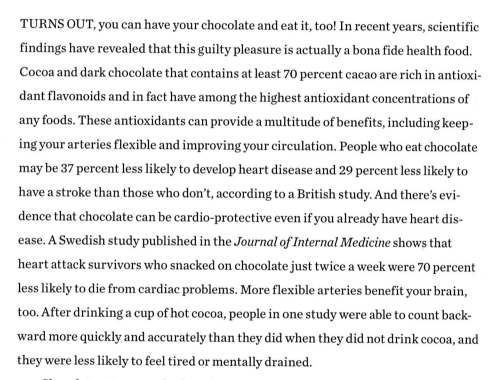

**PROTECTS AGAINST:**
DEPRESSION, DIABETES, HEART DISEASE, AND OBESITY

**KEY NUTRIENTS:**
FLAVONOIDS

TURNS OUT, you can have your chocolate and eat it, too! In recent years, scientific findings have revealed that this guilty pleasure is actually a bona fide health food. Cocoa and dark chocolate that contains at least 70 percent cacao are rich in antioxidant flavonoids and in fact have among the highest antioxidant concentrations of any foods. These antioxidants can provide a multitude of benefits, including keeping your arteries flexible and improving your circulation. People who eat chocolate may be 37 percent less likely to develop heart disease and 29 percent less likely to have a stroke than those who don't, according to a British study. And there's evidence that chocolate can be cardio-protective even if you already have heart disease. A Swedish study published in the *Journal of Internal Medicine* shows that heart attack survivors who snacked on chocolate just twice a week were 70 percent less likely to die from cardiac problems. More flexible arteries benefit your brain, too. After drinking a cup of hot cocoa, people in one study were able to count backward more quickly and accurately than they did when they did not drink cocoa, and they were less likely to feel tired or mentally drained.

Chocolate eaters are also happier, calmer people because daily hits of the treat reduce levels of stress hormones, according to a study in the *Journal of Proteome Research*. Other studies show that the phenethylamine chocolate contains triggers the production of endorphins and results in a feeling of well-being that's similar to falling in love. In one study, couples were connected to brain and heart monitors, given chocolate, and then told to kiss. Both the chocolate and the kissing alone made hearts pound and brains buzz, but the addition of chocolate doubled excitation rates in the brain's pleasure center during the kiss, especially in women.

Paradoxically, giving in to chocolate cravings can help you drop pounds. In one study, people who were offered pizza 2½ hours after eating dark chocolate ate 15 percent fewer calories than they did when they had milk chocolate. And researchers at the University of California, San Diego, conducted a study that made them suspect that the calories in chocolate are metabolized in such a way that they don't lead to weight gain. Dark chocolate lovers were thinner than those who ate very little of the treat, even though they didn't consume fewer calories overall or exercise more. Still, you want to keep your chocolate fix healthy, so stick to small servings and pair it with other antioxidant-rich foods, like fruit or nuts.

# DARK LEAFY GREENS

**PROTECTS AGAINST:**
CANCER, DIABETES, MACULAR DEGENERATION, AND OBESITY

**KEY NUTRIENTS:**
CALCIUM, CAROTENOIDS, FIBER, FOLATE, IRON, VITAMIN C, AND VITAMIN K

NUTRITIONISTS LIKE to talk about "nutrient density"—the amount of nutrients you get from a food relative to its calorie count. From mild-tasting romaine lettuce and spinach, to peppery arugula and mesclun, to pleasantly bitter escarole, kale, Swiss chard, and collards, calorie for calorie, dark leafy greens are among the most nutritious foods on the planet. For instance, 1 cup of cooked kale provides 1,327 percent of your daily vitamin K, 354 percent of your vitamin A (in the form of antioxidant carotenoids), 89 percent of your vitamin C, 9 percent of your calcium, 8 percent of your iron and potassium, 6 percent of your magnesium, 4 percent of your folate and vitamin E, and 3 grams of fiber. It also contains sulforaphane—a cancer-fighting compound found in cruciferous vegetables. All that for just 36 calories. To one degree or another, all leafy greens (even iceberg lettuce) contain the same nutrients. But the darker the green, the more nutritious it is. Iceberg lovers, try romaine: It has the same refreshing crunch, but 9 times the carotenoids, 7.5 times the vitamin C, 4 times the folate, and 3.6 times the vitamin K.

Their carotenoid content makes dark leafy greens potent cancer fighters as well as vision protectors. Lutein, a carotenoid abundant in greens, has been linked to a lower risk of macular degeneration (the leading cause of blindness) and cataracts. Vitamin K is a powerful anti-inflammatory, and some studies suggest that it helps protect against arthritis. It's also an important component of bone health.

The strong flavors of some of the deepest-hued greens make people shy away from them, but there are a few things you can do to make them more palatable. Blanch sturdy greens like kale and collards in boiling water until the color turns vibrant, about 2 to 3 minutes. Then sauté the greens with garlic in a flavorful olive oil. For salads, you can combine milder-tasting greens with peppery ones.

It's worth the effort to learn to love greens. Having just one serving a day (1 cup of raw greens or $\frac{1}{2}$ cup of cooked) cuts your heart attack risk by about 23 percent, according to a report from the Harvard Nurses' Health Study. More is better: Italian researchers found that women who eat 2 ounces of greens a day (about $1\frac{1}{2}$ cups of raw spinach or 1 cup of chopped raw kale) lowered their odds of developing heart disease by about 46 percent. And a study from the University of Leicester found a strong connection between dark leafy greens and a reduced risk of type 2 diabetes. Those who ate at least 1½ servings a day were 14 percent less likely to develop the disease, something the researchers attribute to the high magnesium levels in greens. Need a little extra incentive? Researchers at the University of Munich found that people scored about 20 percent higher on a creativity test when they got a glimpse of the color green beforehand. They believe our brains associate the color with nature, which leads us to think about growth and development. So the next time you're feeling uninspired, toss yourself a dark green salad!

# EGGS

**PROTECT AGAINST:**
CANCER, MACULAR DEGENERATION, AND OBESITY

**KEY NUTRIENTS:**
ANTIOXIDANTS, CHOLINE, OMEGA-3 FATTY ACIDS, AND PROTEIN

WANT TO get cracking in the morning? Have eggs for breakfast. The brain uses the protein they contain to make the neurotransmitters dopamine, norepinephrine, and epinephrine, which boost alertness, energy, and mood. Plus the way their protein is structured makes it easy for your body to absorb. You'll also start your day satisfied. Eggs keep you full a long time, which helps you control your weight. In one study, researchers from the Pennington Biomedical Research Center at Louisiana State University in Baton Rouge gave 20 overweight men and women a breakfast containing either eggs or cereal for a week, and then switched them to the other option. Both meals had exactly the same number of calories and protein, carbohydrates, and fat grams. On two of the days, the participants were brought to the lab for a buffet lunch where they could eat as much as they wanted. While on the egg diet, the participants felt less hungry and ate less at lunch than they did when they had cereal. Eggs increased production of PYY, a hormone that signals fullness, and decreased the amount of ghrelin, a hormone that triggers the urge to eat. Another study from Louisiana State University found that obese people who ate a two-egg breakfast at least five times a week lost 65 percent more weight and had more energy than women who had an equal-calorie bagel.

Eggs are one of the few good sources of choline, a B vitamin that's necessary for proper cell function and also a possible cancer preventer. In one study, women with a high intake of choline cut their risk of breast cancer by 24 percent. Eggs are also a good source of vitamin D, and they're packed with lutein, the carotenoid that helps protect against macular degeneration and cataracts. Researchers at the Jean Mayer USDA Human Nutrition Research Center on Aging at Tufts University in Boston found that although an egg has just 5 percent of the lutein found in $\frac{1}{4}$ cup of spinach, our bodies absorb it three times more effectively because of the fat eggs contain. (Most of the fat is unsaturated.) Some eggs are even good sources of omega-3s, with about 300 milligrams per large egg. Omega-3–rich flaxseed or canola oil is added to the hens' diets to increase this heart-healthy fat in the eggs.

But wait a minute—what about cholesterol? True, eggs contain 184 milligrams apiece, but cholesterol in food doesn't seem to have much of an effect on the levels of cholesterol in your bloodstream. Researchers at Wake Forest University in Winston-Salem, North Carolina, found that when people ate an egg a day for 12 weeks, HDL ("good") cholesterol rose by 48 percent, while LDL ("bad") cholesterol and triglycerides stayed the same.

# MANGOES

**PROTECT AGAINST:**
DIABETES, DIGESTIVE PROBLEMS, HEART DISEASE, AND OBESITY

**KEY NUTRIENTS:**
CAROTENOIDS, FIBER, VITAMIN C, AND VITAMIN E

THE NEXT time someone complains that "healthy foods are bland and boring," hand them a mango and watch what happens. Sweet, juicy, tropical mangoes taste luscious and decadent but are some of the healthiest fruits around. In one study, people who ate $1\frac{1}{4}$ cups of mango daily for a month experienced a 37 percent drop in triglyceride levels, which helps cut heart disease risk. Another heart-healthy perk of mangoes is that they contain antioxidant vitamin E. Mangoes' antioxidant carotenoids not only make them a good source of vitamin A, supplying 36 percent of your daily needs in just 1 cup, but they also help protect against cancer.

Mangoes make a flavorful side dish or topping for poultry, pork, or fish, and they contain enzymes that help your body break down the protein in these foods. One cup also supplies 10 percent of your fiber needs. Both properties ease digestion.

Although the research is preliminary, mangoes may enhance fat burning. Researchers at Oklahoma State University in Stillwater found that mice that were fed mangoes as part of their diets for 2 months weighed the same as mice that were not, but they had less body fat and low blood glucose levels. When glucose is low, the body produces less insulin, a hormone that can boost fat storage. Low glucose also means a lower risk of diabetes. How's that for some sweet news?

# NUTS AND NUT BUTTERS

**PROTECT AGAINST:**
ALZHEIMER'S DISEASE, HEART DISEASE, AND OBESITY

**KEY NUTRIENTS:**
CALCIUM, HEALTHY FATS, MAGNESIUM, PROTEIN, AND VITAMIN E

WHEN IT comes to the nutritional benefits of nuts, the list just keeps growing. In addition to helping your heart, they also boost your brain power. A study published in the journal *Neurology* showed that elderly people who ate diets rich in vitamin E and omega-3 fatty acids were less likely to have brain shrinkage and more likely to perform well on cognitive tests than those who didn't. And those almonds you've been eating? You can subtract about 30 percent from their calorie count, because USDA scientists found that they have only 129 calories per ounce, not 170. Another study by the same group showed pistachios to be lower in calories as well. This trend likely applies to all nuts.

But even before this research was released, nuts were known to be big players in weight control, thanks to the healthy fats, protein, and fiber they contain all in one little package. In a Harvard University study, people who had walnuts at breakfast stayed full all morning and ate fewer calories at lunch. And nuts can rev your metabolism. Researchers from Georgia Southern University in Statesboro found that having a high-protein, high-fat snack increases calorie burn for more than 3 hours afterward!

Still, it's easy to go overboard when eating nuts. Measure out a 1 ounce portion— about ¼ cup of nuts. If one handful just leads to another, try buying unshelled nuts and cracking them yourself. According to a study published in *Appetite*, noshing on pistachios you have to shell yourself can help decrease the number of calories you take in by more than 40 percent. This is probably because shelling the nuts makes you more mindful of how many you're eating and slows you down, giving your brain time to register that your appetite is being satisfied.

Each nut has its own unique nutritional benefit. Almonds are a good source of calcium, walnuts are packed with cardio-protective omega-3s, and just one Brazil nut more than satisfies your daily dose of selenium, a mineral that may help protect against cancer. All nuts have antioxidants, but pecans have the most. Men in an Australian study who ate 12 to 16 macadamias a day experienced an 8 percent rise in HDL ("good") cholesterol levels, probably due to the nut's exceptionally high monounsaturated fat content. Bottom line: As is true for vegetables and fruit, eating a variety of nuts is better than eating just one type.

# OATS

**PROTECT AGAINST:**
DIABETES, HEART DISEASE, AND OBESITY

**KEY NUTRIENTS:**
FOLATE, PROTEIN, AND SOLUBLE FIBER

WHETHER YOU'RE a traditionalist who likes hearty steel-cut oats or someone who prefers the quickness of a bowl of oat-Os cereal, you'll be happy to know that either form of this whole grain serves up valuable nutrients.

Oats are one of the best sources of beta-glucan, a soluble fiber that lowers cholesterol levels. Soluble fiber binds to the cholesterol-based acids in your digestive tract; that means that when the fiber leaves your body, it takes the cholesterol with it. In turn, your liver has to make more of those acids, so it snags cholesterol from your bloodstream, lowering your blood levels of that substance.

In an 8-week University of Connecticut study, men with high LDL cholesterol who got a daily dose of soluble fiber from oats experienced a more than 20 percent drop in cholesterol levels. Other studies show that you need about 3 to 5 grams of soluble fiber a day—1½ cups of cooked oatmeal has 3 grams—to reap this benefit. This protein-rich grain is also high in a type of antioxidant called avenanthramides, which protect LDL cholesterol from oxidation (the first step in the buildup of the arterial plaque that can raise heart attack risk).

The fiber in oats means they're digested slowly, so they keep you full. Oatmeal ranked third in a satiety index developed by Australian researchers who compared 240-calorie portions of various foods. And when Harvard University researchers analyzed the diets of more than 27,000 men over the course of 8 years, they found that the men who added 1 serving of whole grain foods to their daily diets weighed 2.5 pounds less than the men who ate only foods made from refined grains.

Although instant oatmeal has the same amount of soluble fiber ounce for ounce as rolled or steel-cut oats, it is not as filling. That's because when the oats are sliced to cook quickly their glycemic index—the rate at which they are digested and converted to glucose in the bloodstream—rises. Plus, flavored instant oatmeal is often a vehicle for sugar, with about 3 teaspoons of added sugar in each little packet. The truth is that you don't save all that much time with the instant stuff—rolled oats (also called old-fashioned oats) cook up in just 5 minutes and they, too, are perfectly microweavable.

# OLIVE OIL

**PROTECTS AGAINST:**
BONE LOSS, CANCER, HEART DISEASE, OBESITY, AND STROKE

**KEY NUTRIENTS:**
ANTIOXIDANTS, MONOUNSATURATED FAT, AND VITAMIN K

THE CENTERPIECE of Mediterranean cuisine, olive oil is at least partially responsible for the diet's health benefits—but only if you pick the right type. Any olive oil is an excellent source of monounsaturated fat, but getting one with lots of other beneficial compounds takes a little thought. To pick the healthiest oil, don't rely on labels, but trust your taste buds. True cold-pressed extra-virgin olive oil (the kind to buy for both flavor and health) has a slightly bitter, peppery flavor. You should feel a little sting in the back of your throat or the urge to cough when you taste it straight; that's a sign that the oil is rich in anti-inflammatories, polyphenols, and antioxidants.

Olive oil is at its most therapeutic and flavorful when it is as fresh as possible. Light, air, and time decrease the beneficial compounds in the oil, so skip the brands packaged in clear bottles, never buy an olive oil that doesn't have a "best by" stamp and a date a few months away, and don't be tempted by the deal on the 5-gallon can at the warehouse store. You should buy only as much as you will use in a few months. Real olive oil isn't cheap, but a high price is no guarantee of quality. Try to buy your olive oil at a store that will let you taste it beforehand (or return it if you don't like it), and remember that a little goes a long way.

Now that you know how to snag the good stuff, here's why olive oil should be a staple in your kitchen for both cooking and drizzling. For one thing, it will make your heart happy. Monounsaturated fats prevent the oxidation of LDL ("bad") cholesterol, a process that leads to clogged arteries. In one study, people who consumed the most olive oil had a 44 percent lower risk of dying from heart disease (and a 26 percent lower risk of dying from any cause) during the study period compared to those who ate the least olive oil. French researchers found that using extra-virgin olive oil for both cooking and eating lowers stroke risk by 41 percent. While a group of Spanish scientists were studying the effect of the Mediterranean diet on heart disease, they discovered that elderly men who ate olive oil had a dramatic increase in blood markers that signal bone formation, while those who followed a Mediterranean-style diet with nuts and no oil or a low-fat diet did not.

Another reason to stock up on olive oil: The polyphenols and antioxidants it contains have antibacterial properties that kill the bacteria that causes ulcers. Those compounds also have been shown to protect against various cancers.

Finally, foods high in monounsaturated fat help you burn belly fat, and olive oil is no exception. It also appears to be more satisfying than other fats. Researchers at Pennsylvania State University in State College found that a lunch cooked in olive oil keeps you fuller longer than the exact same food cooked in corn oil. Food specialists at the University of Illinois at Urbana-Champaign gave 341 Italian restaurant patrons equal amounts of bread and either olive oil or butter. The olive oil group ate 26 percent more fat on each slice of bread, but the butter eaters ate more bread and therefore consumed about 17 percent more calories. The message here, though, isn't that you should pour olive oil all over everything. At 120 per tablespoon, the calories in olive oil add up quickly, so be sure to measure.

# QUINOA

**PROTECTS AGAINST:**
CANCER, DIABETES, HEART DISEASE, AND OBESITY

**KEY NUTRIENTS:**
ANTIOXIDANTS, FIBER, FOLATE, IRON, MAGNESIUM, PHOSPHORUS, AND PROTEIN

WITH GLUTEN-FREE diets gaining popularity, you may have noticed a new addition to the grain aisle at your local supermarket: quinoa (pronounced KEEN-wah). But quinoa isn't new at all; in fact, it was a staple food for Inca warriors who prized it for its energy-giving powers.

Quinoa is not actually a grain, although it certainly cooks up like one. It's a seed that's botanically related to beets and Swiss chard, and it has some unique nutritional properties among "grains." It's higher in protein, for one thing, and that protein is complete, meaning it has all eight essential amino acids, just like eggs and meat do. All whole grains contain antioxidants, but quinoa is particularly packed with quercetin and kaempferol, anti-inflammatory compounds linked to a lower risk of cancer and heart disease. Quercetin is also a natural antihistamine. Like whole grains, quinoa helps to stabilize blood sugar because it has a low glycemic index and it's high in fiber. That makes it valuable for weight control and diabetes prevention.

There are culinary advantages as well. Quinoa is nuttier and more flavorful than brown rice, and it cooks in just 15 to 20 minutes. Unlike grains, which are soft and chewy, quinoa is both soft and crunchy. When you cook it, the germ of the seed twists out and forms a crunchy "tail." It tastes good hot or cold, can be used in sweet or savory dishes, and comes in three colors: ivory, red, and black. Take any rice or pasta recipe and sub in quinoa. You won't be sorry!

# SALMON, WILD

**PROTECTS AGAINST:**
ARTHRITIS, BREAST CANCER, DEPRESSION, HEART DISEASE, INFERTILITY,
MACULAR DEGENERATION, MEMORY LOSS, AND SKIN CANCER

**KEY NUTRIENTS:**
OMEGA-3 FATTY ACIDS, PROTEIN, SELENIUM, VITAMIN $B_{12}$, AND VITAMIN D

SALMON'S STAR nutrient is omega-3 fatty acids, which are powerful anti-inflammatories. They've been shown to protect your brain, heart, skin, joints, and more. And you don't need to eat much to benefit from this disease-fighting powerhouse: Two $3\frac{1}{2}$-ounce servings a week is what's recommended. Less can be helpful, too. In one study, young women who rarely or never ate fish were 90 percent more likely to develop heart disease than women who ate it just once a week.

Omega-3s are the primary fat in your brain, where they keep cell membranes flexible so the neurotransmitters that regulate mood can flow seamlessly throughout your nervous system. Scientists have long known that depression is less common in cultures that eat a lot of fish, and some studies show that people who get omega-3s from fish or supplements recover from depression faster than those who don't. One study in college students showed that anxiety levels dropped by about 20 percent when study participants were getting omega-3s. At the same time, the students had fewer inflammatory markers in their bodies.

Many of our experts also pointed to salmon's anti-aging powers. Early research suggests that omega-3–rich diets protect telomeres, the ends of cell chromosomes. The longer these "tails" are, the better cells are able to repair themselves. You'll look younger on the outside, too: Omega-3s help keep skin firm and wrinkle free, and a few studies have shown that they may act as an edible sunscreen, blocking the damage that can lead to certain kinds of skin cancer. In men, salmon can improve fertility; omega-3s are necessary for sperm cells to function normally. And increasing fish intake is a smart move for women who want to become pregnant, too. Omega-3s help ensure a healthy pregnancy and proper brain development in infants.

While the omega-3s in salmon get all the attention, this tasty fish is also one of the top natural sources of vitamin D. Just $3\frac{1}{2}$ ounces of salmon contain more than a day's worth of this vitamin. Getting enough D has been linked to cancer prevention and bone health. Salmon is also rich in cancer-fighting selenium.

When it comes to the environment, wild salmon is one of the best catches. According to the Environmental Defense Fund, wild salmon from Alaska is rated "eco-best" because it is caught in a responsible manner and is low in mercury and other contaminants. Farmed salmon, on the other hand, often has high levels of PCBs, and the way these fish are "raised" can pollute waters with waste and chemicals—possibly creating conditions that would lead to disease that may spread to wild fish. Farmed salmon is also less nutritious. It has more fat overall than wild does, but two to three times less omega-3s. Fresh wild salmon can be expensive, but canned Alaskan salmon is nutritionally and environmentally equivalent—and is a fraction of the price. Other less costly omega-3 rich and environmentally safe fish include sardines, mackerel, and herring.

# TEA

**PROTECTS AGAINST:**
ARTHRITIS, BONE LOSS, CANCER, DIABETES, HEART DISEASE, OBESITY, STROKE, AND VIRAL INFECTIONS

**KEY NUTRIENTS:**
CAFFEINE AND CATECHINS

FOR A beverage with such a quiet, meditative, and somewhat fussy reputation, tea certainly packs a powerful health punch. The different varieties of tea—white, green, oolong, and black—all contain antioxidant polyphenols called catechins. The most powerful of these is EGCG, found in highest concentration in green tea. Studies have linked regular consumption of green tea to a lower risk of colon, breast, gastric, lung, and prostate cancers. Researchers at the University of Parma in Italy studied 32 men with a type of precancerous prostate change that develops into cancer within 1 year of diagnosis about 30 percent of the time. The men took 200 milligrams of green tea catechins (the amount in about 1 cup of tea) three times a day for a year, and only one developed prostate cancer. White tea also has disease-fighting properties. A study at Kingston University in London tested 21 plant and herb extracts and found white tea to be the most effective at reducing inflammation, thereby lowering your odds of rheumatoid arthritis, some cancers, and wrinkles.

EGCG is also a metabolism booster. Researchers at the USDA found that people burned an extra 67 calories a day when they drank oolong tea than when they drank the same amount of caffeinated water. They believe that something in the tea other than caffeine, most likely the catechins, encourages the body to burn fat for energy first (rather than carbohydrates). Fat oxidation was 12 percent higher when the study volunteers were drinking tea. In a small Japanese study, men burned 17 percent more fat during a 30-minute workout when they drank green tea beforehand.

But everyday black tea is no health slouch, either. People who drink a cup of it after eating high-carb foods decrease their blood sugar levels by 10 percent for 2½ hours, according to a study published in the *Journal of the American College of Nutrition*. Black tea also reduces blood pressure and helps you combat LDL ("bad") cholesterol, lowering it by up to 10 percent in only 3 weeks.

Your immune system gets a helping hand from tea, too. Drinking a cup zaps viruses, such as the kinds that cause colds and flu, within 10 minutes, scientists at Pace University in New York City found. Have a sinus infection? Researchers at Alexandria University in Egypt found that green tea enhances the action of antibiotics, in some cases by threefold. Even allergy sufferers can get a break: EGCG may block the allergenic response some people have to pollen, pet dander, and dust.

And if all of that's not enough, here's the kicker: Tea can help slow the bone loss that comes with age. An Australian study found that tea-drinking women between the ages of 70 and 85 had greater bone-density than women of the same age who did not drink tea.

Herbal tea doesn't have the same antioxidants that regular tea does, but it does have its own health benefits. For example, chamomile and peppermint can soothe upset stomachs, passionflower helps you sleep, rosemary wards off stress-induced headaches, and thyme alleviates coughing and sinus pressure.

Iced tea is just as powerful as hot tea, if you make it yourself; the bottled stuff varies widely in antioxidant content. And scientists can't seem to agree on the effect milk has on tea's antioxidants. Some studies show that milk protein binds the beneficial compounds, yet others show it doesn't make a difference. Until the jury comes in, drink at least a few of your cups straight up.

# YOGURT

**PROTECTS AGAINST:**
DIGESTIVE PROBLEMS, HEART DISEASE, HIGH BLOOD
PRESSURE, OBESITY, AND OSTEOPOROSIS

**KEY NUTRIENTS:**
CALCIUM, POTASSIUM, PROBIOTICS, PROTEIN, AND VITAMIN $B_{12}$

YOU PROBABLY think of yogurt as a great source of calcium, and you wouldn't be wrong. (There's only one other food that is a better natural source of this mineral than yogurt, and that's ricotta cheese.) A 6-ounce container of nonfat plain yogurt has about 300 milligrams, or 30 percent of what you need each day.

But yogurt supplies so much more. First there's the protein, a hefty 8 grams, surpassing the amount in a large egg or $1/2$ cup of kidney beans. Nonfat Greek yogurt has more protein (18 grams) than regular yogurt, but also less calcium (200 milligrams). Next up is potassium—468 milligrams in 6 ounces, close to the amount in a large banana. Calcium and potassium work together to lower blood pressure. One study found that two servings of low-fat dairy a day cut the odds of developing hypertension by 54 percent.

Turning milk into yogurt requires the addition of healthy bacteria. Two strains—*Lactobacillus bulgaricus* and *Streptococcus thermophilus*—are used for this purpose. Many also contain *Lactobacillus acidophilus,* which is a probiotic, a bacteria that takes up residence in your digestive tract and helps keep you healthy in several ways. (Many yogurt manufacturers add other probiotic strains to their products.) Probiotics have been shown to boost the immune system. In one study, elderly people who ate about 3 ounces of yogurt a day were 2.6 times less likely to catch colds than those who didn't eat yogurt. Antibiotics decrease the number of healthy bacteria in your gut, which can lead to diarrhea. Eating yogurt helps you repopulate the good bacteria and reduces your odds of experiencing this unpleasant side effect by about 60 percent. Probiotics are also being studied for their role in heart disease prevention and weight control.

The calcium and protein combo in yogurt has been shown to make dropping pounds easier. A study from the Harvard School of Public Health that looked at the diet habits of more than 120,000 people for two decades found that consumption of nuts and yogurt was most closely correlated with weight loss. And yogurt seems particularly effective in burning belly fat. University of Tennessee, Knoxville researchers found that women who lost weight eating yogurt had 81 percent less fat around their waists than those who didn't eat yogurt.

All of these weight-loss benefits come from eating *plain* yogurt. The sugar-filled stuff is candy in disguise, in many instances. Some of the sugar in fruit yogurts comes from lactose in the milk itself (anything with -*ose* at the end is a sugar) or from the fruit. Even a plain, unsweetened, low-fat yogurt has 12 grams of sugar in a 6-ounce container. These natural sugars aren't a problem, but fruit and flavored yogurts often contain added sugar in the form of sucrose or high-fructose corn syrup. Different brands add different amounts and both natural and added sugars are lumped together on food labels. Your very best defense is to buy plain yogurt and add your own fruit, or even a little honey, if you like. That way, you control how much sugar you eat. Your second best option is to read labels carefully and pick a flavored yogurt with as close to 12 grams of sugar as possible. If you don't mind sugar substitutes, yogurts made with them will have the same amount of sugar as an equal portion of plain yogurt.

# CHAPTER 4

# Doctors' Diet Orders

A S A PHYSICIAN, I'M USED TO MY PATIENTS ASKING, *WHAT would you do if you were me?* when we're discussing treatment options. Over the past few years, though, they started making different inquiries, too, such as: *What do* you *do to stay healthy? How do you find the time to exercise? Do you lift weights? Do you eat gluten? Fat? Sugar? How do you get your kids to eat vegetables?* And even, *Do you cook?* Clearly, they were craving authoritative guidance on living a healthy lifestyle, but they also wanted to know what worked in the real world. They see me as someone who has a similar lifestyle—like many of my patients, I balance a demanding job and family responsibilities—but who also has insider knowledge of what really works and what isn't worth my (or their) time. And from talking to other health-care professionals, I know that my patients weren't the only ones hungry for this information.

That's why I teamed up with the editors of *Prevention* to write this book. As you'll see in Chapter 6, we got health experts from around the country to share their personal eating, exercise, and stress-reduction tips. We wanted to hear not only what science has found to be effective or the advice they give to their patients, but also what they did in their own lives.

As we combed through their tips, we noticed a pattern. Although personal tastes differ, the brain doctor, the cardiologist, the oncologist, the obstetrician, the registered dietitian, and the exercise physiologist all follow the same fundamental eating principles. It's not one specific diet; rather, they've used their expertise and research know-how to choose the best elements from a number of healthy plans, namely the Mediterranean, anti-inflammatory, semi-vegetarian, and low-glycemic-index diets. And they combine that style of eating with a healthy dose of behavioral and practical tips that help them eat mindfully, so they really enjoy their meals.

We used their tips to create The Doctors' Diet in the next chapter, but before you dig in, you should know the "rules" this eating plan is based on. Think of this list as your cheat sheet to developing a healthy relationship with food and exercise. It's a relationship that will serve you well for life.

## 12 PRESCRIPTIONS FOR HEALTHY EATING

### 1. Eat often.

Nearly all of our experts stress the importance of eating frequently to keep your metabolism and energy up and to avoid becoming so ravenous that you overeat when you finally do sit down to a meal. The "three meals plus two snacks a day" approach appears to be the best one for weight loss and weight maintenance. In a study in the *Journal of the Academy of Nutrition and Dietetics,* researchers found that people who were at a healthy weight and those who had lost weight both regularly ate two snacks a day. Snacking also appears to prevent weight gain. In one study, researchers followed more than 2,300 girls for 10 years (from about age 10 to age 20). Those who ate less frequently had an average increase of 1 body mass index unit and $\frac{1}{2}$ inch in waist size more than girls who ate six times a day.

How does eating often help? There's really no evidence to support the belief that it keeps your metabolism humming, but the opposite is absolutely true: If you cut back too far on calories, you're embarking on a self-defeating proposition: The lack of calories slows your metabolism. Plus, if you're only eating three times a day and trying to be calorie conscious, there is a good chance that you won't eat enough.

Probably the biggest benefit of eating often comes from the effect it has on blood sugar (glucose) levels and, therefore, insulin production. When glucose and insulin are in balance, your appetite is on an even keel. That not only helps reduce hunger but also simply makes you feel better. I know from personal experience that having small meals throughout the day (instead of three squares) keeps me energized. Some experts think that eating at regular intervals leads to less fat storage, too, because your body learns to recognize that food will be available relatively soon. And psychologically, knowing that your next meal isn't far away helps you cope with the biggest fear of people trying to lose weight: the fear of being hungry.

Of course, what you put in your mouth matters. If your snacks consist of potato chips and cupcakes, you aren't doing your health or your waistline any favors. As you'll see, many of the snacks in our plan are more like mini-meals. That's because we see snacking as the perfect opportunity to sneak more nutrients into your diet—and little portions of "real" foods are far more satisfying than the empty calories you'd get from chips and candy. In a study from the University of Illinois, women who had two snacks a day had a higher intake of fiber than those who noshed less often. Additionally, women who snacked in the afternoon had a higher intake of fruits and vegetables than those who snacked in the morning.

One *Prevention* colleague who worked on this book with me learned the importance of balanced snacking firsthand. As our deadline loomed, she found herself working later than usual and thus getting home for dinner later. When she walked in the door after her hour-long commute, she was famished, so she immediately grabbed a container of hummus and a bag of multigrain chips to munch on while she made dinner. (Hey, hummus is healthy, right? And the package said one serving of chips was a good source of fiber.) During this same time, though, she was frustrated because she was having a tough time losing the 5 pounds she had put on over the past few years. We got to talking, and I immediately saw that her predinner snack was the reason why. "You realize," I said, "that you're practically eating one meal on top of another, don't you?" I asked her to measure out the typical portion of hummus and chips she ate ($\frac{1}{3}$ cup hummus and 15 chips), and then I gave her the surprising news: Her healthy snack had 355 calories! She decided to skip her *before-dinner* dinner and started having a piece of fruit and a few nuts about an hour before she left the office, which kept her appetite on an even keel right through dinner prep. The result: 10 pounds gone in 3 months. Having a little something in the afternoon helped keep her appetite under control, but what she ate was important, too. And that brings me to our next rule.

## 2. Pair carbs with protein or fat.

Carbs are not evil. They're essential fuel, and they're your body's preferred energy source. On top of that, foods that are classified as mostly carbs—whole grains, fruits, vegetables—come packed with vitamins, minerals, and phytochemicals that are important for disease prevention. They can also be high in fiber, which helps keep you feeling full and satisfied. However, when you eat carbs by themselves, your body converts them into glucose faster than it would if you were eating something that slowed digestion (such as protein or fat) at the same time. An elevated glucose level causes a spike in insulin, which leads to a crash in blood sugar, which then results in extreme hunger. If that happens on a regular basis, your body switches to starvation mode, slowing your metabolism to conserve energy. Translation: You burn fewer calories in everything you do.

The more refined a carbohydrate food is, the more pronounced this spike-and-crash effect is. That's because refined carbs, like white flour and sugar, are chemically closer to glucose, and therefore they break down quickly. The fiber in whole grains and fruit slows this process somewhat, but the effect could be blunted even more if you combined your carbs with some protein or fat, like my colleague did when she ate fruit and nuts for her afternoon snack. (Beans and vegetables are a little different. Beans are mostly carbs, but they pack a hefty dose of protein, too. And except for potatoes, corn, and peas, the carbs in vegetables are comparatively minimal, even in those that are "sweet," like beets, carrots, and winter squash). Every meal and snack recommendation in The Doctors' Diet is a blend of either carbs and protein or carbs and fat—and sometimes all three.

## 3. Don't fear fat.

According to a survey from the International Food Information Council, just 20 percent of people think that all fats are equal when it comes to health, but 67 percent try to cut as far back on all fats as they can. That's a mistake, because how much fat you eat doesn't really have an impact on your weight or your risk for disease. It's the *type* of fat and the total calories you take in that really matter.

There are four general categories of fat: polyunsaturated, monounsaturated, saturated, and trans. With the exception of trans fat, your body needs all of them. Fat is a major component of every cell in your body. It helps you absorb fat-soluble nutrients from low-fat foods, keeps your skin and hair healthy, and makes your brain work more efficiently. Some types of polyunsaturated and monounsaturated fats also protect against disease and control inflammation. Saturated fat raises cholesterol levels and also increases your odds of developing insulin resistance (which can lead to diabetes), but you still need some of it in your diet. Cholesterol, which is primarily made from saturated fat, is an important building block for hormones.

Trans fat should be avoided, period. Studies show that as little as 1 gram of trans fat a day increases your odds of developing heart disease. Steering clear of it is far easier when you follow a diet that contains few packaged foods. The biggest source of trans fat is partially hydrogenated vegetable oil, which is found in crackers, cookies, cakes, and other processed foods. Many manufacturers have cut it from their products, as evidenced by the labels screaming "Trans Fat Free!" Still, always read the ingredients list, looking for the words "partially hydrogenated." Food manufacturers are allowed by law to say that something is trans fat free if it contains less than 1 gram of trans fat. When all it takes is 1 gram a day to put your health at risk, though, you can't afford to "accidentally" eat three half-gram portions.

One big problem with low-fat diets is that people tend to replace the missing fat with carbs. A body of research done at Harvard University as well as other institutions has shown that this swap unfavorably changes cholesterol levels: "Bad" LDL rises and "good" HDL drops. Replace saturated fat with polys or monos, and you get the opposite outcome. Eating a diet relatively high in unsaturated fats also lowers blood pressure more than a diet relatively high in carbs does.

A study funded by the National Institutes of Health found that low-carb and low-GI diets helped people who lost weight to keep it off. The participants ate three different diets for 4 weeks each. The low-carb diet supplied just 10 percent of calories from carbohydrates. The low-GI diet was similar to a traditional Mediterranean diet—40 percent of the calories came from fat, 20 percent from protein. In the low-fat diet about 20 percent of the calories came from fat. The results: The participants burned an average of 300 and 150 more calories a day on the low-carb and low-GI diets, respectively, than they did on the low-fat diet. This was probably because the low-carb and low-GI diets did a better job at keeping blood sugar levels stable and insulin spikes minimal.

These are all reasons why The Doctors' Diet emphasizes foods low in saturated fats (but not free of them) and incorporates good fats in spades—taking calories into consideration, of course. You might be wondering why, if the low-carb diet revved calorie burn twofold, we don't suggest you eat *that* way? Two reasons: Low-carb diets can be notoriously difficult to stick with for life—not for everyone, but for a lot of people. In addition, such a high-protein diet often means a lot of meat. Meat comes with saturated fat, so the impact on your heart health is problematic.

Here's another important point to keep in mind: Fat makes food taste good. On the one hand, that can cause you to overeat, but on the other, it can help you eat more vegetables and other healthy foods that you should be getting in your diet. I'm pretty sure that even the most strident vegetable lover would admit that a little olive oil, Parmesan cheese, toasted nuts, or even—wait for it—butter on top of steamed asparagus likely makes the asparagus more flavorful.

## 4. Never skip breakfast.

Skip the morning meal and chances are good that you'll end up consuming more calories overall simply because you are hungrier. Think about it: If you finish dinner at 7 p.m. and don't eat again until noon the next day, you have gone without food for *17 hours.* You think you're helping yourself drop pounds because you're cutting out calories, but you're actually causing your body to store *more* fat because it doesn't know when the next influx of energy is coming. In addition, eating breakfast has been associated with lower blood glucose and cholesterol levels, and skipping it is linked to constipation and menstrual pain. In children, breakfast helps boost attention span and learning. (It's not clear if adults get the same benefit.)

Studies have consistently shown that breakfast eaters weigh less than breakfast skippers. Some studies have found that people who have a high-protein meal, like eggs, are more satisfied, while others show that whole grain cereal is most filling. Some of the research suggests that you should have a lot of calories at breakfast, while some say a light meal is what's called for. None of these studies are conclusive, so my advice is just eat *something*, preferably a carb-fat or carb-protein combo. The Doctors' Diet gives you plenty of fast but tasty options.

## 5. Never eat standing up.

At one point or another, we have all stood in front of the refrigerator with the door open, eating leftovers or ice cream right out of the container. And even if you aren't guilty of this little healthy eating blooper, I'll bet you've eaten a meal while doing something else—like watching TV or answering e-mail—that diverts your attention away from what you're putting in your mouth. It's a habit that many of our experts have broken, because when you don't concentrate on your food as you're eating it, it doesn't quite register in your body. You could call it calorie amnesia: You can't really remember what you ate, so you don't get as much satisfaction from it. As a result, you find yourself craving something else not long after your meal. The science bears this out. In a study in the *American Journal of Clinical Nutrition,* researchers had one group of participants eat a meal while playing computer solitaire and another group eat without any distractions. The solitaire group had a hard time remembering what they ate, and they felt less full. What's more, they ate twice as much when cookies were offered half an hour later.

No matter how busy you are, you can afford to take 15 minutes to sit down and eat. Focus on your food and really notice the aromas, flavors, and textures. Eating slowly helps, too. Japanese researchers found that fast eaters have triple the risk of being obese as those who take their time.

## 6. Spend time in the kitchen.

Learning to cook changed my health for the better. I can control the nutritional quality and calorie counts of my meals. I also found that cooking with my kids makes them more likely to try different foods—an observation backed up by a study from the University of Alberta, which found that children who helped with food prep were about 10 percent more inclined to like vegetables.

To say that restaurant portions tend to be large is an understatement. On average, the typical restaurant meal has 50 percent more calories than a home-cooked meal. But those calories aren't the only worrisome things you're being served: A survey of restaurant meals by the RAND Corporation uncovered the sad fact that 96 percent of the nearly 30,000 chain restaurant menu items tested exceeded daily saturated fat and sodium recommendations. And don't think the local bistro is any healthier: Chefs use a lot of salt, oil, and butter in their cooking, and big portions are just as common in independent restaurants.

Cooking at home does not mean that you have to be the next Jacques Pépin or Rachael Ray. Home cooking can be super simple and, in fact, is for many of our experts, as you'll see by their recipes in Chapter 6. Tossing together a salad from fresh greens and vegetables with a little protein counts as home cooking!

## 7. Eat a pound of produce a day.

That's what the World Health Organization recommends, and it's what most of our health pros do. It's not difficult. A large apple, for instance, can easily be one-third of a pound. Tomato sauce counts. So do beans and lentils.

Studies show that people with a high intake of fruits and vegetables weigh less. They also get fiber, vitamins, minerals, and phytochemicals that protect against cancer and heart disease. "Eat the rainbow" has become a bit of a cliché, but it's the best way to think about it. The compounds that give plants their pigments—green, purple, blue, red, orange, yellow—aren't just pretty. They're powerful antioxidants, and you want to eat a variety of them. Even white vegetables are good for you: Every ounce of them you eat each day reduces your stroke risk by 9 percent.

## 8. Have one meatless day a week.

Meatless Mondays, semi-vegetarian, vegifore, vegan until 6 o'clock, flexitarian— these are just some of the words used to describe a way of eating that emphasizes plant foods but doesn't totally eschew dairy, meat, poultry, or fish. Maybe the best way to think about it is to consider yourself a vegetarian most of the time. In fact, one survey found that two out of three people who describe themselves as vegetarians actually eat this way. Most of the people in the Mediterranean (Italy, Greece, and Spain) follow this kind of diet, and study after study has shown that they have lower risks of chronic diseases. Researchers at Loma Linda University School of Public Health in California found that the occurrence of diabetes in semi-vegetarians was about half that of people who ate a typical nonvegetarian diet. Harvard researchers found that limiting red meat intake to no more than $10\frac{1}{2}$ ounces a week could prevent 1 in 10 early deaths in men and 1 in 13 in women. And cutting out one serving of red meat per day lowered the risk of premature death by 7 to 19 percent, depending on whether the meat being eliminated was a burger or a roast or processed red meat. Another study showed that semi-vegetarians live an average of 3.6 years longer.

The Doctors' Diet is semi-vegetarian—mostly plant-based, with some dairy and eggs. Meat, poultry, and fish are included in small amounts no more than once a day. And every week you have one meatless day—it doesn't have to be Monday!

## 9. Go fish twice a week.

Two servings of fish each week is pretty much a universal health recommendation from organizations like the American Heart Association and the USDA. And many of our health pros eat fish more often than that. Fish is the best source of omega-3 fatty acids, a polyunsaturated fat that is anti-inflammatory. Omega-3s lower heart disease risk, protect your brain, and are also important for a healthy pregnancy for both mother and baby. Several of our experts gave us delicious fish recipes, and you'll find them in The Doctors' Diet.

## 10. Desugar your diet.

Evidence that added sugar plays a role not just in weight gain but also in heart disease, diabetes, cancer—and even wrinkles!—is steadily mounting. The average person eats 22 teaspoons, or 88 grams, a day. (Each teaspoon weighs 4 grams.) That's 352 calories' worth. The American Heart Association recommends a maximum daily intake of just 5 teaspoons for women and 6 for men, which means that if you have one soda, you've exceeded your limit. Follow The Doctors' Diet, though, and you likely won't get close to 6 to 9 teaspoons. We use some sugar in our meal suggestions, where it really makes a difference in flavor, but we keep it to a minimum.

Most of the sugar people eat isn't added to food by the teaspoon, though—it's in processed and packaged products. And separating added sugar from naturally occurring sugar in fruits, some vegetables, dairy products, and whole grains isn't easy. The amount of sugar listed on food labels is the combination of both natural and added sugars in one serving of the food. Sugar has many names—high-fructose corn syrup, glucose, sucrose, honey, maple syrup, barley malt, beet sugar, cane juice, and cane sugar, to name a few—so reading the ingredients list can help. The best way to keep your added sugar intake low is to eat real foods.

## 11. Separate your mood from your food.

Stress can ruin the best-laid diet plans. According to a survey by the American Psychological Association, 40 percent of respondents reported emotional eating—that is, eating for reasons other than hunger, such as feeling pressured, anxious, sad, or bored. (Interestingly, studies have found that being happy also causes people to eat more.) Stress appears to change the brain's response to food, making appetizing food more enticing— and it affects where your body stores fat. When your stress hormones are high, you tend to have more abdominal fat, which is linked to an increased risk of heart disease and diabetes. The solution is three pronged. First, eat mindfully (see rule 5). Second, find an outlet for your stress. In a University of California, San Francisco, study, mindful eating and meditation helped women feel less stressed and reduced stress hormones. The women in the study lost belly fat, even though they did not change what they ate. Exercise is also a terrific stress reliever.

Finally, learn to distinguish true hunger from head hunger—the desire to eat because you think you deserve it, because it will make you feel better, or just because the food looks good. How can you do this? Tune in to your body. After you eat a meal, focus for a few minutes on your belly. You should feel satisfied but not stuffed, as though you could eat a few more bites, but you don't need to. (Don't check in too soon, though. Your brain needs 20 minutes to register that your stomach is full.) Once you become familiar with that feeling, ask yourself, "Am I hungry?" every time you want to eat. If the answer is yes, eat. If the answer is no, ask yourself what else is going on. Take 10 minutes to think about it—whatever you are craving will still be there—and then decide. Take a walk, read a book, call a friend—do anything you enjoy that will take your mind off of food. If that doesn't work, have a small portion of the food you want. That's often enough to make you feel satisfied. Whatever you do, though, don't beat yourself up. Even the best eaters give in to head hunger sometimes.

## 12. Move every day.

Okay, this isn't a diet tip, exactly, but exercise and diet are so closely linked that it can't be ignored. The experts in this book may not do formal "exercise" every day, but from climbing the stairs in the hospital to walking their dogs at home, they do move. And being physically active often leads you to eat better. Some of that may just be a natural side effect of wanting to be healthy, but some researchers believe that exercise actually changes your brain so you are better able to resist temptation or so that the hormones that control your appetite are more balanced. People who get $2\frac{1}{2}$ hours of moderate activity a day have lower levels of inflammatory markers in their bloodstreams. And exercisers are more sensitive to insulin (which lowers your risk for diabetes) and are less likely to develop dementia later in life. Exercise helps you sleep better, too, and people who get enough high-quality sleep are more likely to be slim.

Now that you have your orders, let's eat!

# CHAPTER 5

# The Doctors' Diet: 30 Days to a Slimmer, Healthier You

T HE FIRST GOAL OF THIS BOOK IS TO SHOW YOU HOW THE

principles of a semi-vegetarian, anti-inflammatory, low-glycemic-index

diet come together in the real world. We've laid out 30 days of menus

that incorporate all of the health pros' favorite recipes, along with

some simple yet tasty dishes that you can pull together quickly. There are no recipes here that require a culinary degree to make or have so many ingredients that you start thinking, "Where are the take-out menus?" While we did make a special effort to feature all 18 of the healing foods discussed in Chapter 3 (because those are the foods the health pros told us they turn to again and again), there are hard-to-find ingredients in these dishes. They're just delicious, easy, good-for-you meals.

The editors of *Prevention* and I had many discussions about the best way to design an eating plan. We talked about giving you a list of meal suggestions and leaving it to you to mix and match them to fit your needs. While that approach gives you the most flexibility, it also makes it too easy to overlook some of the Doctors' Diet Orders in Chapter 4, such as eat fish twice a week or get a pound of produce a day. You need to get in the rhythm of a new way of eating before you can put all of the healthy elements together effortlessly yourself. That's why we decided on a compromise: We'd spell out what to eat for the main meals of the day, but give you a variety of choices for snacks and desserts.

Being a bit more prescriptive also allows us to achieve our second goal, which is to help you drop pounds without feeling hungry or deprived. To lose weight, you have to reduce the number of calories you take in and increase the number you burn. (Turn to Chapter 7 for our advice on the "burning" part of this equation.) The trick is to eat as much nutritionally rich food as you can for the fewest number of calories. That way, you stay satisfied and supply your body with the nutrients it needs to function at its best and ward off disease. You'll be amazed at how much food you can have on this plan because your options are built around low-calorie, filling, flavorful, *real* foods. And the meals and snacks are nutritionally balanced, so you're never eating carbs alone (another of our Doctors' Diet Orders), which keeps your blood sugar steady and controls your appetite.

Our base diet supplies 1,300 calories a day. That's the level most people need to keep their energy up and their immune systems strong. If that was all you ate, you'd lose weight, but you'd likely be hungry—and that feeling of hunger and deprivation will doom any eating plan. We want you to stick to this style of eating (if not these exact meals) for life, so we've also given you a list of snacks and desserts at different calorie levels. You'll mix and match them with your meals to reach 1,400, 1,600, or 1,800 calories a day. The chart on the next page gives you the right calorie count for your gender, height, activity level, and weight-loss goals.

## THE 30-DAY PLAN

Ready to see what you'll be eating this month? The chart beginning on page 78 gives you an overview. The meals highlighted in **BOLD** are our health pros' favorite recipes. Our meal plan (and the nutritional information provided) assumes that you'll eat one serving of the recipe. (See the individual recipes for preparation instructions and portion sizes.) Instructions for pulling together the other meals are in the Day-

# HOW MANY CALORIES SHOULD I EAT?

| TOTAL CALORIES | RIGHT FOR |
|---|---|
| 1,400 | • Women who want to combine diet with moderate exercise (such as walking 30 minutes a day) to lose weight quickly. |
| | • Women who are under 5′4″ and want to lose weight. |
| | • Women and men who are sedentary and don't need to lose weight, but who want to eat a disease-preventing diet. |
| 1,600 | • Men who want to combine diet with moderate exercise (such as walking) to lose weight quickly. |
| | • Women who are active (following the exercise plan in Chapter 7 or something similar) and who want to lose weight. |
| | • Women who are under 5′4″ and don't need to lose weight, but who want to eat a disease-preventing diet. |
| 1,800 | • Women who don't need to lose weight, but who want to eat a disease-preventing diet. |
| | • Women who are very active (doing more exercise than what's recommended in Chapter 7) and who want to lose weight. |
| | • Men who are active (following the exercise plan in Chapter 7 or something similar) and who want to lose weight. |

Note: Men who don't need to lose weight but who want to eat a disease-preventing diet can eat 2,000 calories a day. Men who are very active and want to lose weight can eat 2,200 calories.

By-Day Menu Planner beginning on page 88. These mini-recipes serve one person, but they are easily doubled, tripled, or quadrupled to feed everyone at your table.

You'll find a list of snack options to pick from starting on page 118. We've grouped them by calorie count, and it's up to you to choose which ones you'll use to complete your day. For example, if you're following the 1,600-calorie plan, you can have three 100-calorie snacks or one 100-calorie snack and one 200-calorie snack. You can choose one option one day and another the next to round out your daily diet.

Take a look at the nutrition stats for each day and you'll see that sometimes the base diet doesn't exactly add up to 1,300 calories. (We could have gotten that precise, but this is real life, not a lab experiment!) And some of the snacks have a few more or a few less calories than the calorie category they're listed in. That means that once you factor in your snacks on the 1,600-calorie plan, for example, you may eat 1,550 calories one day, 1,622 the next, and 1,619 the next. The bottom line is, it's okay if you don't hit the round numbers every day—it all averages out over the course of a week.

If you're a do-it-yourself kind of person, you might not feel 100 percent comfortable committing to even 1 month of planned meals. I'm like that, too—I like to have choices. But this plan appeals to me because it takes the guesswork out of what to eat but still allows me some flexibility. That being said, we've anticipated some questions you may have.

**Can I switch meals around?** If you want to swap meals within the same day—have breakfast for lunch, for instance—feel free! You can also trade entire days, if you like. What gets tricky, though, is substituting one day's breakfast, lunch, or dinner for another day's, even in the same meal slot. Each day's calorie count adds up to about 1,300, but the calorie counts aren't consistent across meal types. And as I said earlier, you need to get into the rhythm of a new way of eating before you can put all of the healthy elements together effortlessly yourself. But if you feel that you can adhere to the principles of the plan outlined in Chapter 4 and you don't mind the math, use the calorie information that follows each meal to create your own 1,300-calorie plan.

**What should I drink?** Water or seltzer (plain or flavored), hot or iced coffee or tea (black or with a splash of milk, but no sugar), and herbal tea are all zero-calorie (or close to it) beverages. (A teaspoon of sugar in your coffee or tea adds 16 calories.) You should sip these "free" drinks the vast majority of the time. Most beverages, including 100 percent fruit juice, provide lots of calories, and many provide little nutritional benefit. For example, a 12-ounce can of cola will cost you 140 calories, all coming from the nearly 9 teaspoons of sugar it contains (usually in the form of high-fructose corn syrup), as well as artificial colors and flavorings. It has absolutely no nutritional value. A cup of orange juice contains 102 calories, but you get a significant amount of vitamin C, potassium, and folate for those calories. (Other fruit juices worth considering for their vitamins, minerals, and antioxidants include pomegranate, tart cherry, and purple grape juice.) Milk (102 calories in 8 ounces of low-fat and 91 in 8 ounces of nonfat) contains protein, calcium, vitamin $B_{12}$, vitamin D, and other nutrients.

When you reach for a drink, though, there's something else you should consider: Beverages don't fill you up. Studies show that your body doesn't register the calories they contain in the same way that it registers the calories in food. In a Purdue University study, men and women were given three sets of meals made up of either food or liquids that differed in their protein, carbohydrate, and fat composition to determine which form was more satisfying. The high-protein test compared cheese and milk; the high-carb, watermelon and watermelon juice; and the high-fat, coconut and coconut milk. On the days they drank the beverages, the study participants took in 12 to 15 percent more calories overall. Bottom line: What they drank didn't quell their appetites as much as what they ate.

This wouldn't really matter, though, if you had just *one* soda a day or a single glass of orange juice. Unfortunately, that's not the case for the majority of

*(continues on page 83)*

---

## RESEARCH REPORT

**FROM THE LAB OF: Karina Martinez-Mayorga, PhD**, Chemistry Institute at the National Autonomous University of Mexico

**HAPPY DIET** Did you ever notice that drinking a cup of tea can calm you down or that eating a piece of chocolate perks you up? It turns out that certain flavor compounds in chocolate, tea, and berries are chemically similar to valproic acid, a drug used in some antidepressant drugs. This study didn't test the effect of these foods on people's moods, but the results may indicate you could quite possibly eat your way happy.

# THE DOCTORS' DIET AT A GLANCE | WEEK 1

| | BREAKFAST | LUNCH | DINNER | DAILY NUTRITION |
|---|---|---|---|---|
| **DAY 1** | Kasha porridge with dates and almonds | Spinach and egg roll-ups | • **Chicken Paillard with Tomato and Fennel** <br> • 3½ oz roasted red potatoes | 1,318 calories, 61 g protein, 128 g carbohydrates, 22 g fiber, 66 g fat, 12 g saturated fat, 1,421 mg sodium |
| **DAY 2** | **Healthy Granola** with yogurt and berries | • **Basil Roll** <br> • **Kale-Cherry Salad with Lemon Vinaigrette** | Whole wheat penne with tomatoes, broccoli, and chickpeas | 1,278 calories, 60 g protein, 139 g carbohydrates, 29 g fiber, 56 g fat, 10 g saturated fat, 846 mg sodium |
| **DAY 3** | Whole grain cereal with fresh fruit | **Turkish Wedding Soup** | **Almond-Encrusted Wild Salmon Fillet on a Bed of Wilted Greens** | 1,277 calories, 71 g protein, 133 g carbohydrates, 27 g fiber, 56 g fat, 8 g saturated fat, 1,052 mg sodium |
| **DAY 4** | Chai Smoothie | • Veggie and cheese pita <br> • 1 cup orange segments with cinnamon | • **Dr. Lynne's Baked Meatballs** (3) with spaghetti <br> • Mixed green salad with beets and edamame | 1,250 calories, 73 g protein, 143 g carbohydrates, 26 g fiber, 46 g fat, 13 g saturated fat, 1,548 mg sodium |
| **DAY 5** | Rosa's Breakfast Pancake | • **Asian Chicken and Walnut Salad** <br> • 1 small pear | Mexican Wrap | 1,279 calories, 84 g protein, 152 g carbohydrates, 31 g fiber, 40 g fat, 5 g saturated fat, 2,397 mg sodium |
| **DAY 6** | **Peanut Butter–Honey Oatmeal** | • Tuna salad sandwich <br> • **Apple and Endive Salad** | • **Veggie Spaghetti** <br> • Fresh mozzarella with tomatoes and olives | 1,298 calories, 59 g protein, 142 g carbohydrates, 28 g fiber, 59 g fat, 12 g saturated fat, 901 mg sodium |
| **DAY 7** <br> Meatless | **Greeno Mojito Smoothie** | Mediterranean bulgur salad | **Spinach, Berry, and Goat Cheese Salad** | 1,279 calories, 62 g protein, 121 g carbohydrates, 24 g fiber, 68 g fat, 20 g saturated fat, 883 mg sodium |

Note: Meals in **bold** are doctor recipes.

# THE DOCTORS' DIET AT A GLANCE | WEEK 2

| | | BREAKFAST | LUNCH | DINNER | DAILY NUTRITION |
|---|---|---|---|---|---|
| DAY | 8 | PB and banana muffin | • **Avocado, Mango, and Shrimp Salad with Miso Dressing** • Melon with honey and mint | • **Chicken Rolls Florentine** • Confetti quinoa • 1 cup cooked carrots | 1,243 calories, 75 g protein, 144 g carbohydrates, 23 g fiber, 45 g fat, 8 g saturated fat, 1,548 mg sodium |
| DAY | 9 | **Muncy Morning Smoothie** | • Spinach and egg roll-up • Fruit with honey-lime glaze | • **Nine-Vegetable Soup with Beef and Barley** • Mediterranean salad | 1,278 calories, 89 g protein, 143 g carbohydrates, 25 g fiber, 45 g fat, 7 g saturated fat, 2,071 mg sodium |
| DAY | 10 | Whole grain cereal with fruit | • **Fish Tacos and Guacamole** • ½ cup sliced pear | • **Vegan Cassoulet** • 1 cup melon balls | 1,267 calories, 68 g protein, 165 g carbohydrates, 34 g fiber, 44 g fat, 6 g saturated fat, 922 mg sodium |
| DAY | 11 | Yogurt with kiwifruit and almonds | Margherita flatbread pizza | • **Juicy Turkey Burger and Baked Sweet Potato Fries** • Arugula and citrus salad | 1,282 calories, 73 g protein, 151 g carbohydrates, 24 g fiber, 46 g fat, 14 g saturated fat, 1,584 mg sodium |
| DAY | 12 | • Cannoli cup • 1 cup raspberries | **Dr. Gwenn's Chicken Taco Salad** | • **Salmon with Noodles** • Spinach with garlic and lemon • Tangy fruit salad | 1,309 calories, 68 g protein, 138 g carbohydrates, 22 g fiber, 56 g fat, 19 g saturated fat, 1,714 mg sodium |
| DAY | 13 Meatless | **Berry-Cherry Oatmeal** | • Veggie and cheese pita • Jicama salad | • Tofu and vegetable stir-fry • **Spiced Edamame** • 1 small Asian pear | 1,319 calories, 59 g protein, 171 g carbohydrates, 34 g fiber, 46 g fat, 11 g saturated fat, 1,680 mg sodium |
| DAY | 14 | • **Fast French Omelet** • **Very Veggie Juice** | • **Quinoa Salad with Almonds and Green Beans** • Strawberries with lime dip | • **Scallops with Lemon-Cilantro Sauce** • **Grilled Mixed Vegetables** • Fresh mozzarella with tomatoes and olives | 1,257 calories, 69 g protein, 115 g carbohydrates, 21 g fiber, 62 g fat, 16 g saturated fat, 1,007 mg sodium |

Note: Meals in **bold** are doctor recipes.

| | BREAKFAST | LUNCH | DINNER | DAILY NUTRITION |
|---|---|---|---|---|
| **DAY 15** | Kasha porridge with raisins and almonds | • **Spicy Chicken Sandwich with Pickled Veggies**<br>• Spring mix salad | • **Anna Maria Tequila-Lime Shrimp**<br>• 2 small slices whole wheat baguette<br>• Zesty green beans | 1,322 calories, 74 g protein, 153 g carbohydrates, 19 g fiber, 47 g fat, 7 g saturated fat, 1,558 mg sodium |
| **DAY 16** | • Poached egg on toast<br>• ½ grapefruit | • **Spinach Salad with Avocado, Fresh Mozzarella, and Strawberry Dressing**<br>• 2 small slices sourdough whole wheat bread | • **Farmers' Market Veggie Pasta**<br>• 1 small apple | 1,266 calories, 59 g protein, 152 g carbohydrates, 25 g fiber, 49 g fat, 15 g saturated fat, 1,942 mg sodium |
| **DAY 17** | **Healthy Granola** with yogurt and cherries | • **Grandma Claire's Chicken Soup**<br>• Greek salad | • **Grilled Salmon with Peach-Mango Salsa**<br>• **Hashed Brussels Sprouts** | 1,300 calories, 97 g protein, 126 g carbohydrates, 25 g fiber, 49 g fat, 12 g saturated fat, 1,662 mg sodium |
| **DAY 18** | Oatmeal with apricots, cranberries, and walnuts | • Spinach and egg roll-up<br>• Melon with honey and mint | • 4 oz grilled sirloin<br>• 1 boiled red potato with dill<br>• **Roasted Winter Vegetables** | 1,301 calories, 67 g protein, 153 g carbohydrates, 22 g fiber, 52 g fat, 10 g saturated fat, 1,057 mg sodium |
| **DAY 19** | PB and apple muffin | • **North Woods Bean Soup**<br>• Cucumber salad<br>• 1 small whole wheat roll | • Spring mix salad<br>• Roast pork with cranberries and pear<br>• 2 fresh figs with 2 oz Brie | 1,331 calories, 67 g protein, 168 g carbohydrates, 35 g fiber, 47 g fat, 15 g saturated fat, 2,437 mg sodium |
| **DAY 20** | **Mocha Protein Shake** | Whole wheat penne with tomatoes, broccoli, and black beans | • **Chicken Tacos with Charred Salsa**<br>• Tangy fruit salad | 1,332 calories, 77 g protein, 176 g carbohydrates, 30 g fiber, 43 g fat, 8 g saturated fat, 621 mg sodium |
| **DAY 21** Meatless | Cannoli cup | • Pita with roasted eggplant hummus<br>• Curried almonds<br>• 1 cup nectarine slices | • **Sweet Potato Ravioli**<br>• Mixed green salad with edamame and beets | 1,285 calories, 46 g protein, 161 g carbohydrates, 23 g fiber, 56 g fat, 13 g saturated fat, 1,885 mg sodium |

Note: Meals in **bold** are doctor recipes.

| | BREAKFAST | LUNCH | DINNER | DAILY NUTRITION |
|---|---|---|---|---|
| **DAY 22** | • **Mark's Açai Smoothie** <br> • 2 slices whole wheat toast, each with 1 tsp almond butter | • **Stir-Fried Kale with Almonds** <br> • 4 oz chicken breast <br> • ⅔ cup brown rice <br> • 1 medium orange | • Pork tenderloin with apricot <br> • Whole wheat couscous with zucchini | 1,270 calories, 77 g protein, 170 g carbohydrates, 25 g fiber, 35 g fat, 5 g saturated fat, 1,648 mg sodium |
| **DAY 23** | • Savory eggs <br> • Tangy fruit salad | • Tomato, cheese, and olive pita <br> • **North Woods Bean Soup** <br> • 1 medium pear | • **Steamed Sole with Creamy Dill Sauce** <br> • **Warm Greens Sauté** <br> • Confetti quinoa | 1,255 calories, 70 g protein, 187 g carbohydrates, 34 g fiber, 29 g fat, 6 g saturated fat, 2,350 mg sodium |
| **DAY 24** | • Whole grain cereal with fresh fruit <br> • 11 almonds | Margherita flatbread pizza | • **Turkey and Broccoli with Couscous** <br> • **Spiced Spaghetti Squash** <br> • Zesty green beans | 1,317 calories, 67 g protein, 172 g carbohydrates, 33 g fiber, 46 g fat, 12 g saturated fat, 1,211 mg sodium |
| **DAY 25** | • **The Sleep Doctor's Smoothie** <br> • 11 almonds | Black bean quesadillas | • **Cajun-Style Grilled Shrimp** <br> • **Mango-Avocado Salad** <br> • ¾ cup cooked brown rice | 1,308 calories, 58 g protein, 179 g carbohydrates, 27 g fiber, 44 g fat, 7 g saturated fat, 1,639 mg sodium |
| **DAY 26** | Oatmeal with apricots and walnuts | Tofu and vegetable stir-fry | **Rigatoni with Turkey and Vegetable Bolognese** | 1,272 calories, 57 g protein, 163 g carbohydrates, 23 g fiber, 46 g fat, 6 g saturated fat, 662 mg sodium |
| **DAY 27** | • French toast with apples <br> • 1 oz low-fat Cheddar cheese | • **Tropical Chickpea Salad** in a 6" whole wheat pita <br> • Yogurt with kiwifruit and almonds | • **Miso-Marinated Chilean Sea Bass** <br> • Sautéed asparagus <br> • Confetti quinoa <br> • 1 cup orange segments | 1,279 calories, 88 g protein, 175 g carbohydrates, 33 g fiber, 29 g fat, 7 g saturated fat, 1,485 mg sodium |
| **DAY 28** Meatless | • Tex-Mex eggs <br> • Melon with honey and mint | **Roasted Beets** in an arugula and goat cheese salad | • Spring mix salad <br> • **Vegetarian Soup with Shirataki Noodles** <br> • Roasted cauliflower | 1,257 calories, 58 g protein, 132 g carbohydrates, 34 g fiber, 62 g fat, 14 g saturated fat, 1,526 mg sodium |

Note: Meals in **bold** are doctor recipes.

|  | BREAKFAST | LUNCH | DINNER | DAILY NUTRITION |
|---|---|---|---|---|
| DAY **29** | Whole grain cereal with fresh fruit | Mediterranean bulgur salad | • **Curried Red Lentils**<br>• Sautéed spinach with garlic and lemon<br>• ½ cup cooked brown rice<br>• 11 almonds | 1,279 calories, 46 g protein, 182 g carbohydrates, 38 g fiber, 51 g fat, 9 g saturated fat, 1,686 mg sodium |
| DAY **30** | **Healthy Granola** with yogurt and berries | • **Black Bean Soup with Avocado Crème**<br>• 1 oz reduced-fat Monterey Jack cheese<br>• 1 small apple | • **Raspberry-Balsamic Glazed Salmon**<br>• Sautéed asparagus<br>• Confetti quinoa | 1,295 calories, 79 g protein, 132 g carbohydrates, 30 g fiber, 53 g fat, 12 g saturated fat, 1,806 mg sodium |

Note: Meals in **bold** are doctor recipes.

Americans. On average, we get 25 percent of our daily calories from drinks. Now, if you *really* like cola or, like the old ad says, a day without orange juice actually *is* like a day without sunshine for you, have just one serving in place of one of your 100-calorie snacks. Love a cold glass of milk with your meals or a latte in the morning? Again—substitute it for one of your snacks.

**What about the occasional cocktail?** We list wine, beer, and liquor in the snack and dessert list (see page 118). One drink a day (defined as 5 ounces of wine, 12 ounces of beer, or 1 ounce of liquor) is the maximum that women should consume. For men, the limit is two drinks. However, I believe that women should limit alcohol to two to three drinks per week. Some studies do suggest that alcohol has a beneficial effect on your heart, but not all scientists agree that the research is clear on that point. And other research links even moderate alcohol consumption to a higher risk of breast cancer in women. Plus alcohol has calories. I would strongly urge you to avoid mixed drinks, such as screwdrivers, rum and colas, cosmos, fruity margaritas, and the like. Those mixers (even straight fruit juice) are packed with sugar, and sometimes even cream—and therefore calories. If you like liquor, stick to tequila with lime juice and club soda, vodka or scotch neat, and martinis—the James Bond kind, not the flavored kind!

**I have to dine out sometimes. What do I do then?** Look at what you are supposed to eat at that meal, and then have something similar. Take a look at the restaurant's Web site to see what your options might be and decide ahead of time what you're going to order—that way you aren't tempted when you sit down. Studies have shown that having soup before a meal takes the edge off your hunger for few calories and it prevents you from overeating during the rest of the meal.

Also don't be afraid to request modifications to your dish. For example, ask for sauce or dressing to be served on the side, for an extra helping of vegetables instead of a starch, or to eliminate an ingredient in the dish, such as the cheese in a salad.

The biggest problem with dining out, though, is the amount of food you're served. Restaurant portions are usually two times (or more) larger than a healthy serving size, so order an appetizer and a salad as your meal, split a meal with a friend, or take half of your meal home.

**I'm worried—will I be hungry?** These meals contain a balance of carbohydrates, protein, fat, and fiber that make them very filling, so my first piece of advice is that you should give it a try for a few days. You might be surprised by how satisfied you are on this plan! Interestingly, many of our health pros, who follow their own versions of this kind of diet, said that they don't get cravings very often. We think you'll discover this is true for you, too, after a few days.

Also ask yourself where the hunger is coming from. You may be bored or upset. If so, try to distract yourself in a nonfood way. Go for a walk, call a friend, or read a book before you reach for a bite of something you'll regret. Or you may be thirsty, so have a cup of tea or a glass of water. It's pretty common for people

---

## RESEARCH REPORT

**FROM THE LAB OF: Brian Wansink, PhD,** Cornell University

## SIDE EFFECTS OF SKIPPING MEALS It's no secret that the

longer you go without food, the hungrier you are when you finally do sit down to eat. But this study showed that fasting also affects *what* you choose to have at your next meal. People who were served a lunch containing starches, meat, and vegetables 18 hours after they last ate were more likely to reach for high-calorie foods first, notably starches, than those who hadn't skipped a meal. What's more, the first food that all the study participants put in their mouths was the food they ate the most of during the lunch. That means that if their first forkful was loaded with vegetables, they consumed fewer calories overall than they did if they started with starch.

> ## RESEARCH REPORT
>
> **FROM THE LAB OF: Urszula Iwaniec, PhD,** College of Public Health and Human Sciences at Oregon State University
>
> **ALCOHOL AND YOUR BONES** Moderate drinking—one-half to two drinks per day—can help midlife women preserve bone and, as a result, lower their odds of osteoporosis. At the start of this study, 40 postmenopausal women who drank alcohol had blood tests to measure the levels of two markers for bone turnover. Then the women abstained from alcohol for 2 weeks then resumed drinking. The tests showed that bone turnover increased, indicating bone loss, when the women did not drink and returned to normal when they began to drink again. So it looks like a glass of milk isn't the only beverage that protects your bones.

to mistake hunger for thirst. Still hungry? Have an additional healthy snack from our list.

**What if this is too much food for me?** Easy—simply drop back to the next lowest calorie level. Just be sure not to eat fewer than 1,300 calories a day.

**What can I substitute for gluten-containing foods?** Many people have gone gluten free, but they feel limited in their food choices. Gluten is a protein found in wheat, barley, oats and rye. Gluten sensitivity requires eliminating or minimizing the "gluten grains." In any of the recipes that call for these grains, substitute a gluten-free alternative, such as quinoa, brown rice, amaranth, teff, or buckwheat (kasha). For example, quinoa and rice pasta are delicious.

**I don't like fish. Do I really need to eat it?** You should, but if we can't convince you to, you can substitute equal amounts of chicken, turkey breast, or pork tenderloin in the fish and shellfish recipes. The food and flavor combinations in those dishes will work with those meats, too. Another option is to eliminate the fish days and repeat another day's worth of meals that includes foods you do like. If you don't eat fish at least twice a week, though, you should take fish oil supplements (unless you are taking an anticoagulant drug or have been told by your doctor not to take fish oil; check with your doctor if you have questions).

**Why isn't there a cheat day on this plan?** My feelings about so-called cheat days are mixed. On the one hand, they give you clear parameters and help you eat healthy 80 percent of the time, as many of our health pros recommend. On the other, they set up the concept of "good" foods versus "bad" foods, which I believe leads to a vicious cycle of cravings and deprivation that makes the psychological part of following a healthy diet more difficult. A better strategy is: Have small treats every day. There are options in the snack and dessert lists starting on page 118. My advice is to follow this plan for a month so you get used to what it feels like to follow a healthy diet, become familiar with portion sizes, and so on. Once you're familiar with it, you'll be better equipped to make judgments about "not everyday" foods.

Of course, if during this plan you have a birthday party or wedding to go to, eat what you're served (try to keep your portions on the small side) and have the cake. Just follow this plan for the rest of the day and get right back on track the next. Life isn't all or nothing, and unless you think of every meal as a celebratory one, a celebratory meal or dessert should be just that. You should enjoy it and not think you've "blown" it. You have the opportunity to reestablish healthy habits at the next meal. The same advice applies if you, for whatever reason, eat an entire pizza or pint of ice cream or stray from this new way of eating in any way. One day does not a health future, or extra pounds, make. It's what you do most of the time that counts. Don't let a lapse turn into a collapse.

---

I don't expect that you'll eat these exact meals month after month for the rest of your life (although you could if you wanted to). But I do think that you'll feel so good

## RESEARCH REPORT

**FROM THE LAB OF: Devina Wadhera**, department of psychology, Arizona State University

**LITTLE PIECES, BIG RESULTS** Could one of the best weight-loss tools be a sharp knife? According to this study, at a Society for the Study of Ingestive Behavior meeting, the answer is yes. College students were given a 3-ounce bagel either whole or cut into four pieces and then were given a free lunch where they could eat as much as they wanted. The amounts of the bagel and the food they ate at lunch were carefully measured. Those who were served the quartered bagel ate less of it *and* fewer calories at lunch than those who got the whole bagel. When food is served in smaller pieces, it's likely that you feel as though you're getting more to eat—and that increases satisfaction.

at the end of 30 days that you'll be convinced that this is the way to eat for pleasure *and* health. You will have more energy, you'll be slimmer (if that was your goal), and you'll see an improvement in blood pressure, cholesterol, and many other health parameters. You'll find some new favorite dishes and flavor combinations, and you'll become more familiar with portion sizes and the kinds of foods that make your body run most efficiently. And most important for long-term success, you'll have the tools and the inspiration you need to create your own healthy meals and be on your way to a lifetime of perfect health.

# DAY 1

## BREAKFAST

### Kasha porridge with dates and almonds          (318 calories)

■ Combine ½ cup water, ⅓ cup 1% milk, and ¼ tsp cinnamon in a small saucepan; bring to a boil. Stir in ¼ cup kasha and ⅛ cup chopped dates; reduce heat to low. Cook, stirring occasionally, for 10 to 12 minutes. Drizzle with 1 tsp maple syrup and ⅛ cup sliced almonds.

## LUNCH

### Spinach and egg roll-ups          (453 calories)

■ Microwave two 6″ whole wheat tortillas one at a time on high for 15 to 20 seconds. Top each with ½ cup baby spinach and 1 chopped hard-cooked egg. Drizzle with 2 tsp olive oil vinaigrette. Roll up each and cut in half.

## DINNER

### Chicken Paillard with Tomato and Fennel          (457 calories)
NICHOLAS DINUBILE, MD (PAGE 182)

### 3½ oz roasted red potatoes with rosemary          (90 calories)

NUTRITION: 1,318 calories, 61 g protein, 128 g carbohydrates, 22 g fiber, 66 g total fat, 12 g saturated fat, 1,421 mg sodium

# DAY 2

## BREAKFAST

### Healthy Granola with yogurt and berries (308 calories)
MARIE SAVARD, MD (PAGE 317)

■ Place 8 oz plain 2% Greek yogurt and 1 cup fresh raspberries in a small bowl; sprinkle with 2 Tbsp Healthy Granola.

## LUNCH

### Basil Roll (1) (134 calories)
TASNEEM BHATIA, MD (PAGE 227)

### Kale-Cherry Salad with Lemon Vinaigrette (331 calories)
MARK MOYAD, MD, MPH (PAGE 311)

## DINNER

### Whole wheat penne with tomatoes, broccoli, and chickpeas (505 calories)

■ Cook 2 oz whole wheat penne until al dente. Drain and return penne to pot. Add ¾ cup chopped plum tomatoes, ½ cup broccoli florets, ½ cup chickpeas (no salt added, drained and rinsed), 1 Tbsp extra-virgin olive oil, minced garlic, chopped basil, and chopped oregano. Cook on medium heat, stirring occasionally until broccoli is cooked but firm, 5 minutes.

NUTRITION: 1,278 calories, 60 g protein, 139 g carbohydrates, 29 g fiber, 56 g total fat, 10 g saturated fat, 846 mg sodium

# DAY 3

## BREAKFAST

### Whole grain cereal with fresh fruit
(300 calories)

■ Combine 1 cup whole grain flakes and ½ cup 1% milk in a small bowl. Top with ½ cup sliced fresh strawberries, ½ small banana (sliced), and ¼ tsp ground cinnamon.

## LUNCH

### Turkish Wedding Soup
(425 calories)

SALLY KUZEMCHAK, MS, RD, LD (PAGE 297)

## DINNER

### Almond-Encrusted Wild Salmon Fillet on a Bed of Wilted Greens
(553 calories)

NICHOLAS PERRICONE, MD (PAGE 140)

NUTRITION: 1,277 calories, 71 g protein, 133 g carbohydrates, 27 g fiber, 56 g total fat, 8 g saturated fat, 1,052 mg sodium

# DAY 4

## BREAKFAST

### Chai Smoothie (310 calories)
**W. CHRISTOPHER WINTER, MD (PAGE 258)**

## LUNCH

### Veggie and cheese pita (346 calories)

▪ Stuff a 6" whole wheat pita with 3 tomato slices, 3 basil leaves, and 1½ oz fresh mozzarella cheese. Drizzle with 1 tsp extra-virgin olive oil and top with ⅛ tsp freshly ground black pepper.

### 1 cup orange segments with cinnamon (85 calories)

## DINNER

### Dr. Lynne's Baked Meatballs with spaghetti (284 calories)
**LYNNE KENNEY, PsyD (PAGE 323)**

▪ Toss 1 cup cooked whole wheat spaghetti with ½ cup low-sodium tomato sauce. Top with 3 Dr. Lynne's meatballs.

### Mixed green salad with beets and edamame (225 calories)

▪ Toss 2 cups mixed salad greens with ½ cup diced, canned beets; ½ cup cooked edamame; ½ cup cucumber slices; ¼ cup grated carrot; 1½ tsp extra-virgin olive oil; and ½ tsp vinegar.

**NUTRITION:** 1,250 calories, 73 g protein, 143 g carbohydrates, 26 g fiber, 46 g total fat, 13 g saturated fat, 1,548 mg sodium

# DAY 5

## BREAKFAST

Rosa's Breakfast Pancake                                    (324 calories)

LARRY LIPSHULTZ, MD (PAGE 172)

## LUNCH

Asian Chicken and Walnut Salad                             (453 calories)

WAYNE WESTCOTT, PhD (PAGE 197)

1 small pear                                                (86 calories)

## DINNER

Mexican Wrap                                               (416 calories)

STEVEN LAMM, MD (PAGE 300)

NUTRITION: 1,279 calories, 84 g protein, 152 g carbohydrates, 31 g fiber,
40 g total fat, 5 g saturated fat, 2,397 mg sodium

# DAY 6

## BREAKFAST

### Peanut Butter–Honey Oatmeal
(425 calories)

ADAM DICKLER, MD (PAGE 166)

## LUNCH

### Tuna salad sandwich
(270 calories)

■ Mix 3 oz canned light tuna with 2 tsp light mayonnaise, $\frac{1}{4}$ tsp curry powder, and 1 Tbsp diced celery. Spread tuna salad on 2 slices whole wheat toast, and top with 2 tomato slices.

### Apple and Endive Salad
(291 calories)

TINA S. ALSTER, MD (PAGE 127)

## DINNER

### Veggie Spaghetti
(199 calories)

MARGARET I. CUOMO, MD (PAGE 163)

### Fresh mozzarella with tomatoes and olives
(113 calories)

■ Combine 1 oz bite-size fresh mozzarella balls with 6 grape tomatoes, 2 pitted kalamata olives, and freshly ground black pepper to taste.

NUTRITION: 1,298 calories, 59 g protein, 142 g carbohydrates, 28 g fiber, 59 g total fat, 12 g saturated fat, 901 mg sodium

# DAY 7

## MEATLESS DAY

### BREAKFAST

Green Mojito Smoothie                                    (290 calories)

FRANK LIPMAN, MD (PAGE 246)

### LUNCH

Mediterranean bulgur salad                              (497 calories)

■ Combine 2 cups chopped Romaine lettuce, 1 cup cooked bulgur wheat, 1 oz
reduced-fat feta cheese, 10 green grapes (halved), ½ cup pomegranate seeds, and
1 Tbsp roasted sunflower kernels in a medium bowl; set aside. Whisk together 1 Tbsp
extra-virgin olive oil, 1 tsp vinegar, and chopped mint, chopped parsley, and freshly
ground black pepper to taste. Drizzle dressing over salad and toss gently.

### DINNER

Spinach, Berry, and Goat Cheese Salad                   (493 calories)

ADNAN NASIR, MD (PAGE 138)

NUTRITION: 1,279 calories, 62 g protein, 121 g carbohydrates, 24 g fiber, 68 g fat,
20 g saturated fat, 883 mg sodium

# DAY 8

## BREAKFAST

### PB and banana muffin (324 calories)

■ Top one toasted whole wheat English muffin with 1 Tbsp natural peanut butter and 1 small banana (sliced).

## LUNCH

### Avocado, Mango, and Shrimp Salad with Miso Dressing (389 calories)
**LORI BUCKLEY, PsyD (PAGE 235)**

### Melon with honey and mint (82 calories)

■ Toss together 1 cup melon balls, 1 tsp honey, ½ tsp fresh lime juice, and chopped mint to taste.

## DINNER

### Chicken Rolls Florentine (274 calories)
**JOHN A. ELEFTERIADES, MD (PAGE 213)**

### Confetti quinoa (98 calories)

■ Cook ⅛ cup quinoa in ¼ cup low-sodium vegetable broth. Mix with ½ cup total of a combination of chopped red bell pepper, corn kernels, chopped onion, chopped carrots, and chopped tomatoes. Sprinkle with ¼ tsp chopped parsley.

### 1 cup cooked carrots with 1 tsp honey (76 calories)

NUTRITION: 1,243 calories, 75 g protein, 144 g carbohydrates, 23 g fiber, 45 g fat, 8 g saturated fat, 1,548 mg sodium

# DAY 9

## BREAKFAST

### Muncy Morning Smoothie (482 calories)
LISA MUNCY-PIETRZAK, MD (PAGE 252)

## LUNCH

### Spinach and egg roll-up (227 calories)

■ Microwave an 8″ whole wheat tortilla on high for 15 to 20 seconds. Top with ½ cup baby spinach and 1 hard-cooked egg (chopped). Drizzle with 2 tsp olive oil vinaigrette. Roll up and cut in half.

### Fruit with honey-lime glaze (146 calories)

■ Toss ¼ cup fresh pineapple chunks, ¼ cup strawberry halves, ¼ cup tangerine sections, ¼ cup sliced banana, and ½ kiwifruit (sliced) with 1 tsp fresh lime juice and ½ Tbsp honey. Top with chopped mint.

## DINNER

### Nine-Vegetable Soup with Beef and Barley (250 calories)
LIZ APPLEGATE, PhD (PAGE 179)

### Mediterranean salad (173 calories)

■ Combine 1 cup chopped romaine lettuce, ½ oz reduced-fat feta cheese, 5 grapes, ¼ cup pomegranate seeds, and 2 tsp sunflower seeds in a medium bowl; set aside. Whisk together 2 tsp extra-virgin olive oil, ½ tsp vinegar, ¼ tsp chopped mint, and ⅛ tsp freshly ground black pepper. Drizzle over salad and toss gently.

**NUTRITION:** 1,278 calories, 89 g protein, 143 g carbohydrates, 25 g fiber, 45 g fat, 7 g saturated fat, 2,071 mg sodium

# DAY 10

## BREAKFAST

### Whole grain cereal with fruit
(330 calories)

■ Combine 1 cup shredded wheat and $\frac{1}{2}$ cup 1% milk in a small bowl. Top with $\frac{1}{2}$ cup blueberries, $\frac{1}{2}$ small banana (sliced), and $\frac{1}{4}$ tsp ground cinnamon.

## LUNCH

### Fish Tacos and Guacamole
(398 calories)
JESSICA WU, MD (PAGE 146)

### $\frac{1}{2}$ cup sliced pear
(41 calories)

## DINNER

### Vegan Cassoulet
(442 calories)
WOODSON C. MERRELL, MD (PAGE 249)

### 1 cup melon balls
(57 calories)

NUTRITION: 1,267 calories, 68 g protein, 165 g carbohydrates, 34 g fiber, 44 g fat, 6 g saturated fat, 922 mg sodium

# DAY 11

## BREAKFAST

### Yogurt with kiwifruit and almonds (252 calories)

▪ Place 8 oz plain 2% Greek yogurt, 1 large kiwifruit (sliced), and 1 Tbsp almonds in a small bowl. Stir and drizzle with 1 tsp honey.

## LUNCH

### Margherita flatbread pizza (395 calories)

▪ Top 1 whole wheat flatbread (3 oz) with 1 tsp extra-virgin olive oil, minced garlic, 1 oz bite-size fresh mozzarella balls, 1 plum tomato (sliced), 1 Tbsp chopped basil, and 1 tsp grated Parmesan cheese. Bake in a 400°F oven until cheese is melted, 12 to 15 minutes.

## DINNER

### Juicy Turkey Burger and Baked Sweet Potato Fries (333 calories)
DAVID PEARSON, PhD (PAGE 188)

### Arugula and citrus salad (302 calories)

▪ Combine 2 cups arugula, ½ cup clementine or tangerine segments, ¼ cup pomegranate seeds, 1 oz Gorgonzola cheese, and ½ tsp chopped mint in a medium bowl. Whisk together 1 tsp extra-virgin olive oil, 1 tsp honey, 1 Tbsp orange juice, and ¼ tsp vinegar. Pour over salad and toss gently.

NUTRITION: 1,282 calories, 73 g protein, 151 g carbohydrates, 24 g fiber, 46 g fat, 14 g saturated fat, 1,584 mg sodium

# DAY 12

## BREAKFAST

Cannoli cup (215 calories)

■ Combine ¼ cup part-skim ricotta cheese with ¼ cup raisins and ⅛ tsp ground cinnamon.

1 cup raspberries (64 calories)

## LUNCH

Dr. Gwenn's Chicken Taco Salad (414 calories)
GWENN S. O'KEEFFE, MD (PAGE 326)

## DINNER

Salmon with Noodles (435 calories)
JORDAN D. METZL, MD (PAGE 186)

Spinach with garlic and lemon (55 calories)

■ Sauté 1 clove garlic (minced) in 1 tsp extra-virgin olive oil. Add 2 cups fresh spinach; sauté until wilted. Season with ½ tsp fresh lemon juice, ¼ tsp freshly ground black pepper, and ⅛ tsp salt.

Tangy fruit salad (126 calories)

■ Toss ½ fresh orange segmented, ⅓ small pear (sliced), ½ small apple (chopped), and 6 red grapes (halved) with ½ Tbsp fresh lemon juice, ⅛ tsp ground nutmeg, and ½ tsp chopped tarragon.

NUTRITION: 1,309 calories, 68 g protein, 138 g carbohydrates, 22 g fiber, 56 g fat, 19 g saturated fat, 1,714 mg sodium

# DAY 13

## MEATLESS DAY

### BREAKFAST

Berry-Cherry Oatmeal                                          (375 calories)
MARYANNE LEGATO, MD (PAGE 302)

### LUNCH

Veggie and cheese pita                                       (346 calories)

■ Stuff a 6" whole wheat pita with 3 tomato slices, 3 basil leaves, and 1½ oz fresh mozzarella cheese. Drizzle with 1 tsp extra-virgin olive oil.

Jicama salad                                                 (82 calories)

■ Combine ¾ cup sliced jicama, ¼ cup chopped red bell pepper, and ½ Tbsp chopped cilantro in a medium bowl. Whisk together ¼ Tbsp extra-virgin olive oil, ½ clove garlic (minced), ¼ Tbsp fresh lime juice, ¼ tsp honey, ¼ tsp lime zest, and ⅛ tsp ground red pepper in a small bowl. Pour over vegetables and toss.

### DINNER

Tofu and vegetable stir-fry                                  (363 calories)

■ Heat 2 tsp canola in a large skillet on medium high. Add ½ cup each firm tofu, broccoli florets, and sliced asparagus. Stir-fry for 5 minutes, or until broccoli is tender. Add ¼ cup sliced mushrooms, 1 clove garlic (minced), 1 tsp white wine, and ½ tsp soy sauce; stir-fry 2 minutes. Top with 1 tsp sesame seeds. Serve with ½ cup cooked brown rice.

Spiced Edamame                                               (101 calories)
ERIC J. TOPOL, MD (PAGE 225)

1 small Asian pear                                           (52 calories)

NUTRITION: 1,319 calories, 59 g protein, 171 g carbohydrates, 34 g fiber, 46 g fat, 11 g saturated fat, 1,680 mg sodium

# DAY 14

## BREAKFAST

Fast French Omelet                 (186 calories)
ROB THOMPSON, MD (PAGE 223)

Very Veggie Juice                (100 calories)
ERIC BRAVERMAN, MD (PAGE 152)

## LUNCH

Quinoa Salad with Almonds and Green Beans    (348 calories)
DAVID KATZ, MD (PAGE 279)

Strawberries with lime dip           (114 calories)

■ Mix together 2 oz plain 0% Greek yogurt, ½ Tbsp honey, ½ tsp lime zest, and ¼ Tbsp fresh lime juice. Serve with 1 cup whole strawberries.

## DINNER

Scallops with Lemon-Cilantro Sauce       (285 calories)
KENNETH M. YOUNG, DDS, PC (PAGE 148)

Grilled Mixed Vegetables          (111 calories)
VONDA WRIGHT, MD (PAGE 201)

Fresh mozzarella with tomatoes and olives    (113 calories)

■ Combine 1 oz bite-size fresh mozzarella balls with 6 grape tomatoes, 2 pitted kalamata olives, and freshly ground black pepper to taste.

NUTRITION: 1,257 calories, 69 g protein, 115 g carbohydrates, 21 g fiber, 62 g fat, 16 g saturated fat, 1,007 mg sodium

# DAY 15

## BREAKFAST

### Kasha porridge with raisins and almonds
(316 calories)

■ Combine ½ cup water, ⅓ cup 1% milk, and ¼ tsp cinnamon in a small saucepan; bring to a boil. Stir in ¼ cup kasha and ⅛ cup raisins; reduce heat to low. Cook for 10 to 12 minutes, stirring occasionally. Drizzle with 1 tsp maple syrup and top with ⅛ cup sliced almonds.

## LUNCH

### Spicy Chicken Sandwich with Pickled Veggies
(350 calories)
KIMBERLY COCKERHAM, MD (PAGE 130)

### Spring mix salad
(84 calories)

■ Toss 2 cups greens with ½ tsp vinegar and 1½ tsp extra-virgin olive oil in a small bowl.

## DINNER

### Anna Maria Tequila-Lime Shrimp
(215 calories)
JOHNATHAN M. LANCASTER, MD, PHD (PAGE 169)

### 2 small slices whole wheat baguette
(150 calories)

### Zesty green beans
(207 calories)

■ Blanch 2 cups sliced green beans for 2 minutes; drain. Heat 1 Tbsp extra-virgin olive oil in a medium skillet and add beans, 1 tsp orange zest, 1 tsp Triple Sec or Cointreau. Add 1 Tbsp low-sodium chicken broth and sauté for 2 to 4 minutes.

**NUTRITION:** 1,322 calories, 74 g protein, 153 g carbohydrates, 19 g fiber, 47 g fat, 7 g saturated fat, 1,558 mg sodium

# DAY 16

## BREAKFAST

### Poached egg on toast
(283 calories)

■ 1 poached egg, 1 slice cooked Canadian bacon, and 1 slice tomato on 1 slice whole wheat toast topped with 1 oz low-fat Cheddar cheese

### ½ Grapefruit
(41 calories)

## LUNCH

### Spinach Salad with Avocado, Fresh Mozzarella, and Strawberry Dressing
(366 calories)

**BARBARA QUINN, MS, RD (PAGE 218)**

### 2 small slices sourdough whole wheat bread
(180 calories)

## DINNER

### Farmers' Market Veggie Pasta
(345 calories)

**CHRISTINE AVANTI, CN (PAGE 256)**

### 1 small apple
(53 calories)

**NUTRITION:** 1,266 calories, 59 g protein, 152 g carbohydrates, 25 g fiber, 49 g fat, 15 g saturated fat, 1,942 mg sodium

# DAY 17

## BREAKFAST

### Healthy Granola with yogurt and cherries (358 calories)

**MARIE SAVARD, MD (PAGE 317)**

▪ Place 8 oz plain 2% Greek yogurt and ⅓ cup dried cherries in a small bowl; sprinkle with 2 Tbsp Healthy Granola.

## LUNCH

### Grandma Claire's Chicken Soup (121 calories)

**TANYA ZUCKERBROT, MS, RD (PAGE 287)**

### Greek salad (327 calories)

▪ Combine 2 cups chopped romaine lettuce, ⅔ cup sliced grape tomatoes, ½ cup cucumber slices, 4 pitted kalamata olives, 1 oz reduced-fat feta cheese, ⅓ cup chickpeas, and 4 artichoke hearts (halved) in a medium bowl. Toss with ½ tsp chopped basil, ½ tsp chopped parsley, ⅓ tsp dried oregano, and ¼ tsp freshly ground black pepper; drizzle with 1½ tsp extra-virgin olive oil and 1 Tbsp red wine vinegar.

## DINNER

### Grilled Salmon with Peach-Mango Salsa (329 calories)

**SHARON CHIRBAN, PhD (PAGE 238)**

### Hashed Brussels Sprouts (165 calories)

**ANDREW WEIL, MD (PAGE 254)**

NUTRITION: 1,300 calories, 97 g protein, 126 g carbohydrates, 25 g fiber, 49 g fat, 12 g saturated fat, 1,662 mg sodium

# DAY 18

## BREAKFAST

### Oatmeal with apricots, cranberries, and walnuts (461 calories)

■ Bring 1 cup soy milk or nonfat milk to a boil in a small saucepan over medium-high heat. Stir in ½ cup old-fashioned oats, 2 Tbsp dried cranberries, 4 dried apricot halves (sliced), and 2 Tbsp chopped toasted walnuts; reduce heat to low. Cook, stirring occasionally, about 4 minutes. Remove from heat, cover, and let stand 2 to 3 minutes.

## LUNCH

### Spinach and egg roll-up (227 calories)

■ Microwave an 8″ whole wheat tortilla on high for 15 to 20 seconds. Top with ½ cup baby spinach and 1 hard-cooked egg (chopped). Drizzle with 2 tsp olive oil vinaigrette. Roll up and cut in half.

### Melon with honey and mint (82 calories)

■ Toss together 1 cup melon balls, 1 tsp honey, ½ tsp fresh lime juice, and chopped mint.

## DINNER

### 4 oz grilled sirloin steak (229 calories)

### 1 boiled red potato with dill (113 calories)

### Roasted Winter Vegetables (189 calories)
ROSHINI RAJ, MD (PAGE 314)

NUTRITION: 1,301 calories, 67 g protein, 153 g carbohydrates, 22 g fiber, 52 g fat, 10 g saturated fat, 1,057 mg sodium

# DAY 19

## BREAKFAST

### PB and apple muffin (291 calories)

■ Top 1 whole wheat English muffin with 1 Tbsp natural peanut butter and 1 cup apple slices.

## LUNCH

### North Woods Bean Soup (235 calories)
TED EPPERLY, MD (PAGE 293)

### Cucumber salad (69 calories)

■ Combine 1 cup cucumber slices with ½ cup grated carrots, ½ cup diced red peppers, ½ cup sliced red onions, and 1 tsp chopped cilantro in a medium bowl. Whisk together 2 Tbsp rice vinegar, 1 tsp toasted sesame oil, ½ tsp light soy sauce, and ½ tsp honey. Toss vegetables with dressing.

### 1 small whole wheat roll (78 calories)

## DINNER

### Spring mix salad (84 calories)

■ Toss 2 cups greens with ½ tsp vinegar and 1½ tsp extra-virgin olive oil in a small bowl.

### Roast pork with cranberries and pear (325 calories)

■ Rub 4 oz pork tenderloin with 1 tsp extra-virgin olive oil, 2 tsp chopped thyme, and ¼ tsp salt. Place in a roasting pan; add 3 Tbsp dried cranberries and 1 small pear (sliced). Roast at 425°F for 15 to 20 minutes or until pork reaches an internal temperature of 145°F.

### 2 fresh figs with 2 oz Brie (249 calories)

NUTRITION: 1,331 calories, 67 g protein, 168 g carbohydrates, 35 g fiber, 47 g fat, 15 g saturated fat, 2,437 mg sodium

# DAY 20

## BREAKFAST

Mocha Protein Shake                                      (264 calories)

ALAN ARAGON, MS (PAGE 263)

## LUNCH

Whole wheat penne with tomatoes, broccoli,
and black beans                                         (563 calories)

▓ Cook 2 oz whole wheat penne until al dente. Drain and return penne to pot. Add
¾ cup chopped plum tomatoes, ½ tsp minced garlic, ⅛ tsp chopped basil, ¼ tsp
chopped oregano, ½ cup broccoli florets, ½ cup black beans (no-salt-added, drained
and rinsed), and ½ Tbsp extra-virgin olive oil. Cook on medium-heat, stirring
occasionally until broccoli is cooked but firm, about 5 minutes.

## DINNER

Chicken Tacos with Charred Salsa                        (379 calories)

ALFREDO QUIÑONES-HINOJOSA, MD (PAGE 157)

Tangy fruit salad                                       (126 calories)

▓ Toss ½ fresh orange (segmented), ⅓ small pear (sliced), ½ small apple (chopped),
and 6 red grapes (halved) with ½ Tbsp fresh lemon juice, ⅛ tsp nutmeg, and ½ tsp
chopped tarragon.

NUTRITION: 1,332 calories, 77 g protein, 176 g carbohydrates, 30 g fiber, 43 g fat,
8 g saturated fat, 621 mg sodium

# DAY 21

## MEATLESS DAY

### BREAKFAST

Cannoli cup                                                    (215 calories)

■ Combine ¼ cup part-skim ricotta cheese with ¼ cup raisins and ⅛ tsp ground cinnamon.

### LUNCH

Pita with roasted eggplant hummus                             (253 calories)

■ Stuff two 4″ whole wheat pitas with 2 Tbsp roasted eggplant hummus and 2 tomato slices.

Curried almonds                                               (97 calories)

■ Combine 11 whole almonds with each ¼ tsp olive oil and ¼ tsp curry powder. Bake in 350°F oven for 3 to 5 minutes.

1 cup nectarine slices sprinkled with fresh basil
and cinnamon                                                  (64 calories)

### DINNER

Sweet Potato Ravioli                                          (431 calories)
JUDD W. MOUL, MD (PAGE 175)

Mixed green salad with edamame and beets                      (225 calories)

■ Toss 2 cups mixed salad greens with ½ cup diced, canned beets, ½ cup cooked edamame, ½ cup cucumber slices, ¼ cup grated carrot, 1½ tsp extra-virgin olive oil, and ½ tsp vinegar.

NUTRITION: 1,285 calories, 46 g protein, 161 g carbohydrates, 23 g fiber, 56 g fat, 13 g saturated fat, 1,885 mg sodium

# DAY 22

## BREAKFAST

Mark's Açai Smoothie                                          (176 calories)
ROMINA WANCIER, MD (PAGE 329)

2 slices whole wheat toast each with 1 tsp almond butter
                                                             (219 calories)

## LUNCH

Stir-Fried Kale with Almonds                                 (125 calories)
SHELBY FREEDMAN HARRIS, PsyD  (PAGE 240)

4 oz cooked chicken breast                                   (129 calories)

²⁄₃ cup cooked brown rice                                    (144 calories)

1 medium orange                                              (62 calories)

## DINNER

Pork tenderloin with apricots                                (232 calories)

■ Rub 4 oz pork tenderloin with ¼ Tbsp canola oil, 1 tsp chopped thyme, and ⅛ tsp salt,
Place in a baking dish with 2 fresh apricots (halved). Roast at 425°F for 15 to 20 minutes or
until pork reaches an internal temperature of 145°F. Mix together ½ tsp Dijon mustard,
½ tsp red wine vinegar, and 1 Tbsp apricot fruit spread in a small bowl. Serve as sauce.

Whole wheat couscous with zucchini                           (172 calories)

■ Combine ½ cup chopped zucchini, 1 Tbsp soy sauce, ½ Tbsp white wine, and
1 garlic clove (minced) in a microwave-safe dish. Microwave covered for 1½ to
2 minutes on medium. Stir in ¼ cup dry couscous, ¼ cup water, and 1 tsp extra-virgin
olive oil. Microwave covered on high for 2½ to 3 minutes.

NUTRITION: 1,270 calories, 77 g protein, 170 g carbohydrates, 25 g fiber, 35 g fat,
5 g saturated fat, 1,648 mg sodium

# DAY 23

## BREAKFAST

### Savory egg wedges (198 calories)

▪ Slice 2 peeled hard-cooked eggs into 4 wedges. Spread each wedge with 2 tsp Dijon mustard mixed with $\frac{1}{2}$ tsp dried basil.

### Tangy fruit salad (126 calories)

▪ Toss $\frac{1}{2}$ fresh orange (segmented), $\frac{1}{3}$ small pear (sliced), $\frac{1}{2}$ small apple (chopped), and 6 red grapes (halved) with $\frac{1}{2}$ Tbsp fresh lemon juice, $\frac{1}{8}$ tsp nutmeg, and $\frac{1}{2}$ tsp chopped tarragon.

## LUNCH

### Tomato, cheese, and olive pita (271 calories)

▪ Stuff a $6\frac{1}{2}$" whole wheat pita with 1 plum tomato (sliced), $\frac{1}{2}$ cup cucumber slices, 2 oz 2% cottage cheese, and 4 jumbo black olives (chopped).

### North Woods Bean Soup (235 calories)
TED EPPERLY, MD (PAGE 293)

### 1 medium pear (103 calories)

## DINNER

### Steamed Sole with Creamy Dill Sauce (168 calories)
MARY JANE MINKIN, MD (PAGE 306)

### Warm Greens Sauté (54 calories)
PAMELA YEE, MD (PAGE 261)

### 1 small whole wheat roll with 1 tsp butter (98 calories)

NUTRITION: 1,255 calories, 70 g protein, 187 g carbohydrates, 34 g fiber, 29 g fat, 6 g saturated fat, 2,350 mg sodium

# DAY 24

## BREAKFAST

### Whole grain cereal with fresh fruit (247 calories)

▣ Combine 1 cup crispy rice whole grain cereal with ½ cup 1% milk in a small bowl. Top with ½ cup raspberries, ½ small banana (sliced), and ¼ tsp ground cinnamon.

### 11 almonds (76 calories)

## LUNCH

### Margherita flatbread pizza (395 calories)

▣ Top a 3 oz whole wheat flatbread with 1 tsp extra-virgin olive oil, ¼ tsp minced garlic, 1 oz bite-size fresh mozzarella balls, 1 plum tomato (sliced), 1 Tbsp chopped basil, and 1 tsp grated Parmesan cheese. Bake in a 400°F oven until cheese is melted, 12 to 15 minutes.

## DINNER

### Turkey and Broccoli with Couscous (227 calories)
JENNIFER MIERES, MD (PAGE 215)

### Spiced Spaghetti Squash (165 calories)
FRANCESCA FUSCO, MD (PAGE 132)

### Zesty green beans (207 calories)

▣ Blanch 2 cups sliced green beans for 2 minutes; drain. Heat 1 Tbsp extra-virgin olive oil in a medium skillet and add beans, 1 tsp orange zest, 1 tsp Triple Sec or Cointreau. Add 1 Tbsp low-sodium chicken broth and sauté for 2 to 4 minutes.

NUTRITION: 1,317 calories, 67 g protein, 172 g carbohydrates, 33 g fiber, 46 g fat, 12 g saturated fat, 1,211 mg sodium

# DAY 25

## BREAKFAST

The Sleep Doctor's Smoothie (122 calories)
MICHAEL J. BREUS, PhD (PAGE 231)

11 almonds (76 calories)

## LUNCH

Black bean quesadillas (365 calories)

■ Top two 6" corn tortillas each with ¼ cup canned black beans (rinsed and drained), 1 Tbsp tomato paste, ⅛ tsp ground cumin, ½ tsp chopped cilantro, 1 Tbsp shredded Cheddar cheese, ⅛ cup salsa, ⅛ cup chopped onion, and 1 clove garlic (minced).

## DINNER

Cajun-Style Grilled Shrimp (285 calories)
STEPHEN GULLO, PhD (PAGE 272)

Mango-Avocado Salad (299 calories)
SUZANNE GILBERG-LENZ, MD (PAGE 243)

¾ cup cooked brown rice (162 calories)

NUTRITION: 1,308 calories, 58 g protein, 179 g carbohydrates, 27 g fiber, 44 g total fat, 7 g saturated fat, 1,639 mg sodium

# DAY 26

## BREAKFAST

### Oatmeal with apricots and walnuts · (488 calories)

■ Bring 1 cup soy milk or nonfat milk to a boil in a small saucepan. Stir in ½ cup old-fashioned oats, 4 dried apricot halves (sliced), and 2 Tbsp chopped toasted walnuts; reduce heat to low. Cook, stirring occasionally, about 4 minutes. Remove from heat, cover, let stand 2 to 3 minutes.

## LUNCH

### Tofu and vegetable stir-fry · (363 calories)

■ Heat 2 tsp canola in a large skillet on medium high. Add ½ cup each firm tofu, broccoli florets, and sliced asparagus, Stir-fry until broccoli is tender, about 5 minutes. Add ¼ cup sliced mushrooms, 1 clove garlic (minced), 1 tsp white wine, and ½ tsp soy sauce; stir-fry 2 minutes. Top with 1 tsp sesame seeds and serve with ½ cup cooked brown rice.

## DINNER

### Rigatoni with Turkey and Vegetable Bolognese · (421 calories)
**TRAVIS STORK, MD (PAGE 283)**

NUTRITION: 1,272 calories, 57 g protein, 163 g carbohydrates, 23 g fiber, 46 g fat, 6 g saturated fat, 662 mg sodium

# DAY 27

## BREAKFAST

French toast with apples                                    (295 calories)

■ Whisk 1 egg with $\frac{1}{4}$ cup water, $\frac{1}{4}$ tsp cinnamon, and 1 tsp vanilla extract. Dip 2 slices of whole grain bread in egg and grill. Top with $\frac{1}{2}$ cup sliced apples and 1 Tbsp maple syrup.

1 oz low-fat Cheddar cheese                                  (71 calories)

## LUNCH

Tropical Chickpea Salad in a 6″ whole wheat pita     (260 calories)
P. MURALI DORAISWAMY, MD (PAGE 154)

Yogurt with kiwifruit and almonds                      (252 calories)

■ Place 8 oz plain 2% Greek yogurt, 1 large kiwifruit (sliced), and 1 Tbsp almonds in a small bowl. Stir and drizzle with 1 tsp honey.

## DINNER

Miso-Marinated Chilean Sea Bass                         (125 calories)
KERI PETERSON, MD (PAGE 143)

Sautéed asparagus                                        (93 calories)

■ Sauté 1 cup sliced asparagus with 2 tsp extra-virgin olive oil, 1 garlic clove (minced), 1 tsp fresh lemon juice, $\frac{1}{4}$ tsp freshly ground black pepper, and $\frac{1}{8}$ tsp kosher salt.

Confetti quinoa                                          (98 calories)

■ Cook $\frac{1}{8}$ cup quinoa in $\frac{1}{4}$ cup low-sodium vegetable broth. Mix with $\frac{1}{2}$ cup total of a combination of chopped red bell pepper, corn kernels, chopped onion, chopped carrots, and chopped tomatoes. Sprinkle with $\frac{1}{4}$ tsp chopped parsley.

1 cup orange segments with cinnamon                      (85 calories)

NUTRITION: 1,279 calories, 88 g protein, 175 g carbohydrates, 33 g fiber, 29 g fat, 7 g saturated fat, 1,485 mg sodium

# DAY 28

**MEATLESS DAY**

## BREAKFAST

### Tex-Mex eggs
(362 calories)

▪ Whisk 2 eggs with 2 Tbsp shredded Cheddar cheese, ¼ cup diced tomatoes, and ¼ cup jalapeño. Cook on medium until firm. Drizzle with 1 tsp extra-virgin olive oil. Serve with 1 slice whole wheat toast.

### Melon balls with honey
(123 calories)

▪ Toss 1½ cups melon balls with 1½ tsp honey, ¾ tsp fresh lime juice, and 1 tsp chopped mint.

## LUNCH

### Roasted Beets with arugula and goat cheese
(419 calories)

PAMELA PEEKE, MD (PAGE 193)

▪ Toss 1 serving Roasted Beets with 2 cups arugula, 1 cup orange segments, 2 tsp extra-virgin olive oil, and 1 tsp balsamic vinegar. Top with 1 oz goat cheese and 1½ Tbsp toasted walnuts.

## DINNER

### Spring mix salad
(84 calories)

▪ Toss 2 cups greens with ½ tsp vinegar and 1½ tsp extra-virgin olive oil.

### Vegetarian Soup with Shirataki Noodles
(242 calories)

SUSAN BOWERMAN, MS, RD, CSSD (PAGE 290)

### 2 cups roasted cauliflower
(97 calories)

NUTRITION: 1,257 calories, 58 g protein, 132 g carbohydrates, 34 g fiber, 62 g fat, 14 g saturated fat, 1,526 mg sodium

# DAY 29

## BREAKFAST

### Whole grain cereal with fresh fruit                          (247 calories)

▓ Combine 1 cup wheat bran flakes and ½ cup 1% milk in a small bowl. Top with ½ cup fresh sliced strawberries, ½ small banana (sliced), and ¼ tsp ground cinnamon.

## LUNCH

### Mediterranean bulgur salad                          (497 calories)

▓ Combine 2 cups chopped Romaine lettuce, 1 cup cooked bulgur wheat, 1 oz reduced-fat feta, 10 green grapes (halved), ½ cup fresh pomegranate seeds, and 1 Tbsp roasted sunflower kernels in a medium bowl; set aside. Whisk together 1 Tbsp extra-virgin olive oil, 1 tsp vinegar, 1 tsp each chopped fresh mint and parsley, and ⅛ tsp freshly ground black pepper. Toss salad with dressing.

## DINNER

### Curried Red Lentils                          (188 calories)
PREDIMAN K. SHAH, MD (PAGE 221)

### Sautéed spinach with garlic and lemon                          (164 calories)

▓ Sauté 3 garlic cloves (minced) in 1 Tbsp extra-virgin olive oil. Add 6 cups fresh spinach; sauté until wilted. Season with 2 tsp fresh lemon juice, freshly ground black pepper, and salt.

### ½ cup cooked brown rice                          (108 calories)

### 11 almonds                          (76 calories)

NUTRITION: 1,279 calories, 46 g protein, 182 g carbohydrates, 38 g fiber, 51 g fat, 9 g saturated fat, 1,686 mg sodium

# DAY 30

## BREAKFAST

### Healthy Granola with yogurt and berries (308 calories)
MARIE SAVARD, MD (PAGE 317)

■ Place 8 oz plain 2% Greek yogurt and 1 cup fresh raspberries in a small bowl; sprinkle with 2 Tbsp Healthy Granola.

## LUNCH

### Black Bean Soup with Avocado Crème (268 calories)
MELINA B. JAMPOLIS, MD (PAGE 275)

### 1 oz reduced-fat Monterey Jack cheese (81 calories)

### 1 small apple (77 calories)

## DINNER

### Salmon with Raspberry-Balsamic Glaze (369 calories)
KERI GLASSMAN, MS, RD (PAGE 268)

### Sautéed asparagus (93 calories)

■ Sauté 1 cup sliced asparagus with 2 tsp extra-virgin olive oil, 1 garlic clove (minced), 1 tsp fresh lemon juice, ¼ tsp freshly ground black pepper, and ⅛ tsp kosher salt.

### Confetti quinoa (98 calories)

■ Cook ⅛ cup quinoa in ¼ cup low-sodium vegetable broth. Mix with ½ cup total of a combination of chopped red bell pepper, corn kernels, chopped onion, chopped carrots, and chopped tomatoes. Sprinkle with ¼ tsp chopped fresh parsley.

NUTRITION: 1,295 calories, 79 g protein, 132 g carbohydrates, 30 g fiber, 53 g fat, 12 g saturated fat, 1,806 mg sodium

# SNACK/DESSERT OPTIONS
## (100 Calories or Less)

Latte with nonfat milk
(4 oz coffee, 4 oz nonfat milk) (43 calories)

1 Mixed Berry Ice Pop (46 calories)
MARY LUPO, MD, FAAD (PAGE 134)

1 oz vodka, gin, rum, or whisky (64 calories)

Watermelon salad (70 calories)
▥ Toss ½ cup watermelon chunks with 2 Tbsp reduced-fat feta cheese and 6 cherry tomatoes (halved).

Stuffed dates (76 calories)
▥ Stuff 2 dates each with 1 tsp blue cheese and 1 whole almond.

Strawberries with lime dip (79 calories)
▥ Dip ½ cup whole strawberries in 2 oz light sour cream mixed with ½ Tbsp honey, ½ tsp grated lime peel, and ¾ tsp fresh lime juice.

2 oz 2% cottage cheese
with ½ cup pineapple chunks (89 calories)

4 oz champagne (92 calories)

1 cup air-popped popcorn with 1 tsp grated
Parmesan and 1 Tbsp roasted peanuts (92 calories)

1 Tbsp dried cherries, 3 dried apricot halves, and
1 Tbsp unsalted roasted pistachios (93 calories)

1 Tbsp dried cranberries and 1½ Tbsp
sunflower seed kernels                                    (94 calories)

Fresh mozzarella with tomatoes and olives          (94 calories)

▤ Toss ¾ oz bite-size fresh mozzarella balls with 6 grape tomatoes, 2 pitted kalamata olives, and ⅛ tsp freshly ground black pepper.

3 Tbsp hummus with ¾ cup raw vegetables          (95 calories)

12 oz light beer                                         (96 calories)

4 oz white wine                                          (96 calories)

Curried almonds                                          (97 calories)

▤ Toss 11 whole almonds with ¼ tsp extra-virgin olive oil and ¼ tsp curry powder. Bake on a baking sheet in 350°F oven for 3 to 5 minutes.

1 oz low-fat Cheddar cheese with 14 grapes          (99 calories)

Bean salad                                               (100 calories)

▤ Toss ¼ cup rinsed and drained canned kidney beans with 1 tsp extra-virgin olive oil, 1 tsp vinegar, 1 Tbsp chopped onion, and a pinch of dried rosemary and oregano.

1 hard-cooked egg and 2 rice crackers               (100 calories)

4 oz red wine                                            (100 calories)

Very Veggie Juice                                        (100 calories)
ERIC BRAVERMAN, MD (PAGE 152)

# SNACK/DESSERT OPTIONS
## (101 to 200 Calories or Less)

**Dark Chocolate Bark with Cranberries, Almonds, and Pecans** (121 calories)
ARTHUR AGATSTON, MD (PAGE 207)

**The Sleep Doctor's Smoothie** (122 calories)
MICHAEL J. BREUS, PhD (PAGE 231)

**Chocolate-coated banana** (123 calories)

■ Roll ½ banana in ½ oz melted dark chocolate and 1½ tsp chopped pecans. Freeze.

**Chocolate Flourless Torte** (130 calories)
WILLIAM DAVIS, MD (PAGE 210)

**1½ oz low-fat Cheddar cheese with 17 grapes** (134 calories)

**½ cup 2% fat cottage cheese with ½ cup pineapple chunks** (140 calories)

**Vanilla sundae** (142 calories)

■ Top ¼ cup vanilla ice cream with ½ cup sliced strawberries and 1 Tbsp chopped hazelnuts.

**¼ cup hummus with 1½ cups sliced raw vegetables** (144 calories)

**Latte with nonfat milk (4 oz coffee, 4 oz nonfat milk) and 1 slice whole grain toast with 1 tsp peanut butter** (145 calories)

**Hard-cooked egg with ½ whole wheat English muffin** (146 calories)

**12 oz regular beer** (157 calories)

### Strawberries with lime dip (158 calories)

■ Dip 1 cup whole strawberries in 4 oz light sour cream mixed with 1 Tbsp honey, 1 tsp grated lime peel, and $\frac{1}{2}$ Tbsp fresh lime juice.

### $\frac{1}{2}$ cup steamed edamame and 1 medium plum (160 calories)

### Toasted pita wedges with avocado and lime (161 calories)

■ Slice a 4″ pita into 4 wedges. Brush with $\frac{1}{2}$ tsp olive oil and sprinkle with $\frac{1}{8}$ tsp paprika. Bake at 350°F until browned, for 5 to 7 minutes. Mash $\frac{1}{4}$ medium avocado in a bowl with $\frac{3}{4}$ tsp fresh lime juice, $\frac{1}{8}$ tsp sea salt, and $\frac{1}{8}$ tsp cumin. Use as a dip for pita.

### Mark's Açai Smoothie (176 calories)
ROMINA WANCIER, MD (PAGE 329)

### 2 cups air-popped popcorn with 1 tsp grated Parmesan cheese and 2 Tbsp roasted peanuts (176 calories)

### Fresh mozzarella with tomatoes and olives (178 calories)

■ Toss 1$\frac{1}{2}$ oz bite-size fresh mozzarella balls with 8 grape tomatoes, 4 pitted kalamata olives, and freshly ground black pepper.

### 2 dried figs and 1 Tbsp roasted pumpkin seeds (179 calories)

### 2 mozzarella string cheese sticks and 1 medium apple (180 calories)

### 2 Tbsp dried cherries, 2 dried apricot halves, and 2 Tbsp pistachios (185 calories)

### $\frac{1}{2}$ cup 2% cottage cheese with $\frac{1}{2}$ medium fresh peach and 1$\frac{1}{2}$ Tbsp walnuts (188 calories)

### 2 Tbsp dried cranberries and 3 Tbsp sunflower seeds (189 calories)

### Apple-fennel salad
(190 calories)

▓ Toss 1 small apple, sliced with ½ fennel bulb, thinly sliced, 2 Tbsp vinegar, 1 Tbsp grated Parmesan cheese, and 1 Tbsp chopped walnuts.

### Yogurt with mixed berries and wheat germ
(190 calories)

▓ Mix 6 oz plain 2% Greek yogurt and ½ cup mixed berries. Sprinkle with 1 Tbsp toasted wheat germ.

### Bread and olive oil
(196 calories)

▓ Mix 1 Tbsp extra-virgin olive oil with a pinch of dried rosemary and oregano and freshly ground black pepper. Use as a dip for 1 slice crusty whole wheat bread.

### Cannoli cup
(199 calories)

▓ Mix ½ cup part-skim ricotta cheese with 1 Tbsp raisins and ⅛ tsp ground cinnamon.

### Yogurt with kiwifruit and almonds
(200 calories)

▓ Mix 6 oz plain 2% Greek yogurt with 1 medium kiwifruit (sliced) and 2 tsp almond.

# SNACK/DESSERT OPTIONS
## (Over 200 Calories)

### Refreshing Rhubarb and Strawberry Pudding
(266 calories)

JACOB TEITLEBAUM (PAGE 320)

### ½ oz dark chocolate, 1 Tbsp raisins, and 1 oz almonds
(273 calories)

# CHAPTER 6

# What Doctors Eat

S AY YOU FIND YOURSELF ON A 5-HOUR FLIGHT TO L.A. AND, IN
the course of conversation with your seatmate, discover that he's one of
the nation's leading cardiologists, or a world-famous cancer researcher, or
a nationally recognized obesity expert. Wouldn't you peek to see which
parts of his in-flight meal he ate—and what he left on his plate? Wouldn't you just
love to ask him—based on his extensive knowledge of disease and its causes—what
he eats every day, how he exercises, what supplements he takes? Like a magician, he
knows the secrets, and you'd like nothing more than to look into his hat.

Well, consider your curiosity satisfied. We rounded up many of the country's
top doctors and other health-care professionals and asked them some pretty personal questions about their daily habits and favorite foods.

The result is an incredible collection of advice (including mine, starting on
page 226) from a variety of experts who focus on everything from anti-aging, to
heart health, to holistic medicine. Use these 300-plus stay-healthy tips and 65
delicious recipes to set yourself on a path toward a longer, leaner, healthier life.

# TINA S. ALSTER, MD

*Founding director of the Washington Institute of Dermatologic Laser Surgery; clinical professor at Georgetown University Medical Center in Washington, DC; and creator of the skin-care line Skin Is In.*

D R. ALSTER IS A DERMATOLOGIST WHO LIVES SMART AND SMALL. Her diet is designed around brain-boosting nutrients, such as antioxidants, and small portions. Her workouts mix personal training strength sessions and Zumba classes, but she only works out four times a week total. And she appreciates the little things in her life: "I'm keenly aware of how fortunate I am, working with patients affected by devastating birthmarks and scars. I'm always happy when I'm busy, and being grateful allows me to be a better physician." Now that's genius!

**FEED YOUR FACE.** "I keep a stash of almonds at my desk. They're a great healthy-skin food, helping to reduce puffiness and dark circles around your eyes, and they diminish fine lines, too."

**LIFT WITH LASERS.** "To keep my skin looking young and healthy, I do anything that is noninvasive and doesn't require recovery—who has the time? My favorite annual combination for skin rejuvenation and tightening is Fraxel laser treatment and Ultherapy, a high-intensity, focused ultrasound treatment that lifts the skin on your face, neck, and even arms."

**SWAP THE SUGAR.** "I love sweets, but I knew I needed to cut down on my daily allotment of gumdrops. I replaced the candy with fruit smoothies. They still satisfy my sweet tooth, but without the refined sugar, and they contain beneficial antioxidants."

**KEEP IT CLEAN.** "I'm mindful about where the shellfish I eat comes from so I can avoid those procured from polluted waters. The bodies of clams, mussels, and the like are simple filters that retain all of the environmental toxins they take in—and that's nothing I want to be putting in my own body."

**WAKE UP SMARTER.** "I don't have a TV or computer in my bedroom. Instead, I love to do crossword puzzles in bed before I turn off the lights. This tires out my brain and guarantees me a good night's sleep so I'm refreshed and sharp in the morning."

# APPLE AND ENDIVE SALAD

"THIS SALAD MAKES FOR A QUICK MEAL. WHEN I WANT SOMETHING MORE SUBSTANTIAL, I ADD SALMON, BUT YOU COULD ALSO TOP THIS WITH GRILLED CHICKEN."

—TINA S. ALSTER, MD

Serves 1

1 head Belgian endive

1 small green apple

1 tablespoon extra-virgin olive oil

1 teaspoon balsamic vinegar

1 tablespoon chopped walnuts

1 tablespoon dried cranberries

1 Peel off the leaves of the endive and chop them into bite-size pieces. Core the apple, then chop it into bite-size pieces. Toss the endive and apple pieces in a medium bowl.

2 Drizzle the salad with the oil and vinegar. Sprinkle with the walnuts and cranberries, and add salt and freshly ground black pepper to taste.

NUTRITION PER SERVING: 291 CALORIES • 3 G PROTEIN • 33 G CARBS • 8 G FIBER • 19 G FAT • 3 G SATURATED FAT • 5 MG SODIUM

# KIMBERLY COCKERHAM, MD

*Associate clinical professor at Stanford University School of Medicine; ophthalmologist in private practice in San Joaquin Valley and Silicon Valley, California; and owner of the online organic skin-care store Your Skin Space.*

CROW'S-FEET, PUFFY EYES, AND DROOPY EYELIDS ARE COMMON consequences of aging. However, according to Dr. Cockerham, making a few minor changes to your diet can help your eyes stay young. "People don't always make a connection between their eye health and their lifestyle," she says. For instance, she recommends limiting sodium (either as salt or MSG) and alcohol at dinner to avoid waking up with bags under your eyes in the morning. Eliminating high-acid foods, such as tomatoes, strawberries, and alcohol, and eating more foods that contain omega-3 fatty acids can alleviate dry eye and redness—and it's a better remedy than eye drops, which can lead to rebound redness and irritation. Itchy eyes? Your diet may be too high in iodine (found mostly in table salt, but also in seafood), which can cause a thyroid imbalance that affects your eyes. And, she says, by taking a few more little steps, you can keep the rest of your body healthy, too.

SLEEP FOR SUCCESS. "The simple way to avoid overeating: Get at least 8 hours of sleep. When you're tired, you're more likely to snack, even if you're not hungry."

BRING A LITTLE ORDER TO YOUR LIFE. "When my house or office gets messy or cluttered, my stress level rises. Straightening up calms me down, and seeing everything organized reminds me that I can take charge of my busy life."

**TREAT YOURSELF KINDLY.** "Put down the magnifying mirror—it's bad for your soul! Only you and the 5x mirror can see your enlarged pores and fine lines. This is not the way others see you."

**GIVE "BAD" BEVERAGES THE BOOT.** "I love diet root beer and I don't like water, but I know water is better for me. To ensure that I make good choices, I keep bottled water in my car and office. I'm more likely to drink water when it's around."

**MOVE TO THE MUSIC.** "I love the feeling I get after a good run, but sometimes knowing what's waiting for me at the end isn't enough to get me to lace up my sneakers. That's why I use shuffle on my iPod; being surprised by my favorite songs is the antidote to exercise boredom."

**STAND UP TO FATIGUE.** "To raise my energy while I'm at work, I walk quickly and sit rarely."

**REFRESH YOUR SPF.** "Micronized zinc oxide powder is a fantastic sunblock that can be applied over face serums, creams, or makeup. It's approved for kids and works well on bald spots, ears, and the back of your hands while you drive."

## "THE SIMPLE WAY TO AVOID OVEREATING: GET AT LEAST 8 HOURS OF SLEEP."

# SPICY CHICKEN SANDWICH WITH PICKLED VEGGIES

"SINCE BECOMING A DOCTOR, I'VE LEARNED TO LOVE SALAD AND VEGETABLES AND TO LIMIT MY RED MEAT INTAKE. YOU CAN PAIR THIS SANDWICH WITH A DARK GREEN SALAD FOR A HEALTHY, VEGETABLE- AND PROTEIN-PACKED LUNCH."

—KIMBERLY COCKERHAM, MD

**Serves 4**

1 medium carrot, thinly sliced

5 radishes, trimmed and sliced

4 tablespoons seasoned rice vinegar

1 pound boneless, skinless chicken breasts, thinly sliced

1 tablespoon extra-virgin olive oil

2 cloves garlic, minced

1/4 cup reduced-fat mayonnaise

1/2 teaspoon Sriracha (Thai hot sauce)

1/4 cup fresh cilantro

1/4 cup fresh mint

4 mini French baguettes, preferably whole grain, split

1 Toss the carrot and radishes with 2 tablespoons of the vinegar in a bowl. Let stand, stirring occasionally, for 15 minutes to pickle.

2 Combine the chicken, oil, garlic, and the remaining 2 tablespoons of vinegar in a resealable plastic bag, massaging to coat the chicken. Let stand for 15 minutes. Mix the mayo and Sriracha in a bowl.

3 Preheat the broiler. Remove the chicken from the marinade (discard the marinade) and place it on a baking sheet. Broil 6 inches from the heat, turning, until golden and cooked through, about 8 minutes. Let stand for 5 minutes before slicing.

4 Layer the chicken, spicy mayo, pickled veggies, cilantro, and mint on the baguettes and serve.

NUTRITION PER SERVING: 350 CALORIES • 29 G PROTEIN • 36 G CARBS • 2 G FIBER • 9 G FAT • 2 G SATURATED FAT • 907 MG SODIUM

# FRANCESCA J. FUSCO, MD

*Assistant clinical professor of dermatology and assistant attending physician at the Mount Sinai School of Medicine, assistant attending physician at Beth Israel Medical Center in New York City, and associate dermatologist at the Wexler Dermatology Group.*

WHILE SUNSCREEN AND RETINOL HAVE KEPT DR. FUSCO'S SKIN smooth and blemish-free, she knows that having healthy skin requires more than just applying topical products. "Your skin reflects your general well-being," says Dr. Fusco. That's why she makes sure to meet with a personal trainer at least twice a week and fills her diet with salmon, green tea, and fruits and vegetables rich in carotenoids to stay healthy on the inside and glowing on the outside.

MAINTAIN BALANCE. "My meals are always a combination of carbs, fat, and protein, which leaves me feeling satisfied. I keep healthy snack bars or nuts with me at all times as fillers between meals."

KNOCK IT OUT. "My trainer, a tough football coach, leads me through a 30-minute boxing routine. This workout is a great way to keep fit and relieve stress."

FIND AN ALTERNATIVE. "I have a wicked sweet tooth, and I love Italian bread and bagels. To keep my in cravings in check I allow myself healthy versions, like whole wheat or spelt bread, and a small amount of dark chocolate now and then."

BE MINDFUL OF YOUR MANE. "Your scalp is an extension of the skin on your face, and it requires just as much care and attention. Proper nutrition, hair care, supplements, and products are essential!"

STAY UPBEAT. "I always use positive words. If I don't feel well, that's what I say—never, 'I'm sick.' I also focus on all of the good things I encounter daily."

# SPICED SPAGHETTI SQUASH

"SPAGHETTI SQUASH IS LOW IN CALORIES AND A GOOD SOURCE OF VITAMIN C. I LIKE IT IN PLACE OF PASTA WITH TOMATO SAUCE, BUT THIS RECIPE ENHANCES THE VEGETABLE'S NATURAL SWEETNESS."—FRANCESCA J. FUSCO, MD

**Serves 4**

1 spaghetti squash (about 2½ pounds), halved and seeded

⅓ cup golden raisins

¼ cup orange juice

2 tablespoons butter

1 teaspoon ground cumin

¾ teaspoon ground cinnamon

⅛ teaspoon ground red pepper

1 teaspoon grated orange zest

1 Preheat the oven to 350°F. Place the squash halves, cut sides down, in a 13" × 9" baking dish. Add enough water to come ½ inch up the sides of the squash. Bake until the squash is fork-tender, 40 to 45 minutes.

2 Remove the pan from the oven and let the squash cool for 10 minutes. Scrape the insides of the squash halves with a fork to remove spaghetti-like strands. Transfer the "spaghetti" to a bowl and set aside.

3 Combine the raisins and orange juice in a small saucepan. Bring the juice to a boil, then remove the pan from the heat and let it stand for 10 minutes.

4 Melt the butter in a large skillet over medium heat. Add the cumin, cinnamon, red pepper, and salt to taste. Cook until the spices are fragrant, about 1 minute. Add the squash, raisins, and any remaining juice and cook until hot and well combined, about 1 minute. Remove from the heat, stir in the orange zest, and serve.

NUTRITION PER SERVING: 165 CALORIES • 2 G PROTEIN • 28 G CARBS • 1 G FIBER • 7 G FAT • 4 G SATURATED FAT • 375 MG SODIUM

# MARY LUPO, MD

*Dermatologist and clinical professor of dermatology at Tulane University School of Medicine in New Orleans, director of Tulane's residents' Cosmetic Clinic, and founding director of The Cosmetic Boot Camp.*

WHAT DOES IT REALLY TAKE TO KEEP YOUR BODY YOUNG INSIDE and out? According to Dr. Lupo, it's not all that complicated. "I'm a big advocate of preventive, noninvasive measures to postpone aging," she says. "Stay out of the sun, use topical retinoids (I've been using them since I was in my twenties) minimize sweets, eat right, and try Botox or fillers if you need or want them." Her best anti-aging secret? "Look on the bright side. Being an optimist is in my DNA."

KNOW YOUR DIET TRIGGERS. "I love ice cream, but it's high in sugar and saturated fat. It would be easy for me to go overboard, so I'm careful about how much I have and how often I eat it. And I always give it up for Lent."

BUILD YOUR "D-FENSES." "When you shun the sun like I do, you have to pay attention to your vitamin D status. (Your body makes vitamin D in response to sunlight.) D keeps bones and muscles healthy, and there's some evidence that it protects against certain cancers. I take a supplement every day, and my blood levels are excellent—despite the fact that I never go out in the sun without sun protection."

SAY NO TO SODA. "I stay away from soft drinks—regular and diet. A 12-ounce can of cola has 140 calories—all from the 9 teaspoons of sugar it contains! And even if you choose sugar-free varieties, drinking too many artificially sweetened sodas can increase your odds of metabolic syndrome (which can lead to diabetes and heart disease) by 50 percent."

SIP AWAY WRINKLES. "Blueberries are rich in antioxidants that help keep skin smooth. In the morning, I'll often whip up a smoothie with lots of blueberries, nonfat Greek yogurt, and a little honey."

SPLURGE IN THE MORNING. "When most people go out for breakfast, they like to have something special. So do I, but instead of pancakes or waffles, my favorite is the Chinese breakfast at the Peninsula Hotel. It's a combination of eggs, steamed pork buns, rice, sesame balls stuffed with red bean paste, chicken, and vegetables. It's a bit indulgent, but it's packed with protein and very satisfying."

NOD OFF NATURALLY. "The perfect combination for a good night's sleep is melatonin, lavender, and the sound of the ocean. Melatonin is a hormone that controls sleep and wake cycles, and your body produces more of it in the evenings. As you get older, you make less of it; supplements can help offset that. Lavender is a soothing scent, and a white noise machine that plays ocean waves blocks disruptive noises and helps you relax."

GO TO THE DOGS. "I love taking my two dogs for long walks. It helps me get my exercise in and it keeps me relaxed and busy."

# MIXED BERRY ICE POPS

"THERE ARE MANY WAYS TO ADD MORE ANTIOXIDANT-PACKED BERRIES TO YOUR DIET— AND THIS IS A FUN ONE. UNLIKE THE ICE POPS YOU PROBABLY HAD AS A KID, THESE AREN'T FULL OF SUGAR AND ARTIFICIAL COLOR AND FLAVORINGS."—MARY LUPO, MD

Makes 6

²/₃ cup blueberries

30 small fresh mint leaves

1¹/₃ cups raspberries

1¹/₂ cups seltzer

2 tablespoons light floral honey, such as acacia

2 tablespoons fresh lemon juice

1 Layer the blueberries, mint, and raspberries evenly in 6 ice pop molds.

2 Combine the seltzer, honey, and lemon juice in a 2-cup measuring cup, stirring gently until the honey dissolves. Very slowly pour the mixture over the berries and mint. (Leave about ¹⁄₂ inch of space at the top of each mold to allow for expansion during freezing. Adjust the amount of liquid you use accordingly.) Insert handles or sticks into the molds.

3 Freeze for at least 4 hours before serving.

NUTRITION PER SERVING: 46 CALORIES • <1 G PROTEIN • 12 G CARBS • 2 G FIBER • 0 G FAT • 0 G SATURATED FAT • 0 MG SODIUM

# ADNAN NASIR, MD

*Medical director of dermatology at Wake Research Associates, professor at Duke University, president of the Nanodermatology Society, and author of* Eczema-Free for Life.

ACCORDING TO DR. NASIR, THERE HAVE BEEN TREMENDOUSLY important new discoveries recently for treating skin cancer, including medications that have high success rates and minimal side effects for advanced forms of the disease. And, he says, there's strong evidence that daily habits, like eating certain foods, play a role in the prevention of skin cancer. "In addition to sunscreen, eating a Mediterranean–style diet—one rich in omega-3 fatty acids from fish, monounsaturated fatty acids from olive oil, and antioxidants from red wine, citrus, tomatoes, and other fruits and vegetables—protects your skin," he says. "These are simple steps that can have a powerful impact—and, as with all diseases, prevention is preferable to treatment."

MAKE A FIST. "A healthy portion is the size of your fist. Meals should be about three portions: one for protein and the other two a combination of whole grains, fruits, and vegetables."

STAY ON SCHEDULE. "Having a daily routine has helped me to consistently get a good night's sleep. I try to avoid caffeine after lunch, and I read in bed every night. When I travel, especially to big cities, I bring a pair of foam earplugs. There's something about blocking out unexpected noises and replacing them with the sound of my own breathing and pulse that never fails to lull me to sleep."

**WALK IT OFF.** "Being sedentary for too long has serious medical consequences; it's something I consider to be the biggest epidemic of our time. I recommend walking at least 10,000 steps a day to avoid high blood sugar and cholesterol. Taking a stroll also helps me cope with stressful situations, burning excess energy and allowing me to clear my head. Taking my walk outside has the extra benefit of exposing me to nature, which I find very relaxing."

**WAKE UP TO WORK OUT.** "Physical fitness is so important for maintaining health and preventing disease. I usually exercise early in the morning, before breakfast. It's a huge relief to know that when I get to work and things begin to get busy, my fitness routine is already done for the day."

**SHOWER AT NIGHT.** "During the day, pollutants, pollen, and dirt accumulate on your skin and in your hair. You should rinse them away before you climb into bed. Be mindful of the temperature of the water—really hot showers can irritate and dry your skin."

**SLOW DOWN AND SET GOALS.** "Life is a marathon, not a sprint. Slow down—when you eat, speak, or think. You'll enjoy everything more, and you'll reap more from every experience. And stay curious. I try to learn something new each year. This year, I'm studying Mandarin."

"BEING SEDENTARY FOR TOO LONG HAS SERIOUS MEDICAL CONSEQUENCES; IT'S SOMETHING I CONSIDER TO BE THE BIGGEST EPIDEMIC OF OUR TIME."

# SPINACH, BERRY, AND GOAT CHEESE SALAD

"THIS SALAD IS PACKED WITH CAROTENOIDS, ANTHOCYANINS, AND VITAMIN C, WHICH PROTECT YOUR SKIN AND YOUR ENTIRE BODY. THE TOASTED WALNUTS AND GOAT CHEESE MAKE IT A FILLING MEAL."—ADNAN NASIR, MD

**Serves 2**

1½ tablespoons extra-virgin olive oil

1½ tablespoons red wine vinegar

2 teaspoons blackstrap molasses

Zest of ½ lemon

6 cups baby spinach

1 cup sliced strawberries

½ cup blueberries

¼ teaspoon freshly grated ginger

¼ cup toasted walnut halves

4 ounces goat cheese

1 Whisk together the oil, vinegar, molasses, and lemon zest in a small bowl. Set aside.

2 Place the spinach, strawberries, blueberries, and ginger in a large bowl. Toss gently to combine. Whisk the dressing again if necessary, then pour it over the salad and toss gently to coat the spinach leaves.

3 Divide the salad between 2 plates or bowls. Top each salad with half of the walnuts, 2 ounces of goat cheese, and freshly ground black pepper, and serve.

NUTRITION PER SERVING: 493 CALORIES • 17 G PROTEIN • 28 G CARBS • 7 G FIBER • 37 G FAT • 14 G SATURATED FAT • 413 MG SODIUM

# NICHOLAS PERRICONE, MD

*Board-certified clinical and research dermatologist and author of* The Perricone Prescription, The Wrinkle Cure, *and* Forever Young.

DR. PERRICONE WAS ONE OF THE FIRST EXPERTS TO PROMOTE AN anti-inflammatory diet for healthy skin and a healthy body, and now he is focused on the cutting-edge science of nutrigenomics. "By manipulating different aspects of your diet and lifestyle, you can switch on protective genes and switch off genes that may have a negative effect on your health. Eating anti-inflammatory foods at every meal—fruits, vegetables, nuts, fish, whole grains—is key," he says.

SKIP SUGAR, AVOID WRINKLES. "Steering clear of foods that cause blood sugar spikes—specifically sugar and white-flour products—controls inflammation, which my decades of research show as the single greatest cause of aging. Inflammation leads to wrinkled, sagging skin, heart disease, diabetes, Alzheimer's disease, and some forms of cancer."

COMMUNE WITH NATURE. "Getting out into the fresh air and seeing the magnificent planet that we're lucky to live on renews my spirits every day. Spending time in a park, at the beach, or even just on a tree-lined street is a safe and very enjoyable way of reducing the deadly, aging effects of stress. A walk outside provides benefits that your treadmill cannot."

MIX WEIGHTS WITH YOGA. "I've incorporated yoga poses into my strength-training sessions so I maintain flexibility while building muscle mass."

**STAY HYDRATED.** "Drink at least 6 glasses of pure spring water and a few cups of green tea each day. Fluid helps your body process nutrients, and the tea contains powerful antioxidants that fight aging and disease."

**GET YOUR VITAMIN D NATURALLY.** "Sunshine triggers your body to produce vitamin D, and it's the best source of this vitamin, which helps reduce the risk of osteoporosis and many cancers. I spend 15 minutes a day in the sun while taking a brisk walk or doing some other activity without wearing sunscreen. Don't go overboard, though. Any longer than that increases your risk of skin damage."

# ALMOND-ENCRUSTED WILD SALMON FILLETS ON A BED OF WILTED GREENS

"THIS DISH IS THE PERFECT RECIPE FOR HEALTHY SKIN. IT CONTAINS GOOD FATS, VITAMIN C, VITAMIN E, AND ASTAXANTHIN—THE CAROTENOID THAT GIVES SALMON ITS REDDISH COLOR. ALL OF THESE HELP CONTROL INFLAMMATION."—NICHOLAS PERRICONE, MD

**Serves 2**

1/2 cup chopped almonds

1/4 cup chopped fresh flat-leaf parsley

1 tablespoon grated organic lemon zest

1/4 teaspoon sea salt

1 large egg

2 wild-caught skinless salmon fillets (6 to 8 ounces each)

2 tablespoons extra-virgin olive oil

4 cups mixed organic baby greens, spinach, or watercress

Lemon wedges

1 Mix the almonds, parsley, lemon zest, sea salt, and freshly ground black pepper to taste in a wide, shallow bowl.

2 Beat the egg in another wide, shallow bowl. Pat the salmon dry with a paper towel.

**3** Dip a salmon fillet into the egg, turning to coat. Transfer the fillet to the bowl with the almond mixture, and press firmly so the almonds adhere. Set aside and repeat with the second fillet.

**4** Warm the oil in a large skillet over medium heat. Add the salmon and cook, turning once, until it's opaque in the center, about 5 to 7 minutes.

**5** Arrange 2 cups of greens per plate and place a cooked salmon fillet on top of the greens. Garnish with lemon wedges and serve immediately.

NUTRITION PER SERVING: 553 CALORIES • 44 G PROTEIN • 10 G CARBS • 6 G FIBER • 38 G FAT •
5 G SATURATED FAT • 340 MG SODIUM

# KERI PETERSON, MD

*Internist in private practice in New York City, author of* Sexy Ever After, *and medical advisor for the health-care Web site HealthiNation.com.*

"YOU CAN'T TURN BACK THE CLOCK, BUT YOU CAN AGE *WELL*," says Dr. Peterson. "I think what's most important is having a balanced life—working to live, rather than the other way around. Spending time with friends and family and having hobbies you enjoy are also key."

PAIR CARBS WITH PROTEIN. "I love carbohydrates and would have a difficult time cutting them out altogether. So I try to add protein whenever I indulge in carbs, and I stick to whole grains as much as possible. You should incorporate lean protein into every meal and limit fat intake to healthy fats only."

DRIVE AWAY STRESS. "Hitting golf balls at the driving range is a great way to relieve tension. It gets me out in the fresh air and allows me to get my body moving and clear my head. Plus, it's fun!"

SLEEP BETTER NATURALLY. "I dim the lights well before bedtime to wind down and allow for optimal production of melatonin, which controls your sleep cycle. I turn off the TV and computer and instead read quietly to decrease excessive stimulation. I make sure my bedroom is very dark and cool. Your body temperature naturally drops when you sleep, and you can wake up if you get too warm."

# MISO-MARINATED
# CHILEAN SEA BASS

"I LIKE TO SERVE THIS FISH WITH ASPARAGUS AND QUINOA FOR A MEAL THAT'S A
PERFECT BALANCE OF OMEGA-3 FATS, A VEGGIE, AND A HEALTHY CARB."

—KERI PETERSON, MD

**Serves 4**

2 teaspoons sake

2 teaspoons mirin

2 teaspoons miso paste

¼ cup minced garlic

1 pound Chilean sea bass

1 tablespoon chopped fresh chives

1 Combine the sake, mirin, miso paste, and garlic in a large bowl. Add the fish, and cover and refrigerate for 1 hour.

2 Heat the broiler. Place the fish in an ovenproof glass dish and drizzle with the marinade. Broil the fish 6 inches from the heat until cooked through, 4 to 5 minutes. Slice the fish into 4 equal portions and sprinkle each portion with chives and serve.

NUTRITION PER SERVING: 125 CALORIES • 21 G PROTEIN • 2 G CARBS • 0 G FIBER • 2 G FAT •
<1 G SATURATED FAT • 184 MG SODIUM

# JESSICA WU, MD

*Dermatologist, assistant clinical professor of dermatology at the University of Southern California Keck School of Medicine, author of* Feed Your Face *and the daily e-newsletter* Dr. Jessica Wu Hollywood Dermatologist, *and developer of Dr. Jessica Wu Cosmeceuticals.*

D R. WU IS THE PERFECT PERSON TO PROVE THAT IT'S NEVER TOO late to get healthy. "I was a chubby, clumsy kid and didn't set foot in a gym until I was 30," she says. "In medical school, I lived on white bread and salad and never exercised." Today, she primarily eats an anti-inflammatory diet—lean protein, fruits, and vegetables, with little sugar and refined carbs—and does three cross-training workouts a week. The result? "I am stronger, fitter, and happier with my figure now in my forties than I was in my twenties."

FUEL UP FIRST THING. "It's easy to skip breakfast when you're rushing to get out of the house in the morning (or if you're trying to cut calories), but you'll be starving by midmorning and more likely to overeat at lunch. That leads to wild swings in blood sugar and insulin levels, which can worsen acne breakouts, wrinkles, and rashes."

EXPLORE YOUR SILLY SIDE. "I love taking improv comedy classes. When I'm in class, I'm using brain 'muscles' that I don't usually use in my day-to-day work life. I can be silly and creative and usually end up doubled over in laughter at some point. Improv has taught me to be present in the moment, which helps me forget about what I should have done yesterday and what I need to do tomorrow."

RETHINK YOUR COFFEE HABIT. "Stop drinking frozen, flavored coffee drinks. I'm convinced these are contributing to our obesity and diabetes epidemic. They're packed with sugar and dairy, both of which can aggravate acne and rashes and speed up aging, in addition to their obvious effects on weight and blood sugar. I tell my patients that I'd rather they drink a plain iced green tea and have a square of dark chocolate than have one of these drinks."

MAKE DINING OUT A "DO." "I enjoy going to restaurants with friends, and I often eat out for business. I don't want to always be the one who orders steamed veggies when everyone else is indulging in drinks and appetizers, but I also don't want to pay the price of being bloated or broken out after eating the wrong foods. My strategy is to pre-eat: An hour before an event I'll have a light but satisfying meal like a grilled chicken and spinach salad or, if I'm on the road, two tangerines and a handful of almonds. That way, I'm not starving at the restaurant, and I can make smarter choices."

PUSH YOUR LIMITS. "To keep myself excited and looking forward to each day, I usually have a goal or project I'm working on that's not related to medicine. This past winter I trained for and became certified as a Canadian ski instructor. My next goal is to compete in an open-ocean stand-up paddleboard relay."

PAMPER YOUR SKIN—FROM WITHIN. "Green and yellow vegetables—such as zucchini and yellow squash, or green and yellow peppers—sautéed in extra-virgin olive oil, are excellent healthy skin foods. They help prevent wrinkles, especially crow's-feet around your eyes. If you're going to eat steak or another high-fat food, pair it with a side of these veggies. New research shows that people who eat a diet high in saturated fat but who also eat lots of green and yellow veggies have fewer wrinkles than people who eat a high-fat diet and few greens."

# FISH TACOS AND GUACAMOLE

"BOTH FISH AND GUACAMOLE CONTAIN OMEGA-3 FATTY ACIDS, WHICH ARE ANTI-INFLAMMATORY AND HAVE BEEN SHOWN TO IMPROVE SKIN CONDITIONS LIKE ACNE, ECZEMA, AND PSORIASIS."—JESSICA WU, MD

**Serves 4**

2 large avocados, pitted, peeled, and halved

1 tablespoon fresh lime juice

½ small red onion, minced

2 plum tomatoes, diced

1 tablespoon chopped fresh cilantro

1 clove garlic, minced

2 tablespoons extra-virgin olive oil

¼ cup fresh lemon juice

1 pound Pacific (Alaskan) halibut

4 whole wheat or gluten-free tortillas (8-inch diameter)

1 cup shredded red cabbage

2 plum tomatoes, coarsely chopped

1 Scoop the flesh from each avocado half into a large mixing bowl. Add the lime juice and salt to taste. Mash the avocados to the desired consistency. Stir in the onion, tomatoes, cilantro, and garlic. Refrigerate until ready to serve.

2 Combine the oil, lemon juice, and salt and freshly ground black pepper to taste in a shallow dish. Add the halibut and marinate in the refrigerator for 30 minutes.

3 Prepare a grill at medium heat. Grill the halibut (discard the marinade), turning once, until it is just opaque, 6 to 10 minutes. Cool the halibut slightly and cut into bite-size pieces.

4 Put the tortillas in microwaveable plastic wrap and heat on high for 1 minute to soften. Evenly distribute the halibut on top of the tortillas. Top with the cabbage and tomatoes. Fold the tortillas over and serve with the guacamole.

NUTRITION PER SERVING: 398 CALORIES • 29 G PROTEIN • 32 G CARBS • 8 G FIBER • 21 G FAT • 3 G SATURATED FAT • 247 MG SODIUM

# KENNETH M. YOUNG, DDS

*Cosmetic and restorative dentist and partner in New Concept Dental Solutions in New York City.*

W HEN YOUR BODY IS HEALTHY, YOUR MOUTH IS HEALTHY, SO Dr. Young pays as much attention to diet, exercise, and stress management as he does to brushing and flossing. "I find that avoiding carbohydrates, reducing serving sizes (think smaller dinner plates), and having lots of fresh fruits and vegetables in my diet all help keep me feeling fit," he says. An avid cook, he does, however, know that food has benefits beyond health. "Food is meant to bring pleasure," he says. Fortunately, healthy food can easily be flavorful food, too.

**HIDE THE SALT SHAKER.** "I love salty foods, but I've learned to break the salt habit. I don't keep salty snacks in the house, and I stash the salt shaker in the back of the spice drawer. That way, sprinkling on the salt isn't automatic."

**UNLEASH YOUR CREATIVITY.** "Painting abstracts on large canvases brings an intellectual sense of serenity to me. Painting may not be for everyone, but everyone should have an outlet for expressing themselves. It helps to keep your mind sharp, too—better than Sudoku!"

**STAGE A PLAQUE ATTACK.** "Chewing crunchy fruits or vegetables, such as apples or carrots, can remove plaque from your teeth, and eating cheese protects teeth against tooth decay. Of course, nothing is a substitute for brushing three times a day for 3 minutes and flossing twice a day."

**GARGLE AWAY GERMS.** "Simply gargling with water a few times a day can help fight off colds and alleviate symptoms."

**EXERCISE FOR YOUR BRAIN.** "Taking a brisk 2-mile walk every day and doing pushups and crunches every other day helps me clear my head, keep focused in my work, and feel ready for whatever comes next. The benefits of a daily exercise routine cannot be overestimated."

**SKIP SODA, SMILE PRETTY.** "Soft drinks are bad for your teeth—and not just because of the sugar they contain. Even diet soda is acidic, and acid wears down tooth enamel."

**JUST BREATHE.** "Meditation is so valuable. When we reach a place where we can truly say that we are not stressed, our health improves, our immunity to disease is enhanced, and we can welcome the challenges that life inevitably tosses our way."

**DON'T GET DISCOURAGED.** "It takes work to stay fit, but I know that my exercise routine and the attention I pay to portion control at meals keep me slimmer than I'd ever be otherwise. Remember to use that smaller dinner plate!"

# SCALLOPS WITH LEMON-CILANTRO SAUCE

"EATING SEAFOOD AT LEAST TWICE A WEEK LED ME TO COME UP WITH A FEW DIFFERENT WAYS OF SERVING IT. THESE SCALLOPS GO WELL WITH ORGANIC BROWN JASMINE RICE."—KENNETH M. YOUNG, DDS

Serves 4

¼ cup chopped fresh cilantro

2 tablespoons fresh lemon juice

1 clove garlic, minced

¼ cup extra-virgin olive oil

1½ pounds dry (not packed in liquid) sea scallops, tough muscle removed

1 large lemon, thinly sliced

**1** Combine the cilantro, lemon juice, garlic, and salt and freshly ground black pepper to taste in a small bowl. Whisk in the oil. Set aside.

**2** Coat a grill pan with cooking spray and heat over medium-high heat. Pat the scallops dry with a paper towel, and sprinkle them with salt and freshly ground black pepper. Add the scallops to the grill pan and cook until the scallops are opaque, about 2 to 3 minutes per side. Divide among 4 plates, spoon the reserved sauce over the scallops, and top with lemon slices.

NUTRITION PER SERVING: 285 CALORIES • 29 G PROTEIN • 7 G CARBS
<1 G FIBER • 15 G FAT • 2 G SATURATED FAT • 775 MG SODIUM

# ERIC BRAVERMAN, MD

*Professor of integrative medicine at Weill Cornell Medical College in New York City; author of* Younger (Sexier) You, Younger (Thinner) You Diet, *and* Younger Brain, Sharper Mind; *and the founder of PATH Medical (www.pathmed.com).*

IF YOU'RE STRUGGLING WITH YOUR WEIGHT, IT MAY BE ALL IN YOUR head. "A healthy brain orchestrates all of the organs and systems in your body," says Dr. Braverman. "But an unhealthy, aging brain cannot do its job as well." The brain and body begin to show the effects of age, including weight gain, as early as age 30, unless you take steps to prevent it. "The key to losing weight and keeping it off forever is to literally replenish lost brain cells, rebalance your brain chemistry, and recreate a younger, more vibrant brain." The steps below will help.

**CHALLENGE THE CHEF.** "Restaurants often use a lot of salt in the foods they prepare. I've written my dietary restrictions on a card that I ask the waiter to give to the chef. That way, I can enjoy a meal out and still stick to my diet."

**GO WILD.** "I'm careful when it comes to fish—it has to be wild and mercury-free. To guarantee this, I order fish from VitalChoice.com and have it shipped to me."

**MAKE TIME FOR TEA.** "Tea contains the nutrient L-theanine, which stimulates the alpha brain waves that are associated with a relaxed but alert mental state. Green tea has the added benefit of boosting metabolism and decreasing appetite. I recommend having a cup of tea after every meal. By doing so, I believe you can lose 5 percent more weight. My suggestion would be to have a cup of green tea after breakfast, within 2 hours of waking. Keep your energy going with a cup of flavored black tea at midmorning, follow lunch with a strong cup of oolong tea, and have pep-permint tea after dinner to help aid digestion."

LEVEL YOUR LEPTIN. "Leptin is a hormone that's produced in body fat tissue. It serves as a metabolic signal and controls appetite. The absence of leptin means that you have nothing signaling your brain that you're full, so you eat far more food than you need. Leptin levels change more when food intake decreases than when it increases—so starving yourself slows metabolism and actually leads to weight gain."

SPICE IT UP. "Herbs and spices are terrific sources of antioxidants. Plus, because of their intense flavors, you don't need salt when you use them. Too much sodium leads to high blood pressure and kidney disease. I try to add three herbs and spices to every meal. You get the most flavor from them when you add them to the finished dish or toward the end of the cooking time."

STIMULATE YOUR SLEEP. "I don't have caffeine after 4 p.m. and I take mag-nesium, which helps you relax, at night. I'm also a big advocate of the cranial electri-cal stimulation (CES) device. It's FDA approved to improve sleep and relieve anxiety and depression. It works by electrically stimulating your neurotransmitters to help you relax."

POWER UP WITH POMEGRANATES. "Each of those tiny, ruby-colored seeds contains important amino acids, lipids, minerals such as zinc and copper, plus anti-oxidants. Pomegranates may lower blood pressure, help prevent skin cancer, slow the progression of prostate cancer, and lower cholesterol, among other things. One hundred percent pomegranate juice is the best way to get a red fix, but make sure it is unsweetened."

GET CLEVER WITH CHOLINE. "Breakfast is my favorite meal of the day. Typically, I have a probiotic yogurt with cinnamon, organic maple syrup, and 1 teaspoon of choline powder mixed in, as well as two eggs, which are high in choline. Choline is a B vitamin; your body uses it to produce acetylcholine, which your brain needs to process and recall information quickly."

# VERY VEGGIE JUICE

"I ALWAYS BLEND A BATCH OF THIS ANTIOXIDANT-RICH JUICE IN THE MORNING AND HAVE IT WITH BREAKFAST."—ERIC BRAVERMAN, MD

Serves 2

4 or 5 baby carrots

1 beet, scrubbed and roughly chopped

$\frac{1}{2}$ cup pomegranate juice

2 or 3 ribs celery, roughly chopped

$\frac{1}{2}$ cup watermelon chunks, seeds removed

$\frac{1}{2}$ apple, cored, roughly chopped

1 Add the carrots, beet, and $\frac{1}{4}$ cup of the pomegranate juice to a blender. Blend until smooth.

2 Add the celery, watermelon, apple, and the remaining $\frac{1}{4}$ cup of pomegranate juice to the blender. Blend until smooth.

3 Pour into 2 glasses and serve. If you prefer a thinner consistency, pour the mixture through a fine-mesh sieve over a medium bowl. Use a wooden spoon to push the mixture through the sieve. Discard any pulp that remains.

NUTRITION PER SERVING: 100 CALORIES • 2 G PROTEIN • 25 G CARBS • 4 G FIBER • 0 G FAT • 0 G SATURATED FAT • 90 MG SODIUM

# P. MURALI DORAISWAMY, MD

*Head of the division of biological psychiatry at Duke University and author of* The Alzheimer's Action Plan.

"I WISH RESTAURANTS POSTED WORKOUT TIME EQUIVALENTS instead of calories on their menus," says Dr. Doraiswamy. "People don't realize how easy it is to take in 500 calories—and how hard it is to burn them off." The Duke University neuroscientist keeps his calories in check and his mind in top condition by following a vegetarian diet. "After seeing the plaque-loaded hearts and brains of heavy meat eaters, becoming a vegetarian was a no-brainer!" And that's just one of the smart, healthy moves he made.

**TRAIN YOUR APPETITE.** "There is an old Okinawan saying, *hara hachi bu:* 'Eat until you are 80 percent full.' The people of Okinawa, a Japanese island, are known for their longevity. I especially keep this in mind when I'm at a buffet or business dinner, as I have a tendency to overeat in those circumstances. Using a small plate and taking just one trip through the buffet line helps me stay in control, too."

**GO HEAVY ON THE CURRY.** "Most Indian vegetarian curries are low in saturated fat, which reduces stroke risk. And curcumin, an ingredient in curry, may protect against Alzheimer's disease."

**WORK YOUR BODY AND YOUR BRAIN.** "I play tennis with a tennis pro three times a week. By hitting with someone much better than me, I'm pushing myself to improve. Tennis isn't just a good cardio workout, it's also a brain workout because it involves coordination and strategy."

**KEEP THINGS IN PERSPECTIVE.** "I keep a miniature smiling baby Buddha on my desk. It reminds me that the real source of happiness is inner peace."

**LET YOUR MIND WANDER.** "Your brain uses five to six times more energy during daydreaming than when it's focused on specific tasks. I also read biographies and science books to expose myself to new ideas and help me overcome my biases."

# TROPICAL CHICKPEA SALAD

"THIS IS BASED ON SUNDAL, A COMFORT FOOD FROM MY CHILDHOOD IN INDIA. IT ALSO HAPPENS TO FIGHT THE PLAQUE BUILDUP THAT CAN DAMAGE BLOOD VESSELS IN THE BRAIN."
—P. MURALI DORAISWAMY, MD

**Serves 4**

1 can (15 ounces) chickpeas, rinsed and drained
¼ cup chopped fresh cilantro
1 teaspoon fresh lemon juice
1 teaspoon extra-virgin olive oil
1 small red onion, thinly sliced

½ cup sliced mango
1 teaspoon shredded coconut
1 to 2 green chiles (optional)
1 sprig fresh curry leaves (optional)
¼ teaspoon asafetida (optional)

1 Combine the chickpeas, cilantro, lemon juice, oil, onion, and mango in a medium bowl. Sprinkle with the coconut and freshly ground black pepper.

2 If using the chile peppers, remove and discard the seeds; chop the peppers (wear plastic gloves when handling). Add with the curry leaves and asafetida, if using, and toss to combine. Chill at least 1 hour before serving.

NUTRITION PER SERVING (ABOUT ¾ CUP): 160 CALORIES • 6 G PROTEIN • 30 G CARBS • 5 G FIBER • 3 G FAT • 0 G SATURATED FAT • 320 MG SODIUM

# ALFREDO QUIÑONES-HINOJOSA, MD

*Professor of neurosurgery and oncology, neuroscience, and cellular and molecular medicine at Johns Hopkins University in Baltimore; director of the Brain Tumor Surgery Program at Johns Hopkins Bayview Hospital, the Pituitary Surgery Program, and the Brain Tumor Stem Cell Laboratory at the Johns Hopkins Hospital; and author of* Becoming Dr. Q.

AN UPBEAT OUTLOOK IS THE KEY TO A HEALTHY BODY AND brain, according to Dr. Quiñones-Hinojosa, or Dr. Q, as he's known to his colleagues and patients. "I don't let myself think negatively, and I love to sit quietly and daydream," he says. Those habits have led him to exciting discoveries in his professional life. For example, he's currently studying brain stem cells—cells left behind when you remove a tumor that may regenerate and develop into another tumor. "I'm very optimistic that we can find ways to target these cells and that one day brain cancer will become a disease you can live with," he says. His outlook helps him follow a healthy lifestyle. "It comes down to three simple things: Rest well, eat well, and enjoy life," he says. "I do my best to work out regularly and avoid diet drinks and processed foods. Those things go a long way toward your overall health."

**TUNE IN**. "Pay attention to your body. Eat when you're hungry, rest when your body asks you to, and exercise when your body demands it."

**STAY ENERGIZED**. "Between surgery, seeing patients, and teaching classes, I don't have a lot of time to sit down to eat, but I make sure I have several small, healthy meals throughout the day so I don't get fatigued. A combination of protein and carbs works best."

**BLOCK STRESS EATING**. "My body seems to demand high-calorie foods when

I'm under a lot of pressure. I try to trick it by eating high-fiber foods like popcorn."

**LET YOUR BRAIN VEG OUT.** "Vegetables are packed with antioxidants, which help keep your brain healthy and may protect against cancer. Fruits do, too, but they have more calories. A cup of broccoli has 31 calories, whereas a cup of orange segments has 81. Eat fruit—just don't get all of your antioxidants from it."

**DECIDE TO BE HEALTHY.** "Your past habits don't matter. You can make better choices starting today. I've only been exercising routinely for a year. I do an intense 30-minute workout three times a week, with 1-hour workouts on Saturday and Sunday. Running gives me stamina and stress relief. I recently finished a half-marathon with one of my patients to raise money for brain cancer research."

# CHICKEN TACOS
# WITH CHARRED SALSA

"FRESH SALSA IS PACKED WITH VITAMIN C AND LYCOPENE, BOTH ANTIOXIDANTS, AND ½ CUP COUNTS AS A VEGETABLE SERVING."—ALFREDO QUIÑONES-HINOJOSA, MD

**Serves 4**

4 limes

¼ cup orange juice

¼ cup + 2 tablespoons chopped fresh cilantro

1 tablespoon + 1 teaspoon minced garlic

½ teaspoon ground cumin

4 boneless, skinless chicken breasts (4 ounces each)

8 plum tomatoes

2 jalapeño peppers

⅓ cup chopped scallions

1 large red onion, thinly sliced

6 whole wheat flour tortillas (8-inch diameter)

¾ cup low-fat sour cream

2 cups finely shredded romaine lettuce

*(continued)*

1 Grate the rind from 3 of the limes into a large bowl. Cut the limes in half and squeeze the juice into the bowl. Discard the limes. Stir in the orange juice, $\frac{1}{4}$ cup of the cilantro, 1 tablespoon of the garlic, and the cumin.

2 Pound the chicken breast to an even thickness of $\frac{1}{2}$". Add to the marinade and turn to coat. Cover and refrigerate for at least 1 hour or up to 4 hours, turning at least once while marinating.

3 Set a large cast-iron skillet over high heat. When it's hot, add the tomatoes and peppers. Cover and cook, turning occasionally, until the vegetables are charred on all sides, 8 to 10 minutes. Remove the pan from the heat and let stand, covered, until the vegetables are cool enough to handle.

4 Remove and discard the pepper skins and seeds (wear plastic gloves while handling). Finely mince the peppers and transfer them to a medium bowl. Cut the tomatoes in half crosswise and squeeze each half to remove the seeds. Coarsely chop the tomatoes and add them to the bowl. Juice the remaining lime and add to the tomatoes. Stir in the scallions, the remaining 2 tablespoons cilantro, the remaining 1 teaspoon garlic, and $\frac{1}{8}$ teaspoon of salt.

5 Coat the skillet with cooking spray and place over medium heat. Add the chicken (discard the marinade) and onion. Cook, turning the chicken halfway through, until the chicken is cooked through and onions are softened, about 6 minutes. Cut the chicken into 1-inch slices.

6 Wrap the tortillas in microwaveable plastic wrap and heat on high for 1 minute to soften. Divide the chicken mixture among the tortillas. Top evenly with the salsa, sour cream, and lettuce. Roll to enclose the filling. Slice tacos in half and serve.

NUTRITION PER SERVING (1$\frac{1}{2}$ TACOS): 379 CALORIES • 34 G PROTEIN • 49 G CARBS • 6 G FIBER •
8 G FAT • 3 G SATURATED FAT • 514 MG SODIUM

# MARGARET I. CUOMO, MD

*Diagnostic radiologist specializing in the diagnosis of cancer and AIDS, and author of* A World Without Cancer.

BOTH PERSONALLY AND PROFESSIONALLY, DR. CUOMO HAS SEEN how devastating cancer can be—to those who have it, and to their families. "Our system to study, diagnose, and treat cancer is fatally flawed," she says. "It is not structured to do what we most need: determine how to prevent the disease." Obesity, poor diet, and lack of exercise account for 30 percent of cancer cases, and we could cut cancer incidence in half if we applied what we know right now, says Dr. Cuomo. "We each have the power to improve our overall health and significantly reduce our cancer risk through better nutrition and increased physical activity, and by never smoking, or quitting if we do smoke."

RELISH FOOD! "Think about your meal as you're eating it. Consider the flavor, texture, and aroma of the food. If you pay attention to the quality of your meal and take the time to enjoy it, you're more likely to feel satisfied by it."

EMBRACE YOUR AGE. "Aging is a part of life, and the alternative is unacceptable! By eating healthfully, supplementing our diets with vitamin D, exercising regularly, limiting alcohol consumption, using sunscreen, and getting enough sleep, each of us can feel and look our best at any age. Being young at heart is the key to longevity and to a better quality of life. Try to do something you enjoy each day. Doing something that helps others is important as well. If you feel good about yourself and the life you lead, and you feel like you're contributing, you'll feel better and look better—and you'll be able to communicate that joy for living to those around you."

BE CONSISTENT. "Regardless of how busy I am, I make time for physical activity each day. That might mean walking instead of taking a subway or driving, or walking several flights of stairs rather than taking an elevator. Physical exercise increases my energy level and enhances every part of my life."

IMPOSE A BAN. "I've eliminated added sugar in food, and I've also eliminated artificial sweeteners. High-fructose corn syrup and trans fatty acids are not a part of my diet, so they've been banned from my kitchen, too."

## BEING YOUNG AT HEART IS THE KEY TO LONGEVITY AND TO A BETTER QUALITY OF LIFE."

# VEGGIE SPAGHETTI

"WHEN I PREPARE A MEAL, THE FOCUS IS ON FRESH AND SIMPLE INGREDIENTS, PREFERABLY ORGANIC. THIS DISH IS A DELICIOUS WAY FOR YOU AND YOUR FAMILY TO ENJOY VEGETABLES. YOU CAN VARY THIS RECIPE BY ADDING PESTO INSTEAD OF MARINARA SAUCE, OR YOU CAN SERVE IT JUST WITH OLIVE OIL AND PARMESAN CHEESE TO TASTE."—**MARGARET I. CUOMO, MD**

**Serves 4**

1 large yellow turnip (rutabaga)

4 large carrots

3 yellow squash

3 green squash (zucchini)

1 tablespoon extra-virgin olive oil

1 cup marinara sauce, homemade or low-sodium bottled

¼ cup grated Parmesan cheese (Reggiano Parmigiano is best)

**1** Scrub the turnip, carrots, and squash well with a vegetable brush. Use a vegetable peeler to peel them into long, thin ribbons. Keep the carrot and turnip ribbons separate from the squash ribbons.

**2** Bring a large pot of salted water to a boil over high heat. Add the carrot and turnip ribbons; cook for 2 to 3 minutes. Add the squash ribbons and continue cooking until the vegetables are tender, but not mushy, 2 to 3 minutes more. Drain the vegetables in a colander and rinse with cold water to stop the cooking.

**3** Return the pot to the stove and add the oil. Warm the oil on medium heat. Add the vegetable ribbons and sauté until heated through, 1 or 2 minutes. Add the marinara sauce and toss gently. Cook until heated through, about 2 to 3 minutes. Divide the vegetable ribbons among 4 plates, top with tomato sauce, sprinkle evenly with the cheese, and serve.

NUTRITION PER SERVING: 199 CALORIES • 8 G PROTEIN • 30 G CARBS • 10 G FIBER • 6 G FAT • 2 G SATURATED FAT • 201 MG SODIUM

# ADAM DICKLER, MD

*Radiation oncologist, national expert in the field of radiation treatment for early stage breast cancer, and medical director at the CyberKnife Cancer Institute of Chicago.*

DR. DICKLER WANTS YOU TO THINK ABOUT THE WAYS YOUR lifestyle affects your health before you have to. "It is easy to make changes when you're sick and undergoing treatment, but maintaining those behaviors and continuing them throughout the rest of your life can be extremely challenging," he says. Dr. Dickler has seen amazing progress in the treatment of diseases like cancer—especially with CyberKnife, a noninvasive alternative to surgery that involves the accurate delivery of high-dose radiation to tumors. His personal view, however, continues to be that diet and lifestyle make as big a difference as scientific advances in cancer treatment.

BE PICKY ABOUT FAT. "Saturated fats and trans fats increase your risk of developing cancer, and unsaturated fats can decrease your risk of cancer. Saturated fats are found mostly in animal products like red meat and dairy. Trans fat can be found in many types of junk food, like potato chips and cookies, and in margarine. Foods high in unsaturated fat include olive oil, canola oil, and nuts."

TAKE A STEP BACK. "Staying positive while seeing so many patients with such serious medical conditions can be truly challenging. When I'm feeling a bit down, I try to focus on those who have been cured of their disease or had their pain controlled as a result of their radiation treatment. I also find that being around pets or children is the quickest way to distract myself. Hanging out with my nieces, Ally and Zoe, quickly helps to put my mind at ease and allows me to refocus on what is really important in life."

**GET OUT OF YOUR DIET COMFORT ZONE**. "I tend to be a very finicky eater. My typical diet includes many items others would consider to be quite bland: egg whites, plain tuna and chicken, sashimi, and lean steak. I'm not a fan of salads or dishes with many ingredients. As a result, my challenge has always been incorporating enough leafy vegetables and variety into my diet. It often takes friends and family reminding me to eat some broccoli or lettuce!"

**PILE ON THE BERRIES**. "They're sweet, but low in calories, high in fiber, and rich in antioxidants, which protect cells from the damage that can contribute to cancer. Blueberries are one of my favorite things to eat, and they also contain one of the highest antioxidant levels of any food."

**GET EXERCISE OVER WITH**. "I like to work out—cardio once or twice a week and weights three or four times a week—in the morning before work, because that gives me energy for the rest of the day and allows me to relax at home after work."

**DINE EN CASA**. "The more I eat at home, the more control I have over what I actually consume. I can choose the type of oil I cook my food in and the amount of salt I add. When I do eat out, I ask for a box to take part of my meal home so that I am not eating such a large serving of potentially unhealthy food at one time."

**"BLUEBERRIES CONTAIN ONE OF THE HIGHEST ANTIOXIDANT LEVELS OF ANY FOOD."**

# PEANUT BUTTER-HONEY OATMEAL

"THIS PROTEIN- AND FIBER-PACKED BREAKFAST TAKES JUST ABOUT 5 MINUTES TO
PULL TOGETHER. YOU CAN ALSO USE ALMOND BUTTER."—**ADAM DICKLER**, MD

**Serves 1**

$\frac{1}{2}$ cup old-fashioned oats

$\frac{3}{4}$ cup vanilla-flavored almond milk

2 tablespoons peanut butter

1 teaspoon honey

$\frac{1}{4}$ teaspoon cinnamon

**1** Mix the oats and almond milk together in a microwaveable bowl. Microwave for
1 minute.

**2** Remove the oats from the microwave and stir in the peanut butter, honey, and
cinnamon. Microwave for an additional 30 to 45 seconds and serve.

NUTRITION PER SERVING: 425 CALORIES • 16 G PROTEIN • 48 G CARBS • 7 G FIBER • 21 G FAT •
4 G SATURATED FAT • 250 MG SODIUM

# JOHNATHAN M. LANCASTER, MD, PhD

*Director of the Center for Women's Oncology in Tampa and chair of the department of women's oncology at the Moffitt Cancer Center.*

N HIS PROFESSIONAL LIFE, DR. LANCASTER COMES ACROSS PLENTY OF cutting-edge research. "Right now we're seeing the potential of molecular medicine for combatting ovarian cancer—something that for decades has been all but a dream," he says. This method uses the genetic fingerprint of a woman's own cancer to help doctors make individualized treatment decisions. "That's a massive advance for patients. As a physician and scientist, it's incredibly exciting to be involved in laboratory research that identifies these molecular fingerprints, and it's even more exciting to be able to enroll patients in clinical trials that test them," he says. The diet and lifestyle strategies he follows in his personal life may be easier to understand, but they're no less state-of-the-art.

**DON'T GO IT ALONE.** "You may not realize it, but the behavior of the people around you can determine whether or not you reach your stay-healthy goals. My wife and I jog together. It's a great way to have time to ourselves, to push each other, and to hold each other accountable."

**BREAK UP WITH A BAD HABIT.** "I love chocolate and candies. My wife and children stay on top of me, as does my assistant, to make sure I don't eat them too often. No sweets in my office! If I do indulge, I only have one piece, and I really savor it."

**KEEP IT SIMPLE**. "If you want to stay lean and healthy, you need to practice two things: portion control and eating several servings of vegetables every day."

**BREATHE**. "If I'm having a tough day, I take a moment, no matter where I am, to focus on my breathing. I feel calmer instantly."

**BE SUPPORTIVE**. "In the field of cancer care, we deal with very delicate situations. If someone close to you is diagnosed with a major disease, it's important that you be as thoughtful as you can. Their mental health can have a big impact on their physical health, both positively and negatively."

**CALL YOUR DOC ONCE IN A WHILE!** "I'm vigilant when it comes to having annual physicals, including cancer screenings. I stress prevention and early detection for myself and my patients, and it starts with being my own advocate for good health."

**GRAB A BUNCH**. "Grapes, grape juice, and even red wine are all excellent sources of resveratrol, an antioxidant that helps prevent damage to blood vessels, reduces 'bad' cholesterol, and prevents blood clots."

> "YOU MAY NOT REALIZE IT, BUT THE BEHAVIOR OF THE PEOPLE AROUND YOU CAN DETERMINE WHETHER OR NOT YOU REACH YOUR STAY-HEALTHY GOALS."

# ANNA MARIA TEQUILA-LIME SHRIMP

"I'LL SERVE THIS PROTEIN-RICH DISH WITH WARM, CRUSTY FRENCH BREAD AND A COLD GLASS OF CRISP WHITE WINE, LIKE A *MUSCADET SUR LIE* FROM THE LOIRE VALLEY."
—JOHNATHAN M. LANCASTER, MD, PhD

**Serves 4**

2 tablespoons tequila

2 tablespoons extra-virgin olive oil

2 tablespoons fresh lime juice

1 tablespoon honey

$\frac{1}{4}$ teaspoon ground cumin

1 pound large shrimp, peeled, tails on

1 lime, cut into 4 quarters

**1** Mix the tequila, oil, lime juice, honey, cumin, and salt and pepper to taste in a glass baking dish. Remove and reserve $\frac{1}{4}$ cup of this mixture, and add the shrimp to the rest. Toss to coat, cover with plastic wrap, and refrigerate for 2 hours.

**2** Remove the shrimp from the baking dish and discard the marinade. Heat a grill and grill the shrimp, turning once, until they're pink and cooked through, 3 to 5 minutes.

**3** Reduce the reserved marinade by half in a saucepan over medium heat. Divide the shrimp evenly among 4 plates, drizzle the sauce over the shrimp, and serve with the lime wedges.

NUTRITION PER SERVING: 215 CALORIES • 23 G PROTEIN • 6 G CARBS • 1 FIBER • 9 G FAT • 1 G SATURATED FAT • 169 MG SODIUM

# LARRY LIPSHULTZ, MD

*Professor of urology and chief of the division of male reproductive medicine and surgery at Baylor College of Medicine in Houston.*

DR. LIPSHULTZ DOESN'T LIKE THE WORD "DIET." "I PREFER TO CALL it a 'way of healthy eating,' and it's one of the three pillars of optimal health," he says. The other two are exercise and hormone balance. If you're a man over 50 who is having trouble losing weight despite eating wisely, Dr. Lipshultz suggests seeing your doctor. "A testosterone deficiency could be the cause," he says. Although, he points out, lifestyle strategies do go a long way as well.

**PACK A SNACK.** "Working in a medical office, I'm surrounded by a barrage of bad snack foods. I bring my own fruit, nuts, and protein bars so I'm not tempted."

**LIE (TO YOURSELF) ABOUT YOUR AGE.** "When you're over 50, just talking about your age can be depressing. But I don't accept the premise that getting older equals feeling bad: Chronological aging is inevitable, but physical aging is not. Pick an age when you felt healthy and vigorous, and keep this as the focal point for the way you want to live your life."

**WIND DOWN AFTER WORK.** "Walking my dog is the best stress reliever. We keep a brisk pace, but I also work with him on sitting, heeling, and staying. This forces me to think about what I'm doing in the moment, rather than revisiting the stresses of my workday."

**WORK OUT SMARTER, NOT LONGER.** "I used to spend an hour at the gym

4 days a week. Counting the time it would take for me to get there and get home, that was 1 hour and 45 minutes a day, and I just looked for reasons not to go. Now I combine weight training and cardio into a single session; between strength sets I run, ride the bike, or climb stairs. My workouts are now 30 minutes and I get the same benefits."

**EAT MORE OFTEN**. "I have six small meals a day, which helps me stay full. Portion control is the key to healthy eating. I've noticed an exponential increase in patients who are overweight, and because obesity affects many of the problems I'm treating them for, including erectile dysfunction, impaired testosterone production, and fertility, I talk to them about making better choices."

**SKIP THE STEAK**. "I stopped eating red meat after considering all we know about endocrine disruptors in the environment and the excess hormones in most processed meat—as well as the increase in prostate cancer in men with red meat–rich diets. I don't miss it, and I actually don't feel as well when I do eat it."

## "CHRONOLOGICAL AGING IS INEVITABLE, BUT PHYSICAL AGING IS NOT."

# ROSA'S BREAKFAST PANCAKE

"I'VE EATEN THIS EGG WHITE AND OATMEAL PANCAKE FOR BREAKFAST EVERY DAY FOR THE PAST 10 YEARS. IT'S A GREAT COMBINATION OF CARBOHYDRATES AND PROTEIN, AND IT HAS ENOUGH FIBER TO KEEP ME FEELING FULL UNTIL MY MIDDAY SNACK."
—LARRY LIPSHULTZ, MD

**Makes 1**

    4 egg whites
    1 very ripe banana
  1/2 cup quick-cooking oatmeal
  1/4 teaspoon vanilla extract
    1 tablespoon applesauce
12–15 fresh blueberries, plus extra for garnish

**1** Put the egg whites and banana in a blender, and blend on high for 5 to 10 seconds. Add the oatmeal, vanilla, and applesauce, and blend on high for an additional 5 to 10 seconds.

**2** Coat an 8" nonstick lidded skillet with cooking spray and place over high heat. Pour the banana-oatmeal mixture into the heated skillet and drop the blueberries evenly across the top of the batter. Cover and reduce the heat to low. Cook until the bottom of the pancake is firm and browned, about 3 to 5 minutes.

**3** Flip the pancake, cover the pan, and cook until firm, about 1 to 2 minutes. Transfer to a plate and serve topped with additional blueberries.

NUTRITION PER SERVING: 324 CALORIES • 21 G PROTEIN • 56 G CARBS • 7 G FIBER • 4 G FAT • <1 G SATURATED FAT • 221 MG SODIUM

# JUDD W. MOUL, MD

*Professor of surgery in the division of urologic surgery, and director of the Duke Prostate Center at Duke Cancer Institute at Duke University Medical Center.*

D R. MOUL BELIEVES THAT IF HE HADN'T BECOME A DOCTOR, HE might have been part of the obesity epidemic. "I grew up in a Pennsylvania Dutch area, where most people eat a steady diet of meat and potatoes," he says. "My weaknesses are bread and potatoes, but my medical experience tells me that excess carbs and processed sugars are responsible for weight gain. I don't avoid them entirely, but I do practice portion control." In his urology practice, he has seen an increase in the number of men who are very overweight. "Obesity contributes to cancer growth, and in some cases, it makes prostate cancer difficult, or impossible, to treat. Maintaining a healthy weight is one of the best things you can do for your body."

**TEAM UP.** "My wife, Ellen, and I encourage each other to eat well. We avoid hydrogenated and trans fats and sodium, which can lead to heart disease. Reading food labels is crucial. If something contains hydrogenated fat, we skip it."

**GO FOR THE REAL STUFF.** "Eat butter (in moderation), not margarine. Whole foods, even those that aren't typically considered 'health' foods, are always better for you than processed foods are."

**LEAVE WORK AT WORK.** "I love my job, but having downtime is important for keeping stress in check. My wife and I both try not to bring work stress home. I'm blessed to have married my soul mate, and talking to her helps keep life in balance. And we have two beautiful cats. There's no better stress reliever than pets."

**DEFY AGING**. "I just turned 55, and now is when the real test of following a healthy lifestyle begins. Most of our biggest killers are diseases of aging. Embracing healthy eating and maintaining exercise are more important now than ever."

**TAKE AN ACTIVE VACATION**. "At home, my wife and I walk in the evenings after work. When we go away, we pack comfortable shoes because we do a lot of our sightseeing on our feet."

**GET SCREENED**. "Recently, prostate cancer screening has come under fire, with some saying that it is not accurate and that it leads to too many older men whose cancer is slow growing and may not need treatment being treated. However, the PSA test is pretty accurate, and even more so in young men. Both the American Urological Association and the National Comprehensive Cancer Network recommend that all men have a baseline PSA at age 40. Doing so will help doctors determine a man's future risk."

**"READING FOOD LABELS IS CRUCIAL. IF SOMETHING CONTAINS HYDROGENATED FAT, WE SKIP IT."**

# SWEET POTATO RAVIOLI

"FIBER-RICH SWEET POTATOES ARE VERY FILLING AND THEY ARE AN
EXCELLENT SOURCE OF BETA-CAROTENE."—**JUDD W. MOUL, MD**

*Serves 4*

1 large sweet potato
$\frac{1}{2}$ cup walnut halves,
   toasted and chopped
1 egg yolk
$\frac{1}{2}$ cup grated Parmesan cheese
$\frac{1}{8}$ teaspoon ground nutmeg

24 wonton wrappers
1 tablespoon unsalted butter
2 tablespoons extra-virgin
   olive oil
1 tablespoon chopped fresh sage
1 tablespoon fresh lemon juice

**1** Place the sweet potato in a microwaveable bowl and cook on high power until soft, about 5 minutes. Cool for 5 minutes, then mash until smooth.

**2** Stir in the walnuts, egg yolk, $\frac{1}{4}$ cup of the cheese, nutmeg, and $\frac{1}{8}$ teaspoon of freshly ground black pepper.

**3** Arrange 12 wonton wrappers on a work surface. Drop 2 slightly rounded teaspoons of filling onto the center of each. Wet the edges of the wrapper with a finger dipped in water. Fold one corner of the wrapper diagonally over the filling to form a triangle. Gently press out any air and squeeze the edges to seal. Repeat with the remaining filling and wrappers.

**4** Melt the butter in a small skillet over medium-high heat. Add the oil and sage and cook for 1 minute. Turn the heat to low and add the lemon juice, $\frac{1}{4}$ teaspoon of salt, and $\frac{1}{8}$ teaspoon of freshly ground black pepper. Keep warm.

**5** Bring a large pot of water to a boil. Add the ravioli a few at a time and cook for 2 minutes. Drain, transfer to a large bowl, and toss with the butter mixture. Sprinkle with the remaining $\frac{1}{4}$ cup of cheese.

NUTRITION PER SERVING (6 RAVIOLI): 431 CALORIES • 12 G PROTEIN • 45 G CARBS • 4 G FIBER •
23 G FAT • 6 G SATURATED FAT • 598 MG SODIUM

# LIZ APPLEGATE, PhD

*Director of sports nutrition and professor of nutrition at the University of California, Davis; author of* Eat Smart, Play Hard *and five other books on nutrition and fitness; and columnist for* Runner's World.

D R. APPLEGATE'S NUTRITION 101 COURSE IS ONE OF THE MOST popular classes at UC Davis. She teaches 2,000 students per year and counsels 500-plus student athletes—so she'd better know a lot about healthy eating and walk the talk herself! "I stay lean and fit by doing what I talk about in class—finding a diet and workout routine that works for me and following it regularly," she says. "Big shifts in eating (pigging out and then fasting) or working out feverishly for days and then being a couch potato don't cut it. You have to take care of your one and only body so it lasts a long time!"

**JOIN THE PROBIOTIC REVOLUTION.** "We're beginning to unfold the role of gut bacteria in immune health, intestinal tract function, and weight control. Have kefir [a fermented milk drink that has a tangy taste] every day. Like yogurt, it's high in protein and calcium, but it contains more healthy bacteria than yogurt, and it's low in lactose. Choose one that's fortified with vitamin D."

**GIVE YOUR WORKOUT A JOLT.** "I swim for an hour six mornings a week, and I find that caffeine gets me going. Afterward, I make sure to have both carbs and protein. One of my go-to breakfasts is steel cut oatmeal with 1 cup of plain low-fat kefir; dried tart cherries; a handful of chopped nuts; and sliced banana on top."

**PRIORITIZE PROTEIN.** "Have high-quality protein—low-fat dairy, lean meats

FITNESS

or fish, a hard-cooked egg—at every meal or snack. It keeps you satisfied so you're less likely to reach for sugar or chips."

**SEE THE BIG PICTURE.** "The toughest diet recommendation for me to stick to is having just 5 ounces of wine a day—that's the amount that's considered moderate for women. I like two 5-ounce servings! So I remind myself of the importance of moderation in the overall scheme of my health and well-being."

**KEEP YOUR BODY GUESSING.** "'Mix it up' is my strategy to eating and fitness. I eat different veggies, try different grains, use different cooking methods (and kitchen gadgets), and try different workouts. I think we all benefit from change, newness, and experimentation. No ruts for me!"

> "BIG SHIFTS IN EATING (PIGGING OUT AND THEN FASTING) OR WORKING OUT FEVERISHLY FOR DAYS AND THEN BEING A COUCH POTATO DON'T CUT IT."

# NINE-VEGETABLE SOUP
# WITH BEEF AND BARLEY

"I LOVE A HEARTY SOUP MADE WITH FIVE TO NINE DIFFERENT VEGGIES,
A WHOLE GRAIN, AND A LITTLE BIT OF MEAT. IT'S SO EASY—EVERYTHING IS IN ONE POT!
I CAN MAKE THIS ON A WEEKEND AFTERNOON AND HAVE IT FOR THE WEEK."

—LIZ APPLEGATE, PhD

Serves 8

3 tablespoons cold-pressed
sesame or peanut oil

16 ounces grass-fed beef tenderloin
or sirloin, cut into 1" cubes

2 medium sweet onions, chopped

2 carrots, chopped

2 cups cubed butternut squash

3 ribs celery with leaves, chopped

1 large baking potato, peeled
and chopped

2 small zucchini, chopped

2 cups green beans,
cut into segments

7 cups low-sodium
chicken broth

2 medium tomatoes, chopped

1 bay leaf

8 leaves Swiss chard,
finely shredded

1 cup cooked black or
regular barley

1/4 teaspoon ground nutmeg

**1** Warm the oil over medium-high heat in a large pot. Add the beef and onions and cook until the beef starts to brown and the onions are translucent, 7 to 10 minutes.

**2** Add the carrots, butternut squash, celery, potato, zucchini, and beans. Stir in the broth and tomatoes and bring to a boil. Reduce the heat and add the bay leaf, 1 teaspoon salt, and 1/8 teaspoon freshly ground black pepper. Cover and simmer for 45 minutes.

**3** Discard the bay leaf. Stir in the chard, barley, and nutmeg. Adjust the seasoning, if desired. Simmer for 5 minutes and serve.

NUTRITION PER SERVING (ABOUT 2 CUPS): 251 CALORIES • 19 G PROTEIN • 30 G CARBS • 5 G FIBER •
7 G FAT • 1 G SATURATED FAT • 484 MG SODIUM

# NICHOLAS DINUBILE, MD

*Clinical assistant professor in the department of ortho-paedic surgery at the Hospital of the University of Pennsyl-vania in Philadelphia and author of* FrameWork: Your 7-Step Program for Healthy Muscles, Bones, and Joints *and the* FrameWork Active for Life *book series.*

A LIFELONG INTEREST IN HEALTH, WELLNESS, AND EXERCISE LED Dr. DiNubile to become both an athlete and a physician. His tenure as an orthopedic consultant to the Philadelphia 76ers and the Pennsylvania Ballet, as well as his personal experience and that of his patients, has taught him the impor-tance of what he calls 3-D fitness. "Cardiovascular, strength, and flexibility train-ing should be just the beginning," he explains. "Balance, agility, and hand-eye coordination are also key. Activities like tennis help provide functional 3-D fit-ness in ways that gym workouts alone cannot." Healthy eating is another compo-nent of his fit lifestyle.

SWEETEN YOUR FOOD NATURALLY. "Refined sugar and trans fat cause inflammation that can negatively affect your joints. I do my best to stay away from processed foods and sugar. This isn't always easy when you're busy, skip meals, and are looking for a quick fix until your next healthy meal. One of my go-to options: plain yogurt with strawberries and bananas instead of sugar-filled fruit yogurt."

BUILD MUSCLE. "Strength training is essential for optimal health at all stages of life. In fact, it may actually be more important for women and the elderly than for a pro football lineman. Having muscle protects your frame from injury, improves body function in everyday life and sports, and is important for weight control, as it raises metabolism. Lifting weights doesn't only increase muscle mass, it also strengthens your ligaments, tendons, and bones (which prevents osteoporosis). Make sure you work the front and back muscles of your arms and legs equally, and include core exercises."

FUEL YOUR BODY RIGHT. "Proper pre- and post-workout nutritional choices are a must. After a hard workout or endurance event, you want to get the right blend of carbohydrates and protein into your system within 30 to 60 minutes. Low-fat chocolate milk has been shown to be a good choice for muscle recovery and growth."

NIX THE EXCUSES. "'I don't have time' is the number one reason my patients give for not working out. I tell them that exercise is a great time investment, as it comes back to you in spades. If you exercise regularly, you are more efficient in your everyday activities. You sleep more restfully and require less sleep, so time is actually freed up. And as my good friend Arnold Schwarzenegger has often said: Every minute you exercise is one less hour you'll have to spend at the doctor's office."

GET BACK SAVVY. "Strengthening your core, especially your lumbar extensor muscles and abdominal obliques, protects against back pain. I do a range of spine mobility and stability exercises, including planks and Supermans, an exercise I invented and named many years ago."

PREVENT A SPORTS INJURY. "Warming up before exercise is important—especially as you age. Start slow and build in intensity until you break a sweat—that's how you know your body is ready for action. I love to play tennis, and before a match I do jumping jacks, windmills, stretching, and a variety of mini tennis drills before I start hitting hard."

# CHICKEN PAILLARD WITH TOMATO AND FENNEL

"VEGETABLES AND OLIVE OIL CONTAIN ANTIOXIDANTS AND OTHER COMPOUNDS THAT HELP CONTROL INFLAMMATION, WHICH CAN CAUSE HEART DISEASE, JOINT PROBLEMS, AND OTHER AILMENTS. LEAN PROTEIN, LIKE CHICKEN BREAST OR FISH, HELPS BUILD MUSCLE."

—NICHOLAS DINUBILE, MD

Serves 4

1 cup extra-virgin olive oil

4 (4-ounce) boneless, skinless chicken breasts, pounded flat to about 1/2" thick

4 large garlic cloves, thinly sliced

4 plum tomatoes, diced

2 fennel bulbs, thinly shaved

1 cup sliced button mushrooms

1/3 cup sliced black olives

2 tablespoons capers

4 sprigs fresh thyme

1/4 cup chopped fresh flat-leaf parsley

1 Preheat the oven to 400°F. Line a baking sheet with foil and brush with a little oil.

2 Season the chicken breasts on both sides with salt and freshly ground black pepper, and place them in a single layer on the prepared baking sheet.

3 Toss the garlic, tomatoes, fennel, mushrooms, olives, capers, and thyme in a small bowl. Drizzle in the remaining oil, stir to coat, and season with salt and freshly ground black pepper to taste.

4 Place 1/4 of the vegetable mixture on top of each chicken breast. Bake until the chicken is cooked through, 10 to 12 minutes.

5 Top each chicken breast with fresh parsley and a drizzle of the olive oil that has accumulated on the baking sheet, and serve.

NUTRITION PER SERVING: 457 CALORIES • 28 G PROTEIN • 15 G CARBS • 6 G FIBER • 33 G FAT • 5 G SATURATED FAT • 566 MG SODIUM

# JORDAN D. METZL, MD

*Sports medicine physician at the Hospital for Special Surgery in New York City; author of* The Young Athlete, Sports Medicine in the Pediatric Office, *and* The Athlete's Book of Home Remedies; *and medical columnist for* Triathlete *magazine.*

WHETHER YOU'RE NEW TO EXERCISE OR YOU'RE A MARATHON veteran, Dr. Metzl believes the diet rules are the same. "Eat if you're hungry and try to have natural food, if you can," he says. And having completed 29 marathons and nine Ironman Triathlons himself, he speaks from experience! But can it possibly be that simple? "You don't have to stress about food," he says. "Having a blend of healthy carbs and fats and lean protein at every meal will give you the nutrients you need."

GIVE ME 30. "I exercise at least once a day, every day, and I encourage everyone to do the same. I believe it makes me a better doctor and a better citizen. But exercise doesn't have to take a ton of time; I usually do 30-minute workouts. To avoid injury and make sure I'm having fun, I mix up what I do—swimming, cycling, running, plyometrics, yoga, and Pilates—and I vary the intensity."

PUSH YOURSELF A LITTLE. "Every year I like to choose a goal that I'm somewhat scared of. I also try to do at least one Ironman and one marathon every year. Two of my brothers also compete, and our rivalry pushes me to go faster. I don't want to lose to them—especially Jamie, the younger one!"

COLOR YOURSELF HEALTHY. "My freezer is full of blueberries. For breakfast, I sprinkle a handful on top of Greek yogurt and add some granola and honey.

The antioxidants in the berries help me maintain a strong immune system. That's important because as a sports physician, I'm exposed to a lot of germs—I touch skin, shake hands, and meet new people all day, every day."

FUEL WITH REAL FOOD. "You don't need protein bars and sports drinks—athletes and active people alike can get what they need from whole foods. Before I exercise I have a little carbohydrate, like some fresh fruit. For long workouts, I pack dried fruit and nuts in the pocket of my bike jersey. I mix dried mangoes, apricots, and dates with salted, roasted almonds. The high-fiber dried fruits keep my blood sugar levels up and provide a slow, steady burn; the almonds provide healthy fats and replace the sodium I lose through sweat. Within a half hour after my workout, I have protein, carbs, and a bit of fat—my go-to meal is two egg whites on whole wheat toast and a fruit salad—to help my muscles recover."

RECRUIT YOUR FRIENDS. "When you have a busy life, finding time to exercise can be tough, so I make it a social outing."

"YOU DON'T NEED PROTEIN BARS AND SPORTS DRINKS—ATHLETES AND ACTIVE PEOPLE ALIKE CAN GET WHAT THEY NEED FROM WHOLE FOODS."

# SALMON WITH NOODLES

"SALMON WITH PASTA AND A SIDE OF STEAMED SPINACH WITH LEMON IS MY FAVORITE MEAL."—**JORDAN D. METZL, MD**

Serves 4

4 (4-ounce) skinless wild salmon fillets

8 ounces egg noodles

Zest of 1 lemon

2 tablespoons fresh lemon juice

1 tablespoon butter

1 teaspoon extra-virgin olive oil

1½ teaspoons poppy seeds

**1** Preheat the oven to 450°F and coat a rimmed baking sheet with cooking spray. Season the salmon with ½ teaspoon of salt and ⅛ teaspoon of freshly ground black pepper.

**2** Put the salmon, skin side down, on the baking sheet and bake for 12 to 15 minutes. Meanwhile, cook the egg noodles according to the package directions.

**3** Drain the noodles and toss them with the lemon zest, lemon juice, butter, oil, poppy seeds, and salt and freshly ground black pepper.

**4** Divide the noodles among 4 plates, top them with a salmon fillet, and serve.

NUTRITION PER SERVING: 435 CALORIES • 31 G PROTEIN • 42 G CARBS • 2 G FIBER • 15 G FAT • 4 G SATURATED FAT • 384 MG SODIUM

# DAVID PEARSON, PʜD

*Professor of exercise physiology and associate chair of the School of Physical Education, Sport, and Exercise Science at Ball State University in Muncie, Indiana.*

"LIFE IS MEANT TO BE LIVED IN MOTION," SAYS DR. PEARSON. "IT doesn't matter where you start on your road to fitness because it is a way for you to travel through life." The winner of numerous awards and the author of several articles on sport performance and sport nutrition for scientists and athletes, Dr. Pearson also promotes the power of the right dietary choices to stay fit.

**KEEP FITNESS REAL.** "Too often, the goals we have are too lofty, and we set ourselves up for failure. Remember: This is your time and your body. I've learned to listen to my body on a daily basis and to stop thinking I'm still in my twenties. After years of workouts geared toward competing in power lifting events, I have left the heavy stuff behind. Now I'm most interested in cardiovascular health and maintaining the muscle I currently have; I just don't need that level of muscle mass and strength anymore."

**SIP YOURSELF STRONG.** "I'm a big believer in milk as a great source of protein. But I drink a lot of water, too. Even being just a little dehydrated negatively impacts your muscles and strength."

**PROTECT YOUR JOINTS.** "If I could build a time machine and go back with a lot of glucosamine to my heavy lifting days, I would do it. I helped develop a recovery product called Nutri-Build IV, which is a post-exercise supplement shown to be effective at helping with the growth and repair of muscle."

*(continued on page 190)*

# JUICY TURKEY BURGERS AND BAKED SWEET POTATO FRIES

"MOST OF THE TIME, I'LL CHOOSE A TURKEY BURGER OVER A BEEF ONE. I'VE ALSO SWITCHED TO SWEET POTATO FRIES, BUT I ONLY EAT THEM OCCASIONALLY. ALTHOUGH THEY'RE HIGHER IN ANTIOXIDANTS THAN REGULAR FRIES, THEY'RE STILL FRIES. HOWEVER, IF YOU MAKE 'BAKED' FRIES AT HOME, YOU GET THE CRISPY TEXTURE WITHOUT SO MUCH FAT AND SODIUM."—**DAVID PEARSON, PhD**

**Serves 4**

- ¾ pound ground turkey breast, 90% to 93% lean
- 1 large egg white
- 2⅓ tablespoons finely chopped sweet onion
- 2 medium sweet potatoes, peeled and cut into 12 equal wedges
- 1 tablespoon + 2 teaspoons extra-virgin olive oil
- Pinch of ground red pepper
- 4 whole wheat hamburger buns, toasted

1 Combine the turkey, egg white, onion, ½ teaspoon salt, and ¼ teaspoon freshly ground black pepper in a medium mixing bowl. Using a fork, mix until thoroughly blended. Moisten your hands so the turkey does not stick to them and form the mixture into four 1" thick patties.

2 Preheat the oven to 425°F. Place the sweet potatoes on a rimmed baking sheet. Drizzle with 2 teaspoons of the oil and toss gently to coat. Spread in an even layer and sprinkle with the red pepper, ¼ teaspoon of salt, and freshly ground black pepper to taste. Bake until the fries are lightly browned and crispy, about 15 to 20 minutes.

3 Warm the remaining 1 tablespoon of oil in a heavy, medium-size skillet over medium-high heat. Add the burgers, leaving at least 1 inch between them. Cook until the burgers are browned on the bottom, about 5 minutes. Turn and cook for another 5 minutes, or until the juices run clear. Place the burgers on hamburger buns and serve hot with the fries.

NUTRITION PER SERVING (1 BURGER AND 6 SWEET POTATO FRIES): 333 CALORIES • 22 G PROTEIN • 34 G CARBS • 5 G FIBER • 13 G FAT • 3 G SATURATED FAT • 751 MG SODIUM

**FIND THE KID IN YOU.** "My best stress reliever is swimming, but going to a sports card sale is one of my favorite ways to unwind. I collect a number of sport icons, and spending an hour or two sorting through cards is fun and relaxing. You have to find what makes the little boy—or girl—in you happy."

**GET [A] PHYSICAL.** "It frightens me that so many guys have not had a physical since they played high school sports and were told, 'Turn your head and cough.' As part of your exam, ask that a testosterone test be conducted while they are doing your normal blood work. Low testosterone levels are very common in men and account for numerous conditions, including the possible onset of type 2 diabetes."

**DON'T FALL FOR FADS.** "When it comes to new workout trends, I always ask myself, 'Why should I do this?' before diving in. Even if it is new and exciting, there may be no reason for you to be doing it. Extremely short, painful workouts that result in you throwing up are not badges of honor, nor do they have a long-term positive effect on your health. Finding an exercise routine you can consistently do for 30 minutes 3 days a week is far more beneficial."

**"I DRINK A LOT OF WATER. EVEN BEING JUST A LITTLE DEHYDRATED NEGATIVELY IMPACTS YOUR MUSCLES AND STRENGTH."**

# PAMELA PEEKE, MD

*Internist, assistant professor of medicine and Pew Foundation Scholar in nutrition and metabolism at the University of Maryland in College Park, and author of* Fight Fat After Forty, Body for Life for Women, Fit to Live, *and* The Hunger Fix.

DR. PEEKE IS KNOWN AS "THE DOC WHO WALKS THE TALK"—AND boy does she ever! A triathlete and a marathoner, she swims three times a week, bikes twice a week, lifts weights, and runs with her German shepherd almost every day. However, Dr. Peeke doesn't expect her patients to follow the same demanding workout schedule. "I simply ask them to get up and assume the vertical as much as they can every day," she says. She's found that sharing her enthusiasm for exercise inspires her patients. "An athletic attitude is infectious, and my patients feel more motivated knowing I'm out there slugging it out just the way I'm telling them to," she says. When it comes to healthy eating, she has one main rule: "If it's made *in* a plant, run. If it's made *by* a plant, grab it."

**PLAN AHEAD.** "Plan your weekly meals and snacks the weekend before so that you're always prepared with healthy, whole foods throughout your busy days. If you fail to plan, you plan to fail!"

**COOK YOUR WAY HAPPY.** "My mother cooked well enough to feed five rambunctious kids; however, it was never her passion. I had to learn myself as the years went by, and it's been an adventure. I love the sensuousness—the smell, colors, and feel—of working with whole foods. As an expert in nutrition, I always want to keep learning and experimenting with food."

HANG OUT WITH MOTHER NATURE. "I look for any excuse to smell fresh air and be distracted by the serenading of birds as I walk, run, bike, hike, or swim. Being in nature is a humbling yet rejuvenating way to put your life's stresses into perspective."

VEG A LITTLE. "Every once in a while I'll do some mindless TV watching on my iPad and just allow my brain to enjoy the ride and the rest."

POWER SNACK. "My favorite snacks are carrots and hummus, peanut or almond butter on a sliced apple, cottage cheese and blueberries or blackberries, and 2 to 3 ounces of poultry or salmon on a whole wheat Wasa cracker. These are all combinations of protein and fiber, which take a long time to break down, keeping your stomach full and telling your brain that you're satiated."

GIVE YOURSELF A BREAK. "It takes time to integrate new habits, so be patient with yourself. Don't give up too easily. I often write my patients a prescription for the "Peeke Performance Patience Pill" and order them to take it three times a day!"

FUEL YOUR FIRE. "Peanut butter is my go-to food before a workout. It really sticks to your ribs. I eat it in a variety of ways, from right out of the jar to spread on a whole wheat Wasa cracker, apple slices, or a banana. After a workout, there's a golden window of time (about an hour) during which you need to replenish your glucose levels. Try eating citrus fruits, bananas, nuts, or a smoothie made with whey protein, skim milk or water, and fruit."

GO OUT FOR RECESS. "Adults need this active break, too—we don't play enough. Play in the kitchen, play with your kids, create fun and adventure. Don't turn living a healthy lifestyle into a grind."

# ROASTED BEETS

"I LOVE BEETS. THEY'RE SWEET, LOADED WITH FIBER, AND RICH IN ANTIOXIDANTS. THEY'VE EVEN BEEN FOUND TO IMPROVE ATHLETIC PERFORMANCE! AND DON'T TOSS THE BEET GREENS WHEN THEY'RE NOT USED IN A RECIPE; THEY'RE RICH IN CALCIUM AND DELICIOUS SAUTÉED WITH GARLIC IN OLIVE OIL."—**PAMELA PEEKE**, MD

**Serves 4**

2 pounds small fresh beets, skin on, scrubbed and greens trimmed

2 teaspoons extra-virgin olive oil

1 Preheat the oven to 400°F. Place a piece of foil inside a 9″ × 9″ baking dish. Add the beets to the baking dish and fold the foil over the beets. Roast until tender, about 45 minutes.

2 Let the beets cool. When they're cool enough to handle, remove the skins and quarter the beets. Warm the oil in a large skillet over medium-high heat. Add the beets and cook, stirring frequently, to reheat. Season with $\frac{1}{4}$ teaspoon of salt and $\frac{1}{4}$ teaspoon of freshly ground black pepper. Serve immediately or refrigerate for use in a salad.

NUTRITION PER SERVING: 86 CALORIES • 2 G PROTEIN • 15 G CARBS • 4 G FIBER • 3 G FAT • 0 G SATURATED FAT • 409 MG SODIUM

# WAYNE WESTCOTT, PнD

*Fitness research director at Quincy College in Quincy, Massachusetts, strength-training consultant for the American Council on Exercise and the National Sports Performance Association, and author of* Get Stronger, Feel Younger *and* Strength Training Past 50.

D R. WESTCOTT LIKES BIG PORTIONS. "MY BODY WANTS LOTS OF food, so I satisfy my appetite by having large servings of fruits and vegetables at meals," he says. "They're rich in nutrients, and the fiber and water they contain helps fill me up for very few calories." Consider this: For the same 100 calories in a 1-ounce slice of Cheddar cheese, you could have a large grapefruit, 3 plums, 5 medium tomatoes, or 2 cups of carrots. "I avoid calorie-dense processed foods and high-fat foods—such as whole-milk dairy and red meat—both for my overall health and so I can eat as much as I want."

**REVIVE YOUR MUSCLES.** "My research and other studies show that having extra protein after a strength-training workout boosts muscle development and fat loss. Liquid forms of protein seem to be absorbed best, so I drink a protein shake every time I lift weights."

**PUMP UP THE PROTEIN.** "After age 30, women need more protein to build and maintain muscle, and it's important for them to get a concentrated dose at a single meal—at least 20 grams. That's about what you'll find in a $3^{1}/_{2}$-ounce chicken breast or salmon fillet, 2 eggs and 2 slices of whole wheat toast spread with 1 tablespoon of peanut butter, 1 cup of plain 0% Greek yogurt, or 1 cup of lentils mixed with $^{1}/_{2}$ cup of cooked brown rice."

CUT 200 CALORIES. "For many people, the difference between a healthy weight and an unhealthy one comes down to the little things. You don't have to starve yourself. If you ate 200 fewer calories every day, you'd lose about 2 pounds in a month. Ramp up your calorie burn by the same amount at the same time, and you'll drop about a pound a week. A combination of diet and exercise is best, because when you lose weight through calorie restriction alone, 25 to 50 percent of it is muscle and that muscle loss slows your metabolism."

ADD SOME WEIGHT. "When we put people on a 12-week strength-training program, they lost 4 pounds of fat and gained 3 pounds of muscle, on average. Although the net loss was just 1 pound, from a body composition perspective, they were less 'fat.' They looked leaner, and because muscle burns more calories than fat, they boosted their metabolism."

KEEP IT SHORT. "A 20-minute focused weight-training session can be just as effective as 60 to 90 minutes of unfocused training. I train in a time-efficient manner, typically doing circuit strength training and interval endurance training."

REST! "Your body rebuilds itself during sleep, so getting enough is important if you want to get fitter and stronger. But taking a day off between strength-training workouts is also key, because muscle growth takes place during the recovery phase."

## "I SATISFY MY APPETITE BY HAVING LARGE SERVINGS OF FRUITS AND VEGETABLES AT MEALS."

# ASIAN CHICKEN AND WALNUT SALAD

"I LOVE A LARGE TOSSED SALAD WITH DARK GREENS, FRUIT, NUTS, AND CHICKEN OR TUNA. IT'S A GOOD MIX OF FIBER AND PROTEIN IN A SINGLE TASTY BOWL."

—WAYNE WESTCOTT, PhD

**Serves 4**

¼ cup wasabi-flavored mayonnaise

¼ cup low-fat plain yogurt

4 cups chopped cooked chicken breast

2 ribs celery, sliced

2 carrots, cut into strips

6 cups Asian salad greens

1 cup seedless red grapes, halved

½ cup toasted walnuts

1 Stir together the mayonnaise and yogurt in a medium bowl. Add salt and freshly ground black pepper to taste.

2 Add the chicken, celery, and carrots and toss to combine.

3 Arrange the greens on 4 plates. Top with the chicken salad, grapes, and walnuts.

NUTRITION PER SERVING: 453 CALORIES • 44 G PROTEIN • 16 G CARBS • 3 G FIBER • 25 G FAT • 3 G SATURATED FAT • 941 MG SODIUM

# VONDA WRIGHT, MD

*Orthopedic surgeon specializing in sports medicine at the Center for Sports Medicine at the University of Pittsburgh Medical Center, member of Dr. Oz's advisory board, and author of* Fitness After 40 *and* Dr. Wright's Guide to THRIVE.

D R. WRIGHT LEARNED THE IMPORTANCE OF FOOD BALANCE during her surgical training. "After 7 years of residency and fellowship, when you don't know when your next meal is coming, I got into the habit of eating every time food was available, whether I was hungry or not," she says. Although not everyone has to deal with the rigors of performing 12-hour operations, many people get too busy to eat during the day and end up skipping meals and overdoing it at night. "Feast-or-famine mode isn't good for your health or your weight," says Dr. Wright. "To break out of it, keep food simple. That doesn't mean eating from a package, though; whole, unprocessed food can go quickly from your fridge to your plate."

**MAINTAIN YOUR FOCUS.** "I like to work with no distractions for a few hours so I can tangibly measure my progress. That way, I can relax and enjoy family time and playing without worrying about the things that still need to get done."

**CREATE A VISION.** "You have to strategically plan your health in the same way that you plan your career, education, and vacations. Good health is no accident! See yourself healthy, and plot out the steps that will get you there."

**CONFUSE YOUR MUSCLES.** "After only a couple weeks of a new regimen, your muscles will be stronger and the routine will become easier. As a sports doc, I'm an advocate of total body cross-training. Although I studied classical ballet until I was 20 and still love a great barre workout or salsa night, I am also a runner from a family of runners, and I have raced, often with my father, for as long as I can remember."

BELIEVE THAT YOU ARE AN ATHLETE. "There is never an age, skill, or activity level that prevents you from taking control of your health via exercise and smart nutrition. Our bodies are amazing adaptable machines and will respond to the positive stress of mobility to build a strong body and brain. Six years ago I founded an initiative called PRIMA (Performance and Research Initiative for Masters Athletes), specifically focused on athletes and active people over 40. People in their late thirties, forties, and beyond are remaking the rules of play and winning races and competitions all the time."

PROTECT YOUR SLEEP TIME. "When I was a surgical resident, I was on call every third night and usually stayed up all night and into the next day. This stress altered my thinking, my weight, and my perspective on life. So now I really cherish those 7 solid hours! I'm a morning person, so I get up between 4 a.m. and 6 a.m. and I'm in bed by 9 p.m., when my daughter goes to sleep."

BE A CHRONIC EXERCISER. "Exercise is literally the fountain of youth, right down to our cells. Old muscle stem cells will begin to behave like young cells again after just 2 weeks of exercise! A study I recently published demonstrated that chronic high-level exercise was capable of preserving the muscle mass, strength, and function of active agers even into their eighties."

# GRILLED MIXED VEGETABLES

"GRILLED VEGETABLES WITH GRILLED FISH AND A WHOLE GRAIN
IS ONE OF MY FAVORITE WEEKNIGHT MEALS. IT'S FAST AND EASY; I SAVE THE
COMPLICATED RECIPES FOR THE WEEKENDS."—VONDA WRIGHT, MD

Serves 4

1 red bell pepper, quartered

1 yellow squash, sliced lengthwise
    into ½"-thick pieces

1 zucchini, sliced lengthwise
    into ½"-thick pieces

1 Japanese eggplant, sliced
    lengthwise into ½"-thick pieces

4 cremini mushrooms

4 large asparagus spears

3 scallions

2 tablespoons extra-virgin
    olive oil

1 tablespoon balsamic vinegar

1 garlic clove, minced

1 tablespoon chopped
    fresh flat-leaf parsley

1 tablespoon chopped
    fresh basil

1 teaspoon finely chopped
    fresh rosemary

1 Place a grill pan over medium-high heat or prepare the grill for medium-high heat. Brush the bell pepper, squash, zucchini, eggplant, mushrooms, asparagus, and scallions lightly with some of the oil.

2 Place the vegetables in a single layer on the grill, working in batches if necessary. Cook until they're tender and lightly charred all over, about 8 to 10 minutes for the pepper; 7 minutes for the squash, zucchini, eggplant, and mushrooms; and 4 minutes for the asparagus and scallions.

3 Whisk together the vinegar, garlic, parsley, basil, rosemary, the remaining oil, and salt to taste. Drizzle the herb mixture over the vegetables. Season to taste with freshly ground black pepper. Serve warm or at room temperature.

NUTRITION PER SERVING: 111 CALORIES • 3 G PROTEIN • 10 G CARBS • 4 G FIBER • 7 G FAT •
1 G SATURATED FAT • 157 MG SODIUM

# WHAT DOCTORS TAKE

**WHEN IT COMES TO DIETARY SUPPLEMENTS**—vitamins, minerals, herbs and the like—our experts all agree: food comes first. Pills can't compensate for a poor diet and they simply don't contain the intricate combination of micronutrients and fiber that food does. That said, some of our pros do think there's a place for supplements.

"I have a whole regimen of supplements that combat aging and inflammation. I use them myself, and I recommend them to my patients. Among these are **vitamin D**, **fish oil**, **choline powder**, and **curcumin**."
—ERIC BRAVERMAN, MD

"Find a source of **omega-3s** that works for you. If you don't like fish, you can take a **fish and flax oil** pill; the combination helps prevent that fishy-burp aftertaste."
—KIMBERLY COCKERHAM, MD

"**Vitamin D** is a supplement that nearly everyone needs. Have your vitamin D level (25(OH)D) assessed at least once a year through a simple blood test ordered by a doctor. The amount of vitamin D you take should be enough to bring your blood levels to 40 to 60 ng/ml. Vitamin D and **calcium** work together to promote bone health and reduce cancer risk. Vitamin D also boosts your immune system and helps prevent colds and infections."
—MARGARET I. CUOMO, MD

"If there is one supplement that holds the key to multiple facets of health, it's **vitamin D**. Getting 1,200 milligrams of a combination of **EPA and DHA omega-3** fatty acids from fish oil is also important if you have heart disease, high cholesterol, or high triglycerides. I never use the prescription form because the much less expensive over-the-counter form is equal or superior."—WILLIAM DAVIS, MD

"Some research questions the effectiveness of **glucosamine** and **chondrotin**, but I still think there's strong evidence that a high-quality brand can help reduce joint pain and inflammation without some of the side effects of NSAIDs. Look for a supplement certified by NSF International (Certified for Sport) or United States Pharmacopeia."
—NICHOLAS DINUBILE, MD

"Every day I take a **multivitamin**, **calcium**, **vitamin D**, and **fish oil**. If you don't eat a variety of foods and lots of fruits and veggies on a daily basis, a multi helps fill in the gaps. I also recommend calcium to all women over the age of 30 and vitamin D if their levels are low. (See your doctor for a blood test to determine your levels and establish the proper dosage to get you back on track.) Fish oil is great because it has anti-oxidant and cholesterol-lowering properties."
—KERI PETERSON, MD

"I take 1,000 milligrams of **vitamin C** and **fish oil** every day because there appears to be some evidence of a health benefit. However, today's pill of the moment is tomorrow's reject: There is no magic pill."
—JOHN A. ELEFTERIADES, MD

"Evidence shows that **chasteberry** is helpful for PMS and midlife menstrual-associated changes. I take that along with a **woman's multi**, **vitamin D**, **fish oil**, and **magnesium**."
—SUZANNE GILBERG-LENZ, MD

"As a woman with a strong family history of osteoporosis, I keep up with **calcium**. I also take **vitamin D**. Like so many other Americans, I was surprised to find that my vitamin D levels were low. Vitamin D is an all-around excellent anti-oxidant, and it may help prevent cancer, as well. To keep my heart strong, I take **CoQ10** and **fish oil**. And I add in a **biotin** supplement for healthy hair and nails."—PAMELA PEEKE, MD

"I make sure I get enough of **vitamins B₁₂** and **D**, and **calcium**. I also take a high-quality **multivitamin**, every day. And **biotin** is useful to keep nails and hair in good shape."
—MARYANNE LEGATO, MD

"I take a **daily multivitamin** because it won't hurt, and there's a slight chance it might help. I also take **magnesium**, which is an important nutrient that's underdosed in multivitamins and relatively scarce in our diets. **Vitamin D₃** is another nutrient that we're not getting enough of. Finally, I take **fish oil** because I don't eat fatty fish as often as I'd like to."
—ALAN ARAGON, MS

"Although I recommend a healthy diet, I think that the amount of stress and toxins in our environment make supplements essential. The basic ones I recommend and take daily myself are a good **multivitamin**, **fish oil**, **vitamin D**, and a **probiotic**."—FRANK LIPMAN, MD

"I love to run, but I have bad knees, so I take **glucosamine** daily. I take 1,000 IU of **vitamin D**, 500 milligrams of slow-release **niacin**, and some **fish oil**. I drink about a quart of milk a day, so I don't need to take calcium, but I recommend 1,200 milligrams of **calcium** a day for my patients who don't consume dairy products."
—MARY JANE MINKIN, MD

"If someone wants to take a **multivitamin**, I recommend a **children's formula** because less is more based on the evidence. I don't like to use supplements unless they are for a medical condition or for someone at higher risk of a specific medical condition."
—MARK A. MOYAD, MD

"There's good evidence to support the benefits of **fish oil** for cardiovascular and brain health. It may also have some benefit for skin diseases like psoriasis, and possibly even reduces the risk of certain cancers."—ADNAN NASIR, MD

"As a thin woman, I'm at higher risk for osteoporosis, so I take **calcium** and **vitamin D** supplements to maintain bone strength. **Probiotics**, or beneficial bacteria, are a fascinating new development in gastro-enterology. I recommend them for many of my patients who complain of bloating, bowel irregularity, or abdominal pain. I use them myself if I need to take antibiotics and when I'm traveling."—ROSHINI RAJ, MD

"All of the supplements I take, I also recommend to my patients: **Pycnogenol** (pine bark extract that's a powerful antioxidant), **vitamin D**, **digestive enzymes** and **probiotics**, cocoa (an excellent source of flavonoids), and **chia seed**."
—STEVEN LAMM, MD

"I'm still convinced that a **multivitamin** provides a safety net for things potentially missing from my diet. Men and postmenopausal women should take one without iron. Getting 1,000 to 2,000 IU of **vitamin D** a day is a good move, too. And your brain and heart need the **omega-3** fatty acids that are abundant in cold-water fish, but our diets often lack them, so I take two capsules of **DHA/EPA** daily."—MARIE SAVARD, MD

# ARTHUR AGATSTON, MD

*Cardiologist and medical director of wellness and prevention for Baptist Health South Florida, and author of* The South Beach Diet *series.*

THE AUTHOR OF THE BESTSELLING *SOUTH BEACH DIET* SERIES HAS A confession: "When it comes to sweets, I have the least willpower of anyone in my family," says Dr. Agatston. "My wife helps me stick to the South Beach Diet Three-Bite Rule: Three bites of any dessert satisfies you without triggering your desire to keep eating." And he notes that sticking to his signature approach—good carbs, good fats, lean protein—has meant he craves sugary or starchy foods far less often than he used to.

**EAT BREAKFAST EVERY DAY.** "People who skip the morning meal tend to have higher cholesterol and insulin levels and a larger waist circumference—all risk factors for heart disease."

**KNOW WHAT THE ANIMAL YOU'RE EATING ATE.** "An animal that was grass-fed in pastures is leaner and its meat has more 'good' omega-3 fats and less 'bad' saturated fat than one that was fed grain, kept in a pen, and given antibiotics and hormones."

**GO GLUTEN-FREE FOR A MONTH.** "As healthy as whole grains are, I realized not long ago that certain ones might be problematic for some people—including me—who can't tolerate gluten, the protein found primarily in wheat and barley. When I eat fewer foods containing gluten, I have more energy in general and less joint pain after exercise. Giving up gluten is not for everyone, but I advise many of my patients to try it for a month and see how they feel. Quite a few report that their gastrointestinal problems, skin rashes, and other health issues resolve."

GO TO BED! "My patients know that eating right and exercising are critical to good health, but many think of sleep as a luxury, not a necessity. Insufficient or poor sleep taxes your body and raises your risk of diabetes, heart disease, depression, and weight gain. You don't metabolize food properly and have less willpower to stave off cravings for sugary and starchy carbohydrates."

MIX UP YOUR DIET—AND YOUR WORKOUT. "There are literally thousands of healthful micronutrients in fruits, vegetables, whole grains, and legumes that protect not just your heart but your entire body. They interact in complicated ways that we have been unable to reproduce in a pill. Similarly the more varied your exercise routine, the better off you'll be. Focus on core strengthening and resistance and interval aerobic training, switching them up on different days."

SNACK ON NUTS. "Regular strategic snacking is one of the best ways to promote and sustain weight loss. A protein- and fiber-rich snack keeps you energized, gives your body a steady stream of good nutrients to digest (which keeps your metabolism revved), and leaves you less vulnerable to blood sugar swings. Almonds, my favorite, have vitamin E, protein, and more fiber than any other nut."

## "THREE BITES OF ANY DESSERT SATISFIES YOU WITHOUT TRIGGERING YOUR DESIRE TO KEEP EATING."

# DARK CHOCOLATE BARK WITH CRANBERRIES, ALMONDS, AND PECANS

"I'M A CONFIRMED CHOCOHOLIC, AND THIS TREAT PROVIDES ANTIOXIDANTS (IN THE CRANBERRIES AND CHOCOLATE) AND GOOD UNSATURATED FATS (IN THE PECANS AND ALMONDS). EATING DARK CHOCOLATE IN MODERATION LOWERS BLOOD PRESSURE AND INFLAMMATION IN YOUR BODY."—**ARTHUR AGATSTON, MD**

**Serves 15**

6 tablespoons coarsely chopped almonds

6 tablespoons coarsely chopped pecans

6 tablespoons coarsely chopped dried cranberries

9 ounces bittersweet chocolate chips

**1** Line a baking sheet with foil. Combine the almonds, pecans, and cranberries in a small bowl.

**2** Melt the chocolate chips in a medium bowl set over hot, but not boiling, water. Stir until the chocolate is smooth. Remove it from the heat and stir in the cranberry-nut mixture.

**3** Spread the chocolate mixture evenly over the prepared baking sheet. Refrigerate for 10 minutes, or until firm but not brittle. Cut or break the bark into about 30 jagged pieces and serve, or store in an airtight container in the refrigerator for up to 2 weeks.

NUTRITION PER SERVING (2 PIECES): 121 CALORIES • 2 G PROTEIN • 15 G CARBS • 1 G FIBER • 8 G FAT • 2 G SATURATED FAT • 0 MG SODIUM

# WILLIAM DAVIS, MD

*Cardiologist in Wisconsin, author of* Wheat Belly, *and founder of the online program for heart health Track Your Plaque (www.trackyourplaque.com).*

FOR DR. DAVIS, THERE IS NO DIETARY CHANGE YOU CAN MAKE THAT can help your health more than eliminating wheat. "Modern wheat is the 2-foot-tall plant created by geneticists in the 1970s to increase yield, and it has a multitude of peculiar effects on humans who consume it." One of the consequences: excess flab. "Wheat contains a powerful appetite stimulant that causes you to consume far more calories than you need—about 440 a day extra, on average," he says. "Patients who stop eating wheat often lose weight and find relief from acid reflux, irritable bowel syndrome, joint pain, low mood, brain fogginess, and skin rashes."

SACK THE SUGAR. "I minimize exposure to junk carbohydrates—anything made with cornstarch, sugar, or high-fructose corn syrup. That includes soft drinks. After wheat, these are the greatest dangers to your diet, and no one should be consuming them. Fructose distorts metabolism and increases deep abdominal fat accumulation. I avoid any substantial source of fructose, including honey, maple syrup, and agave."

MAKE FITNESS FUN. "My rules for exercise, physical activity, and fitness are painfully simple: Sweat a little bit and have a good time. My wife is a triathlete, and my daughter is a professional tennis player, so I'm very familiar with what it takes to achieve high—even elite—levels of endurance, speed, and precision. But ideal health can be achieved with less intense levels of effort."

GRAB A HANDFUL. "I snack on raw nuts like almonds, walnuts, pecans, pistachios, and Brazil nuts. I'll also have dark chocolate—85 percent or greater cacao content. Sometimes I make my own chocolate, sweetened with stevia and erythritol (a sugar alcohol). I like to dip pieces of my homemade chocolate in almond, sunflower seed, or natural peanut butter."

GET YOUR FIX OF FAT. "I don't limit my fat intake. I don't hold back on olive oil, coconut oil, nuts, or the fat found in meat, poultry, and fish—provided those meats are organic, free-range, or wild. The healthy fats in these foods can actually protect your heart and support your overall health."

> "I MINIMIZE EXPOSURE TO JUNK CARBOHYDRATES—
> ANYTHING MADE WITH CORNSTARCH, SUGAR, OR
> HIGH-FRUCTOSE CORN SYRUP. AFTER WHEAT, THESE
> ARE THE GREATEST DANGERS TO YOUR DIET."

# CHOCOLATE FLOURLESS TORTE

"A FAVORITE AMONG CHOCOHOLICS, IT'S NATURALLY WHEAT FREE SINCE IT'S MADE WITHOUT FLOUR (HENCE, THE NAME). BUT THIS VERSION ALSO KEEPS BLOOD SUGAR IN CHECK BY USING XYLITOL INSTEAD OF THE USUAL MANY CUPS OF SUGAR."

—WILLIAM DAVIS, MD

**Serves 16**

1 tablespoon cocoa powder

$^3/_4$ cup ground almonds

$^1/_3$ cup xylitol*

6 eggs, yolks and whites separated

$^1/_2$ teaspoon cream of tartar

$^1/_2$ cup reduced-fat sour cream

6 ounces bittersweet chocolate, melted

1 teaspoon cinnamon

**1** Preheat the oven to 350°F. Coat a 9″ springform pan with cooking spray and dust with the cocoa powder.

**2** Combine the almonds and 2 tablespoons xylitol in a blender or food processor until ground finely. Set aside.

**3** Beat the egg whites and cream of tartar in a large bowl with an electric mixer until foamy. Gradually add the remaining xylitol, beating until stiff peaks form.

**4** Beat the egg yolks in another bowl until thick. Add the sour cream, chocolate, cinnamon and beat to blend well. Fold in the almonds. Gently stir $^1/_4$ of the egg whites into the chocolate mixture. Fold in the remaining whites in 2 batches.

**5** Pour into the pan and bake for 45 to 50 minutes, or until a knife inserted in the center comes out clean. Cool the cake completely before slicing.

NUTRITION PER SERVING: 130 CALORIES • 5 G PROTEIN • 11 G CARBOHYDRATES • 2 G FIBER • 10 G FAT • 4 G SATURATED FAT • 30 MG SODIUM

*XYLITOL is a sugar alcohol that is as sweet as sugar but has far fewer calories. You can buy it in some supermarkets and health food stores.

# JOHN A. ELEFTERIADES, MD

*Cardiologist, William W. L. Glenn professor of cardiac surgery and director of the Aortic Institute at Yale–New Haven Hospital, and author of* Your Heart: An Owner's Guide *and the novel* Transplant.

WHAT'S THE PERFECT RECIPE FOR A HEALTHY HEART? "EAT less, walk more, and eat oat-based cereals," says Dr. Elefteriades. "My favorite heart-healthy breakfast is oat-Os, grapes, and 1% milk. It has enough fiber and protein to carry me through a long operation." No matter what kind of diet you follow, he says the key thing is to keep your weight in check. But he also stresses the importance of finding balance in your life. "I want my patients to concentrate more on themselves, rather than totally devoting their lives to their careers."

DITCH THE DELI. "Some studies show that processed meats can harm your health. I avoid them, but I must admit, about twice a year I can't resist a Nathan's hot dog on a fresh bun."

DOUBLE YOUR WEEKEND WORKOUTS. "During the week, I exercise in the evenings, alternating between the treadmill, rowing machine, and weight lifting; mixing it up keeps me interested. On the weekends, I do two workouts a day—and if the weather is good, I'll swap a cardio session for a bike ride."

SCALE DOWN YOUR TREATS. "After a nighttime workout, before going to bed, I may allow myself one scoop of ice cream—the 'real' stuff. The imitations seem hardly worth it. And I love chocolate cake, so I indulge in a small slice occasionally."

# CHICKEN ROLLS FLORENTINE

"ONE OF MY FAVORITE MEALS IS SOLE FLORENTINE—IT'S A GOOD SOURCE OF HEALTHY FATS, AND THE SPINACH IS NUTRIENT RICH. IF YOU DON'T LIKE FISH, THIS IS A GOOD SUBSTITUTE."

—JOHN A. ELEFTERIADES, MD

Serves 4

    8 ounces fresh spinach

1 1/2 teaspoons extra-virgin olive oil

    1 clove garlic, minced

    1 shallot, minced

    1 tablespoon minced fresh rosemary

  1/4 cup dried bread crumbs

  1/4 cup crumbled feta cheese

    1 egg, beaten

    4 (4-ounce) boneless, skinless chicken breast halves, pounded flat to about 1/4" thick

1 Wash the spinach. Transfer the wet leaves to a large saucepan. Cover and cook over medium heat until the spinach is just wilted, about 2 minutes. Drain. When cool enough to handle, finely chop and set aside.

2 Rinse out the saucepan and place it over medium-low heat. Add the oil, garlic, and shallot. Sauté until the shallot is soft, about 4 minutes. Add the spinach and sauté for 2 minutes.

3 Transfer the mixture to a large bowl. Add the rosemary, bread crumbs, cheese, and egg, and mix well. If the mixture does not hold together, add more bread crumbs.

4 Spread equal amounts of filling on each of the 4 breasts. Carefully roll up each breast to enclose the filling. Secure with toothpicks, if necessary.

5 Bring 1 inch of water to a boil in a large saucepan. Set each chicken roll on a small piece of parchment paper or foil, then transfer all 4 to a steaming rack. Set the rack in the saucepan. Cover and steam until the chicken is no longer pink when tested with a sharp knife, 15 to 18 minutes.

NUTRITION PER SERVING: 274 CALORIES • 36 G PROTEIN • 11 G CARBS • 2 G FIBER • 9 G FAT • 3 G SATURATED FAT • 381 MG SODIUM

# JENNIFER H. MIERES, MD

*Medical director at the Center for Learning and Innovation at North Shore–LIJ Health System; professor of cardiology and population health at Hofstra North Shore–LIJ School of Medicine in Long Island, New York; and author of* Heart Smart for Black Women and Latinas.

EVEN THOUGH SHE'S A CARDIOLOGIST AND ONE OF THE COUNTRY'S leading experts on heart disease in women, Dr. Mieres wants her patients to question her advice. "Individuals really have to be in charge of their own health. You want to be a 50-50 partner with your doctor, so ask questions and be sure you understand everything." One thing you can take complete charge of immediately is changing your diet and lifestyle to impact your disease risk and longevity.

**OUTSMART YOUR SWEET TOOTH.** "Desserts are a challenge for me. I keep on top of my desire for them by eating almonds between meals and having an apple every day. This keeps my blood sugar level steady and helps me control my sweet tooth."

**NEVER GO HUNGRY.** "Eat small meals every 3 hours and always include some protein. When you allow yourself to get too hungry, that's when you overeat."

**FIND BALANCE.** "I use the acronym FEAST to remind myself of the elements of a healthy lifestyle: Family and Friends, Eat healthy, Activity, Stress reduction, and Take control of your life."

**LAUGH IT OFF.** "I recommend 5 minutes of hearty laughter every day. It's the best stress reliever and it's good for your heart."

**CLEAN UP YOUR DIET.** "High-sodium processed foods and sugary beverages never cross my lips. They have little or no nutritional value. Sodium raises blood pressure, and sugar provides empty calories that contribute to weight gain—both of which are risk factors for heart disease."

**EAT THE RAINBOW.** "Colorful fruits and vegetables are the ultimate heart-healthy foods—low in calories, high in antioxidants. I add different colors to my plate at every meal."

# TURKEY AND BROCCOLI WITH COUSCOUS

"THIS IS A GREAT COMBINATION OF PROTEIN AND CARBS, AND IT CONTAINS ONE OF THE SUPER VEGETABLES: BROCCOLI!"—**JENNIFER H. MIERES, MD**

Serves 4

½ red bell pepper, cut into thin strips

2 tablespoons chopped yellow onion

1 pound boneless, skinless turkey cutlets, rinsed, dried, and sliced into 2″ strips

1 teaspoon dried sage

1 cup low-sodium chicken broth

2 cups broccoli florets

½ cup couscous

1 Coat a deep skillet with cooking spray and heat the skillet on medium.

2 Add the bell pepper, onion, and freshly ground black pepper to the skillet and cook, stirring frequently, until the onion is slightly translucent, about 2 minutes.

3 Add the turkey and sage. Cook for 2 minutes. Add the broth and broccoli. Bring to a boil for 1 minute.

4 Stir in the couscous. Cover the skillet and remove it from the heat for 5 to 10 minutes, or until the couscous has absorbed all of the broth. Stir and serve.

NUTRITION PER SERVING: 227 CALORIES • 33 G PROTEIN • 21 G CARBS • 3 G FIBER • 1 G FAT • 0 G SATURATED FAT • 131 MG SODIUM

# BARBARA QUINN, MS, RD

*Clinical dietitian/diabetes educator for the diabetes and nutrition therapy program at the Community Hospital of the Monterey Peninsula in Monterey, California, and the author of* The Diabetes DTOUR Diet *and* Diabetes DTOUR Diet Cookbook.

EVEN IF YOU'VE BEEN DIAGNOSED WITH A SERIOUS ILLNESS LIKE diabetes, you don't have to sacrifice flavor to protect your health. "Food is meant to be enjoyed—not dreaded," says Quinn, who helps people with diabetes eat healthfully and pleasurably every day. "I follow my own advice and look at food as an incredible vehicle to provide nutrients in just the right balance for my body. Of course, as my grandfather used to say, 'Too much of anything is not good for you,' but food is not the enemy."

**CHILL OUT WITH CALCIUM.** "I can't prove it scientifically, but taking a calcium supplement before bed seems to help me rest (especially if I haven't gotten my calcium quota that day). Exercise is also important; I always sleep better on days that I've worked out. Knowing that keeps me motivated to stay active."

**TAKE 5.** "You don't want to obsess over every pound, but I aim to stay within 5 pounds of the weight where I feel the best. If it creeps up more than that, I cut out extra snacks and increase my exercise until I'm back to where I'm comfortable."

**FIND YOUR BLISS.** "The best way to relax is to do what you love. For me, it's spending time with my horse, Cal. Sometimes just raking manure and hauling a wheelbarrow can put my mind right back where it needs to be. And after a ride, I feel like I'm 20 years old again."

**LET YOUR SURROUNDINGS INSPIRE YOU.** "I swim 2 or 3 nights a week in an outdoor pool (one of the benefits of living in California). I get to look at the stars and moon and unwind as I exercise. It's a perfect antidote to stress eating."

**TEA UP.** "There are incredible health benefits to foods we often take for granted. Tea is a good example. It contains an array of flavonoids, potent antioxidant compounds that protect your heart and may even guard against infection. A preliminary study suggests that green tea may even help control autoimmune diseases, such as rheumatoid arthritis. I take out my prettiest tea cup and brew a pot in the evenings, when I feel like snacking on foods I shouldn't be eating."

**NIBBLE WISELY.** "I love M&M's. If they're around, it's easy for me to mindlessly eat too many of them. When I want some, I buy a single-serving package and really pay attention to enjoying them. That keeps me satisfied with less."

> "TOO MUCH OF ANYTHING
> IS NOT GOOD FOR YOU,
> BUT FOOD IS NOT THE ENEMY."

# SPINACH SALAD WITH AVOCADO, FRESH MOZZARELLA, AND STRAWBERRY DRESSING

"WHEN I GET HOME AT THE END OF A LONG DAY, I WANT SOMETHING SIMPLE. A SPINACH SALAD WITH A PIECE OF MY HOMEMADE SOURDOUGH BREAD AND A GLASS OF COLD, LOW-FAT MILK IS PERFECT. IT'S A MEAL RICH IN MAJOR NUTRIENTS AND FIBER, BUT EASY TO PREPARE."—BARBARA QUINN, MS, RD

Serves 4

- 2 cups hulled and sliced strawberries, divided
- 2 tablespoons extra-virgin olive oil
- 2 tablespoons honey
- 1 tablespoon + 1 teaspoon balsamic vinegar
- 1 bag (6 ounces) baby spinach
- 1 ripe medium mango, pitted, peeled, and cut into small chunks
- 5 ounces fresh mozzarella cheese, cut into small chunks
- 1 avocado, pitted, peeled, and cut into small chunks
- 3 tablespoons toasted chopped almonds

1 Place $^1/_2$ cup of the strawberries, the oil, honey, and vinegar in a blender or food processor. Blend or process until smooth. Scrape into a salad bowl and stir in $^1/_2$ teaspoon of salt and $^1/_8$ teaspoon of freshly ground black pepper.

2 Add the spinach, mango, and the remaining $1^1/_2$ cups of strawberries to the dressing and toss to mix well. Sprinkle the cheese, avocado, and almonds over the top, and serve.

NUTRITION PER SERVING: 366 CALORIES • 10 G PROTEIN • 34 G CARBS • 6 G FIBER • 23 G FAT • 7 G SATURATED FAT • 469 MG SODIUM

# PREDIMAN K. SHAH, MD

*Shapell and Webb professor and director of cardiology at Oppenheimer Atherosclerosis Research Center at Cedars-Sinai Heart Institute in Los Angeles, and professor of medicine at Cedars-Sinai and UCLA.*

TO PROTECT YOUR HEART, YOU DON'T HAVE TO EAT A BLAND, boring diet or go fat-free or vegan. Dr. Shah says that olive oil, juicy tomatoes, toasted nuts, fresh fish, and even pasta are all cardio-protective. "A Mediterranean-style diet lowers heart disease risk and is delicious and satisfying," he says. In fact, a Spanish study showed that following a Mediterranean diet is linked to better quality of life. So follow Dr. Shah's lead and you won't just be healthier, you'll be happier!

**KEEP A STASH.** "I always have mixed unsalted nuts in my office. They're heart healthy and high in protein and fiber, so they fill you up. If I get hungry in the middle of the day, I can have a handful of those instead of being tempted to have something that's not so good for me."

**LAUGH IT OFF.** "Watching a funny movie always seems to make me feel less stressed. The benefits of laughter are innumerable!"

**CLIMB YOUR WAY TO FITNESS.** "I'm on my feet all day at work, but I still try to use the stairs instead of the elevator. I walk up 103 steps several times a day at the hospital, and it helps me stay fit and energized."

**CREATE A "NO TEMPTATION" ZONE.** "We don't generally keep unhealthy foods in the house, but occasionally you will find pistachio ice cream in the freezer. I treat myself to a couple of scoops once in a great while."

**EAT TOGETHER, STAY TOGETHER.** "Our family is very close, and we spend a lot of time with each other. Staying connected is important for your health. My wife and I encourage our grown children to have dinner with us at least once a week."

**MAKE MEAT A TREAT.** "I avoid not only processed meats but also red meat in general to keep my cholesterol and cancer risk low. But I do love a good Kashmiri lamb dish once in a great while. It's rich and very flavorful, so you don't need to eat a lot of it. Plus the spices used in Indian cooking are rich in antioxidants."

**GO BANANAS.** "Bananas are portable and packed with potassium, which helps keep blood pressure in check. The best way to get enough potassium in your diet is to eat a variety of fruits and vegetables."

## "I ALWAYS HAVE MIXED UNSALTED NUTS IN MY OFFICE. THEY'RE HEART HEALTHY AND HIGH IN PROTEIN AND FIBER."

# CURRIED RED LENTILS

"SPICY BEAN-BASED DISHES LIKE THIS ONE SUPPLY PROTEIN AND HEALTHY CARBS ALONG WITH A WHOLE LOT OF BENEFICIAL MICRONUTRIENTS."—**PREDIMAN K. SHAH, MD**

**Serves 4**

$\frac{3}{4}$ cup red lentils, sorted and rinsed

1 tablespoon extra-virgin olive oil

$\frac{1}{2}$ cup chopped onions

$\frac{1}{2}$ cup chopped scallions

1 green bell pepper, diced

1 tablespoon chopped, canned, mild green chile peppers

1 tablespoon all-purpose flour

2 teaspoons curry powder

Ground red pepper

$\frac{3}{4}$ cup low-sodium chicken broth

1 teaspoon reduced-sodium soy sauce

1 teaspoon rice vinegar

1 tablespoon chopped fresh cilantro

**1** Combine the lentils with $1\frac{3}{4}$ cups of water in a medium saucepan and bring to a boil over medium-high heat. Reduce the heat to low, cover, and simmer until the lentils are tender, about 25 to 30 minutes. Drain.

**2** Heat the oil in a large nonstick skillet on medium. Add the onions, scallions, bell pepper, and chile peppers. Cook, stirring frequently, until the peppers are tender, 2 to 3 minutes. Stir in the flour, curry powder, and red pepper to taste, and cook for 1 minute.

**3** Whisk in the broth, soy sauce, and vinegar. Add the lentils and cook until the mixture is heated through and begins to thicken, about 2 minutes. Sprinkle with the cilantro and serve.

NUTRITION PER SERVING: 188 CALORIES • 11 G PROTEIN • 28 G CARBS • 7 G FIBER • 4 G FAT • <1 G SATURATED FAT • 151 MG SODIUM

# ROB THOMPSON, MD

*Seattle-based cardiologist and author of five books, including* The Glycemic Load Diet *and* The Sugar Blockers Diet.

A S A PREVENTIVE CARDIOLOGIST, DR. THOMPSON WOULD GIVE patients diet and exercise advice, but it wasn't until he was diagnosed with diabetes himself that he started to actually *follow* that advice. He had no problem figuring out which lab tests and medications he needed, but he realized that changing his diet was harder than he'd thought it would be. "If you could stop eating carbs altogether, there's no doubt you'd lose weight, and if you have diabetes, your blood sugar would be a cinch to control. But cutting carbs is easier said than done," says Dr. Thompson. "However, there are good carbs and bad carbs, and only a few—those with high glycemic loads—cause your blood sugar to spike." Following a low glycemic diet helps people with diabetes or heart disease, as well as anyone looking to prevent those diseases, lose weight, and increase energy. Want proof? "I've lost 25 pounds without really even trying," he says, "and I eat heartier now than I ever did."

START SMALL. "Thirty years of practicing medicine has taught me that when it comes to diet, humans are capable of making only a few changes. Don't rely on willpower to help you meet unrealistic goals. If you're trying to change, choose something you know you can stick with—for good."

TAKE A DIFFERENT ROUTE. "Six years ago I gave up my parking spot and started walking to work—2½ miles each way, 3 days a week. I also stay active at home. I don't see the sense in going to a gym for exercise and then paying others to do work around the house. I'm my own gardener, carpenter, and general contractor, and that helps keep me fit."

**ELIMINATE EMPTY CALORIES**. "Starch—the main component of bread, potatoes, and rice—is a filler food, a cheap way to supply calories. However, it all turns to sugar in your digestive tract. At restaurants, I build a starch pile on one side of my plate. At the end of the meal, if I want some, I'll eat some. By then, the other food has had a chance to reach my bloodstream, and all that starch doesn't look so good."

**CRACK A NUT**. "I'm addicted to nuts. It seems that the more of them I eat, the less I weigh. They're loaded with unsaturated fats, omega-3 fatty acids, fiber, and protein."

**DON'T GO INTO OVERTIME**. "I was raised in a blue-collar town where the kinds of jobs people did were dirty and hard. They put in 8 hours, punched out, and went home. That's my rhythm: 8 hours is enough! I rarely miss dinner with my wife and kids, and I leave myself plenty of time for having fun and being with my friends and family."

# FAST FRENCH OMELET

"WHEN I WAS IN PARIS, I WAS SERVED AN UNUSUAL OMELET. IT WASN'T THE TYPICAL VEGETABLE-AND-CHEESE CONCOCTION YOU USUALLY GET IN THE US—IT WAS SIMPLY A BOWL OF EGG COOKED TO PERFECTION."—**ROB THOMPSON, MD**

**Serves 1**

2 large eggs

1 tablespoon milk

1 teaspoon butter

1 Whisk the eggs and milk in a small microwaveable bowl. Microwave for 3 minutes and 30 seconds at 40 percent power.

2 Remove the eggs from the microwave and top with the butter and salt and freshly ground black pepper to taste.

NUTRITION PER SERVING: 186 CALORIES • 13 G PROTEIN • 2 G CARBS • 0 G FIBER • 14 G FAT • 6 G SATURATED FAT • 148 MG SODIUM

# ERIC J. TOPOL, MD

*Cardiologist, director of Scripps Translational Science Institute, chief academic officer of Scripps Health, professor of genomics at the Scripps Research Institute, and co-founder and vice chairman of the West Wireless Health Institute.*

D R. TOPOL HAS A SIMPLE RECIPE FOR STAYING WELL. "MAKE YOUR health your number one priority," he says. "Eat a balanced diet, exercise regularly, and find a way to cope with life's inevitable stressors. It's the same old story, but it's true!" Named one of the Top 100 Most Influential People in Health Care in 2011, Dr. Topol shares his personal tips for staying heart healthy and happy.

**GO MEATLESS—AT LEAST PART-TIME.** "For both health and environmental reasons, I stopped eating red meat just before graduating medical school in 1979. Red meat has been linked to various cancers, especially colon cancer, which runs in my family. Instead of meat, my diet centers on fish and vegetables. I eat wild salmon for dinner once or twice a week, usually grilled, sometimes with dill and mustard."

**RELEASE TENSION.** "Stress can increase your heart attack risk, so I try to keep it in check. I find outdoor activities to be especially relaxing and mood boosting. I'll hit golf balls, ride my mountain bike, hike the Pacific Crest Trail, or shoot nature photos."

**POWER UP YOUR SNACKS.** "Use snack time as an opportunity to increase your whole grain, fruit, or vegetable intake. There are plenty of healthy finger foods that feel snacky. Some of my favorites are unbuttered, lightly salted popcorn; rice crackers; dried fruit; and edamame."

**FIND YOUR RHYTHM.** "I do rigorous 30-minute intervals on an elliptical trainer 5 days a week. It gives me the cardio benefits of running without pounding my knees. Music helps me keep my pace. I listen to Marvin Gaye, Lionel Richie, and Beyoncé. The faster the beat, the faster I go."

**KEEP A RECORD.** "I step on the scale every morning and write down what I weigh. I also use a device with an accelerometer, such as Fitbit Ultra Tracker, to make sure I take 10,000 steps a day or more. You can also track your steps with a simple pedometer. Having all this information motivates me."

# SPICED EDAMAME

"EDAMAME (GREEN SOYBEANS) IN THE POD MAKE A GREAT SNACK. THEY'RE FUN TO EAT AND PACKED WITH PROTEIN AND FIBER."–**ERIC J. TOPOL**, MD

Serves 6

2 teaspoons coarse sea salt

¾ teaspoon Szechwan peppercorns or ½ teaspoon ancho chili powder, Chinese five-spice powder, or dried lavender

1 bag (1 pound) frozen edamame in the pod

**1** Combine the sea salt and your choice of seasoning in a small skillet. Toast over low heat until fragrant. Set aside.

**2** Bring 1 inch of water to a boil in a large saucepan. Set a steaming rack in the saucepan and cook the edamame in the steamer for 4 to 5 minutes. Remove from the steamer, transfer to a bowl, and toss with the salt and spice mixture while the beans are still hot. Let them cool, and serve.

NUTRITION PER SERVING: 101 CALORIES • 8 G PROTEIN • 9 G CARBS • 4 G FIBER • 3 G FAT • 0 G SATURATED FAT • 670 MG SODIUM

# TASNEEM BHATIA, MD

*Integrative health expert; medical director/founder of the Atlanta Center for Holistic and Integrative Medicine; and columnist for* Prevention.

AS SHE DISCUSSED IN CHAPTER 1, DR. BHATIA HAS COME TO SEE food as medicine for both herself and her patients. "Chinese and Ayurvedic medicine have always put nutrition front and center, not just for its powers to heal, but also to ensure that you feel your best every day," she says. "For example, eating the right foods in the right ways can give you more energy and when you're feeling good, you're more motivated to exercise and do other things that help your health." In the future, she says, it's very likely that analyzing genes will lead to the development of an optional, individualized diet for everyone, but until then she relies on these strategies to stay healthy and balanced.

**LOOK FOR THE MEANING BEHIND YOUR CRAVINGS.** "When I want sweets and salt, I know my body is overworked and stressed out. The connection between what you eat and how your body feels is strong, so I tackle these urges by simply relaxing. Once my stress level is in check, eating 'right' just comes naturally."

**RETHINK THAT DRINK.** "So many of my patients relax with a few glasses of wine at night, but they forget that all alcohol is ultimately sugar. An occasional drink is fine, but if you are using alcohol for stress relief, find other ways to wind down. Try a cup of tea, deep breathing, or spending 10 minutes with a magazine or a good book."

**TIME YOUR TRIPS TO THE TABLE.** "I make sure that I eat every 3 to 4 hours.

That way, I'm less inclined to make poor food choices out of desperation. Plus, my energy level stays high all day."

GO UNDER THE NEEDLE. "I'm aggressive about managing stress, and acupuncture is one of my favorite ways to do so. It not only relaxes the body, but I believe that it's responsible for keeping my skin looking young."

HEAL WITH HERBS. "Astragalus and olive leaf are antiviral. Take them when you first begin to feel 'bad'; they can prevent the progression of colds and the flu."

FIGHT FAT WITH FOOD. "For me, diet plays a much larger role than exercise in keeping me lean. I avoid refined carbohydrates and excessive salt because I feel best after eating meals with lean protein, lots of fresh fruits and vegetables, and no gluten."

TAILOR YOUR SUPPLEMENTS. "Having an integrative practice, I match supplements to individual needs. I take a high dose of B complex, 2 grams of omega-3s, 30 milligrams of iron, and iodine for my thyroid every day."

# BASIL ROLLS

"THESE ROLLS ARE EASY TO MAKE AND TASTE DELICIOUS. MY 4- AND 3-YEAR-OLDS LOVE TO HELP ME ROLL THESE UP, AND THEN THEY HAPPILY EAT WHAT THEY'VE PREPARED!"

—TASNEEM BHATIA, MD

Serves 4

1 tablespoon peanut or canola oil

1/2 pound boneless chicken breast, cut into bite-size pieces

16 medium shrimp, peeled and deveined

2 cups dark leafy greens (such as romaine, spinach, or kale), chopped fine

1/2 cup chopped fresh mint

1/2 cup chopped fresh cilantro

8 round rice paper (spring roll) wrappers (8-inch diameter)

24 fresh basil leaves

1/4 cup low-sodium soy sauce

1/4 cup hoisin sauce

*(continued)*

**1** Preheat a large skillet over high heat. Add the oil, and heat it until it smokes. Add the chicken and stir-fry until nearly cooked through, 5 to 7 minutes. Add the shrimp and continue stir-frying until the shrimp turns pink, 2 to 3 minutes more. Let it cool slightly, then chop the shrimp into bite-size pieces. Place the cooked chicken and shrimp in a medium bowl and set aside.

**2** Toss the greens, mint, and cilantro in a large bowl.

**3** Fill a pie plate with warm water. Working with one wrapper at a time, dip one side of the wrapper in the water for 30 seconds, then the other side. The wrapper will be pliable, but still firm. (If the wrapper is very soft, either the water is too warm or you kept the wrapper in the water for too long.)

**4** Transfer the wrapper to a flat surface. Starting about $\frac{1}{2}$ inch from the bottom of the wrapper, spread $\frac{1}{3}$ cup of greens horizontally across the wrapper. Place about $\frac{1}{8}$ cup of the chicken and 2 shrimp on top of the greens. Top with 3 basil leaves.

**5** Fold the bottom of the wrapper up over the greens, tightening as you fold. Then fold in the sides, and continue rolling up from the bottom. Set the completed wrapper on a plate, and cover it with plastic wrap.

**6** Repeat steps 3 through 5 with the remaining 7 wrappers.

**7** Whisk together the soy sauce and hoisin sauce. Slice the rolls in half on the diagonal and divide them among 4 plates. Serve with the sauce for dipping.

NUTRITION PER SERVING (2 ROLLS): 268 CALORIES • 28 G PROTEIN • 26 G CARBS • 1 G FIBER • 6 G FAT • 1 G SATURATED FAT • 1,248 MG SODIUM

# MICHAEL J. BREUS, PHD

*Psychologist and sleep expert, author of* Beauty Sleep *and* The Sleep Doctor's Diet Plan, *and creator of the Dr. Breus Bed.*

TO DROP POUNDS, IT'S JUST AS IMPORTANT TO SPEND TIME IN BED as it is to spend time at the gym. "Sleep deprivation makes it more difficult to lose weight and can even cause you to gain," says Dr. Breus. "If you need motivation to set a regular sleep schedule, thinking about how much slimmer you'd be should do the trick." Going to bed and getting up at the same time every day is the best way to train your body to sleep well, but what you eat also has a big impact.

**EAT LESS, MORE OFTEN.** "Try to eat small, regular meals throughout the day; they should be made up of about 40 percent protein, 50 percent complex carbs, and 10 percent (or less) fats. Good choices include hummus or goat cheese spread on crackers and oatmeal made with 1% milk instead of water, topped with blueberries."

**AVOID WEIGHT CREEP.** "I've lost weight since my med school days by doing little things, like not using salad dressing and drinking my coffee black. It all adds up."

**LET THE SUN SHINE.** "Getting outside for 15 minutes in the morning helps reset my body clock, so I sleep better at night. And in the middle of the day, it's rejuvenating to spend some time in the sun. Plus, sunlight helps with vitamin D production."

**WALK OFF FATIGUE.** "Everyone's core body temperature drops between 1 p.m. and 3 p.m.—that's what makes you feel sleepy midafternoon, not what you had for lunch. A walk outside increases light exposure and increases body temperature to help wake you up."

**SEE THE UPSIDE.** "My father once told me that 'it takes just as much energy to be happy as it does to be sad.' I'm a pretty positive person, but when I'm faced with a problem, I break it down into manageable chunks to develop a strategy to overcome it. When all else fails, I hang out with my kids. They're awesome, and they always cheer me up."

**FIND A HEALTHY FAVORITE.** "I love blueberries. I could have them in just about anything. I also love ice cream—but I limit my intake of that to two or three servings a week, using it as a reward for other healthy behaviors."

# THE SLEEP DOCTOR'S SMOOTHIE
(Photo on page 328)

"TART CHERRY JUICE CONTAINS MELATONIN—THE HORMONE THAT HELPS REGULATE SLEEP AND WAKE CYCLES. SOME STUDIES SHOW THAT IT ALSO HELPS WITH MUSCLE SORENESS AND RECOVERY AFTER A WORKOUT. I OFTEN HAVE THIS SMOOTHIE ABOUT AN HOUR AND A HALF BEFORE BED TO HELP ME NOD OFF."—**MICHAEL J. BREUS**, PhD

*Serves 2*

1 cup tart cherry juice

½ cup soy milk

1 banana

¼ teaspoon pure vanilla extract

5 ice cubes

Place the juice, soy milk, banana, vanilla extract, and ice in a blender. Process until smooth. Pour into 2 glasses and serve.

NUTRITION PER SERVING: 122 CALORIES • 3 G PROTEIN • 25 G CARBS • 1 G FIBER • 1 G FAT • 0 G SATURATED FAT • 22 MG SODIUM

# LORI BUCKLEY, PsyD

*Clinical psychologist and certified sex therapist in Los Angeles, advisory counsel member for the Sinclair Institute, and columnist for* Health *magazine.*

S THERE A CONNECTION BETWEEN HEALTHY EATING AND A HEALTHY relationship? Absolutely, according to Dr. Buckley. "My general advice is this: Stop multitasking and decrease or eliminate distractions," she says. "This advice applies to many things—it improves relationships and sexual pleasure. When it comes to eating, it allows you to savor every bite, which helps you automatically cut a significant number of calories."

**EAT FOR PLEASURE.** "I focus on what I can eat and what I can do that feels good, rather than thinking about what I can't have or what I have to do. Turn on your senses and eat slowly to really enjoy your food. Notice how it looks, smells, tastes, and feels in your mouth."

**FEED YOUR RELATIONSHIP.** "Finger foods make for the ideal romantic meal. A platter of cheese, prosciutto, and fruit is fun, sensual, delicious, and light—just right before a night of lovemaking."

**STOP FOOD FIGHTS.** "He's a meat-and-potatoes type, you're a vegetarian. Don't worry, this relationship *can* be saved. Couples with incompatible eating habits have to find what they both enjoy and incorporate it into their lives. For example, maybe you both love pizza—so have a pizza night. But even if you're eating different meals, the most important thing is that you eat them together."

LAUGH A LITTLE. "When couples have fun together and don't take things too personally or seriously (although there are times when that's appropriate, of course), they communicate better, want to spend more time together, feel more connected, and have more enjoyable (and therefore more frequent) sex."

CUDDLE UP—OFTEN. "When people are under pressure, they often think they're too stressed for sex. But it's one of the best ways to relax and take your mind off your worries."

IMPROVISE A STIR-FRY. "Stir-fries are easy, fast, cheap, healthy, and versatile. I cut up whatever veggies I have on hand—asparagus, mushrooms, broccoli—and cook them in a hot wok with a little peanut oil, some garlic, and a few red pepper flakes. Alone or over brown rice, it makes a perfect weeknight meal."

EXERCISE WITH OTHERS. "I love Spinning classes. The music, the challenge, the energy—it's all very motivating. Plus Spinning burns a lot of calories in a relatively short period of time."

> "I FOCUS ON WHAT I CAN EAT AND WHAT I CAN DO THAT FEELS GOOD, RATHER THAN THINKING ABOUT WHAT I CAN'T HAVE OR WHAT I HAVE TO DO."

# AVOCADO, MANGO, AND SHRIMP SALAD WITH MISO DRESSING

"I ALWAYS HAVE A BOWL OF WASHED SALAD GREENS AND A JAR OF THIS DRESSING IN MY REFRIGERATOR, SO IT'S READY TO GO WHEN I GET HOME."—**LORI BUCKLEY, PsyD**

**Serves 4**

1/4 cup organic seasoned rice vinegar

2 tablespoons white, low-sodium miso paste

1 teaspoon Dijon mustard

Juice of 1/2 lemon

1/4 cup extra-virgin olive oil

12 ounces large shrimp, peeled and deveined

6 cups chopped romaine lettuce

1/2 head radicchio, chopped

1 avocado, pitted, peeled, and cubed

1 mango, pitted, peeled, and cubed

1/4 cup toasted sliced almonds

1 Make the dressing by whisking together the vinegar, miso, mustard, and lemon juice in a large salad bowl. Slowly whisk in the oil. Season with freshly ground black pepper. Place 2 tablespoons of the dressing in a medium bowl. Refrigerate the dressing in the large bowl.

2 Preheat the grill. Marinate the shrimp in the medium bowl for 5 minutes. Place the shrimp on the grill and cook for 1 minute. Turn the shrimp and grill until opaque, 1 to 2 minutes more, and set aside.

3 Remove the large bowl from the refrigerator and add the romaine and radicchio. Toss with clean hands until the leaves are evenly coated. Add the avocado and mango, and toss gently.

4 Divide the salad among 4 plates. Top each plate with the shrimp and almonds. Season to taste with freshly ground black pepper.

NUTRITION PER SERVING: 390 CALORIES • 22 G PROTEIN • 23 G CARBS • 5 G FIBER • 24 G FAT • 3 G SATURATED FAT • 635 MG SODIUM

# SHARON CHIRBAN, PhD

*Psychology instructor at Harvard Medical School and Boston University, staff psychologist at Boston Children's Hospital, and registered sports psychologist with the US Olympic Committee.*

A DESIRE TO BECOME HEALTHIER, NOT SLIMMER, MOTIVATED Dr. Chirban to make a few lifestyle changes. "I found out that I had high cholesterol when I was in my early thirties, so I started running regularly and made a commitment to cleaner eating. I haven't looked back since!" (Once a week she runs the Harvard Stadium stairs!) She discovered that her mind benefited from the changes as much as her body did, and she's passed that wisdom on to her patients. "As a psychologist, I prescribe exercise to address moderate mental health issues. If I can get people who are coping with stress, anxiety, and depression to use better eating and more exercise as part of their treatment, I feel that I'm providing them with a solution for life."

NIX THE EXCUSES. "I make it a point not to let my hectic schedule divert me from eating right. I've really tried to become more aware of what I put in my mouth. You can find good-for-you options almost anywhere—convenience stores sell both Kashi bars and Snickers bars!"

BREAK THE ASSOCIATION. "I'm working on weaning myself off diet cola because I think all sorts of poor food choices go along with drinking it. I believe that cleaner drinking can lead to cleaner eating."

SPLURGE WITHOUT REGRET. "When I make a less-than-ideal food choice, I do it consciously. Being aware helps me limit myself to a regular serving size of whatever I'm craving and then move on. I think of it as a part of life—not every moment of eating needs to be perfectly nutritionally balanced."

**CONCENTRATE ON WHAT YOU'RE GOOD AT**. "Feeling competent is a big self-esteem strengthener. Taking the time to perform tasks or activities that make you feel effective will lead you to better mental health."

**TAKE A STEP BACK**. "When things get challenging and life presents a crisis, I stay in the present and try not to exaggerate a bad situation. Just because this one thing is giving me trouble doesn't mean my life is a mess! Perspective is the key to solving problems."

**COUNT YOUR BLESSINGS**. "I keep a gratitude list—I write down the things I'm grateful for. I focus on my gifts and talents and I cherish the people I love. Reminding myself of the positive elements in my life leaves my brain open to possibility. We have more mental flexibility to solve problems and to treat ourselves well when we keep an optimistic attitude."

> "WHEN I MAKE A LESS-THAN-IDEAL FOOD CHOICE, I DO IT CONSCIOUSLY. BEING AWARE HELPS ME LIMIT MYSELF TO A REGULAR SERVING SIZE OF WHATEVER I'M CRAVING."

# GRILLED SALMON
# WITH PEACH-MANGO SALSA

"SALMON IS MY FAVORITE HEALTH FOOD."–SHARON CHIRBAN, PhD

**Serves 4**

1 jalapeño pepper

1½ cups chopped fresh tomatoes

¾ cup peeled, chopped fresh peaches

½ cup chopped red onion

½ cup chopped yellow bell pepper

½ cup peeled, chopped mango

3 garlic cloves, minced

1½ teaspoons fresh lime juice

½ teaspoon minced fresh cilantro

2 whole wheat pitas

2 tablespoons extra-virgin olive oil

1 pound wild salmon, skin removed

Lemon wedges

**1** Seed and chop the jalapeño pepper (wear plastic gloves when handling). Combine the tomatoes, peaches, onion, bell pepper, mango, garlic, lime juice, cilantro, and jalapeño pepper in a medium bowl. Cover and refrigerate for at least 1 hour, or up to 24 hours.

**2** Preheat the oven to 425°F. Slice each pita into 8 pieces and brush the pieces lightly with 1 tablespoon of the oil. Bake until crispy, about 3 to 5 minutes.

**3** Preheat the grill. Brush the salmon with the remaining 1 tablespoon of oil and sprinkle with salt. Grill the salmon until just opaque, about 15 to 20 minutes. Let stand for 5 minutes, then cut into 4 even servings.

**4** Place about ½ cup of the salsa on each plate and top with a piece of the salmon. (Store the remaining salsa covered in the refrigerator for up to 3 days.) Serve with the lemon wedges and pita crisps.

NUTRITION PER SERVING: 329 CALORIES • 28 G PROTEIN • 25 G CARBS • 7 G FIBER • 15 G FAT • 2 G SATURATED FAT • 220 MG SODIUM

# SHELBY FREEDMAN HARRIS, PsyD

*Director of the Behavioral Sleep Medicine Program at the Sleep-Wake Disorders Center at Montefiore Medical Center, and assistant professor of neurology and psychiatry at the Albert Einstein College of Medicine, both in Bronx, New York.*

WANT TO WAKE UP FEELING REFRESHED AND ENERGIZED EVERY morning? Sleep expert Dr. Harris says you have to set the right mood the night before. "Falling asleep and waking up are not as simple as flipping a switch off and on," she says. She recommends winding down for at least an hour before your bedtime. "We're always on the go in our society, and we need time before bed every night to quiet our minds and bodies to help signal that sleep is coming." A balanced, healthy diet can also promote better rest. "I read food labels carefully," says Dr. Harris. "If I can't pronounce an ingredient, I don't buy that food."

**BREAK THE SUGAR HABIT IN STEPS.** "I'm trying to overcome my major sweet tooth. I've stopped using sugar and artificial sweeteners in my daily cup of green tea. I now use a small amount of stevia, an herbal sweetener with no calories. Every week I use a little less, and soon I hope I won't need any."

**BE A GOAL GETTER.** "After graduate school, I was out of shape and overweight. I wanted to do something to change my life, so I decided to train for and run the Marine Corps Marathon. I joined a local running club and raised money for cancer research. Setting a goal and being accountable to others was so motivating."

**STRENGTHEN YOUR SOCIAL NETWORK.** "I've made a lot of friends in my running club. It's also a great way to spend time with my son. I put him in a jogging stroller and run 2 miles to the park. We play for a while, and then I run the 2 miles back home. The combination of exercise, mommy time, and fresh air does wonders!"

**LIGHT THINGS UP.** "Soaking in at least 15 minutes of bright sunlight in the morning can really help you sleep better at night. Likewise, it's important to dim your lights at home an hour before going to bed."

**HEAL WITH GINGER.** "To settle an upset stomach, I steep a piece of fresh ginger in some hot water to make ginger tea. It's soothing and flavorful."

**SAVE MEAT FOR THE WEEKENDS.** "I eat a lot of plant-based meals during the workweek. Having too much red meat has been linked to heart disease and cancer."

# STIR-FRIED KALE WITH ALMONDS

"I HAVE DARK LEAFY GREENS TWICE A DAY. THEY'RE A GREAT SOURCE OF FIBER AND ANTIOXIDANTS. KALE IS MY FAVORITE. I SAUTÉ IT WITH GARLIC AND OLIVE OIL, BAKE IT INTO KALE CHIPS, OR USE IT FRESH IN SMOOTHIES."—**SHELBY FREEDMAN HARRIS**, PsyD

Serves 6

2 tablespoons extra-virgin olive oil

1 large clove garlic, finely chopped

1 teaspoon grated ginger

¼ cup slivered almonds

1½ pounds kale, stems removed, chopped (about 6 cups)

1 tablespoon tamari

2 tablespoons low-sodium vegetable broth

**1** Warm the oil in a large skillet over medium-high heat. Add the garlic and ginger and cook for 30 seconds.

**2** Reduce heat to medium. Add the almonds and cook for 1 minute. Add the kale, tamari, and broth. Cook until the kale is wilted but not soggy, about 5 minutes.

NUTRITION PER SERVING: 126 CALORIES • 5 G PROTEIN • 13 G CARBS • 3 G FIBER • 8 G FAT • 1 G SATURATED FAT • 212 MG SODIUM

# SUZANNE GILBERG-LENZ, MD

*Obstetrician and gynecologist at Women's Care of Beverly Hills in California, board-certified in integrative and holistic medicine, ayurvedic specialist, and co-founder of Cedars-Sinai Medical Center's Green Committee.*

"TAKE TIME FOR YOURSELF." YOU MAY HAVE HEARD THIS HEALTH tip before, but Dr. Gilberg-Lenz isn't convinced it's sinking in. "We need to readjust our expectations. Our culture and lifestyles are very fast paced, and we can't keep up. This is making us sick—we need to resist the tempting illusion that we can be everything to everyone," she says. Realizing that as a physician and a mother she's an example to others, she tries to follow her own advice. "I allow myself to be a human and not push so hard all of the time," she says. Dr. Gilberg-Lenz has a few ways she tries to counteract her often demanding and stressful life: "I insist on getting regular exercise, eating right, and making family time a priority. But most of all, I try to forgive myself for not being perfect!"

**EAT SENSUALLY.** "Thanks in part to my ayurvedic training, I've become more mindful at meals. As much as possible, I sit quietly and breathe deeply before I start eating, and I don't rush. I try to use this as an antidote to the busy, stressful 'go-go' lifestyle that I and many of my patients lead. When you scarf down your food, you get so much less out of it. It definitely doesn't satisfy, and that leads to overeating. It also causes heartburn and bloating."

**REMEMBER: ORGANIC JUNK FOOD IS STILL JUNK FOOD!** "I'm all for organic produce and dairy products (pesticides and hormones concentrate in fat), but I avoid processed foods, even if they're labeled organic, and GMO foods whenever possible. I eat lots of greens—in salads, smoothies, cooked, you name it. I support local farmers, and I'm not afraid of butter!"

PUT YOUR FEET UP. "At the end of a long day, I'll come home and get into my favorite restorative yoga pose—*viparita karani,* or Legs-Up-the-Wall. Sit with your knees bent and the left side of your body against a wall. Place your palms on the floor next to each hip. Then turn your hips to the left and swing your legs up the wall as you lower your torso and head back to the floor. (Place a pillow under your upper back if that is more comfortable.) Stretch your arms out to your sides, palms facing up, and relax for 2 to 20 minutes. If you have high blood pressure or glaucoma, check with your doctor before performing this pose."

WORK YOUR CORE. "Abdominal exercises aren't just important for improving posture, protecting your back, and getting a toned tummy—they also promote pelvic strength and stability. That improves your sex life and guards against incontinence."

BE A GUINEA PIG. "Check out the local acupuncture training program or other holistic medical training program, if you are lucky enough to have one in your hometown. It's a great, affordable way to learn more about non-Western modes of healing and health. Though you will be treated by student practitioners, they are supervised by master teachers."

CHECK IT BEFORE YOU WRECK IT. "When you feel angry or upset, take 10 deep breaths and check in with yourself before you react. You might realize that it's you, not them (as in, 'I feel like crying for no reason' or 'I feel like I want to kill this person—ah, yes, my period is coming'), and even if it *isn't* you, taking those breaths will help you respond to the situation calmly."

# MANGO-AVOCADO SALAD

"THIS RECIPE IS A GREAT SNACK, STARTER, SIDE, OR LIGHT LUNCH. ACCORDING TO AYURVEDIC PRINCIPLES, IT BALANCES ALL MIND-BODY CONSTITUTIONS. ADDITIONALLY, THE SPICES AID IN DIGESTION." —**SUZANNE GILBERG-LENZ**, MD

**Serves 2**

1 large mango, pitted, peeled, and cut into chunks

2 small avocados, pitted, peeled, and cut into chunks

1 tablespoon freshly squeezed lime, lemon, or orange juice

½ teaspoon ground coriander or cumin

Sea salt

Ground red pepper (optional)

1 tablespoon chopped fresh cilantro (optional)

**1** Toss the mango, avocado, and juice in a medium bowl.

**2** Sprinkle with the coriander or cumin, sea salt, and red pepper (if using). Toss to combine. Sprinkle with cilantro (if using) and serve.

NUTRITION PER SERVING: 299 CALORIES • 3 G PROTEIN • 29 G CARBS • 10 G FIBER • 21 G FAT • 3 G SATURATED FAT • 306 MG SODIUM

# FRANK LIPMAN, MD

*Internist and holistic physician, founder and director of Eleven Eleven Wellness Center in New York City, creator of health programs and supplements line Be Well by Dr. Frank Lipman, and author of* Revive *and* Total Renewal.

M ORE THAN 3 DECADES AGO, DR. LIPMAN TRAVELED TO POOR, rural areas of his native South Africa and discovered the powers of integrative medicine. The healing practices he witnessed abroad were unlike anything he'd learned in medical school. Today, his approach combines elements of Western and traditional, holistic medicine. "My goal is to restore internal balance and empower people to handle the stresses of modern life," he says. "Making the right food choices is a big part of that."

**THINK BEYOND THE LABEL**. "Although it's important to know how to read a food label, most of your diet should be made up of foods that don't *have* a label— grass-fed meat, organic poultry, fruits, vegetables, nuts, and seeds. When you do buy a packaged food, keep in mind that the longer the ingredients list, the further away from nature—and therefore, the less healthy—that food is."

**STRIKE A POSE**. "Yoga has become a 'workout,' which is fine. But restorative yoga has equally powerful effects. In this form of yoga, you're supported by props and you can stay in the same pose for 15 to 20 minutes, which lets you truly relax into it. I practice twice a week to unwind and stretch my body."

**SIT QUIETLY**. "Meditation sounds difficult, but it's simply clearing your mind. Just focus on your breath, and eventually your mind and body will reap the benefits. Taking time to meditate has helped me discover more about myself."

**CONTROL YOUR OWN DESTINY**. "We used to think that you couldn't change the genes you were born with, but new research shows that most of our genes can be turned on and off. That means diet, exercise, and even what we think and believe determine how our genes are expressed. So if you want to change your life, be conscious of what you eat, how often you move, and what you think."

**DITCH THE DOUGH**. "The bread our ancestors ate is far removed from what we eat today. Modern wheat has been hybridized and crossbred so much that just about the only thing that remains the same is the name. That's not what I call a *natural* food! I've given up wheat and gluten, the protein that wheat contains, and I feel much better."

**HAVE A BALL**. "I use a tennis ball to release tight muscles and fascia (the connective tissue surrounding muscles). You can roll it over any part of your body, and it makes a great foot massager!"

**LOVE WHAT YOU DO AND DO WHAT YOU LOVE**. "I feel so blessed to love my work, whether I'm helping out at a nonprofit in South Africa or seeing patients at my practice in New York City. And I try not to take myself too seriously—most of the time, anyway."

**TURN BACK THE CLOCK**. "I avoid sugar and gluten—two of the most pro-aging 'foods.' By eliminating them from my diet I'm not only healthier, but I feel younger, too. I don't miss the wheat, but I still struggle with sugar cravings. To stop them before they start, I drink protein shakes and eat lots of salads."

# GREEN MOJITO SMOOTHIE (Photo on page 328)

"PROTEIN SMOOTHIES ARE DELICIOUS, SATISFYING, FILLING AND HEALTHY. THIS ONE, DEVELOPED BY MY WIFE, IS MY FAVORITE."—**FRANK LIPMAN, MD**

**Serves 1**

1 packet of my Be Well Recharge powder

¼ avocado

1 teaspoon vanilla extract

¼ cup chopped fresh mint

Juice of 1 lime

3 or 4 ice cubes

1 tablespoon raw honey

Combine the powder, avocado, vanilla, mint leaves, lime juice, ice cubes, honey (to taste), and ¾ cup of filtered water in a blender or food processor. Blend or process until smooth.

NUTRITION PER SERVING: 290 CALORIES • 29 G PROTEIN • 28 G CARBS • 2 G FIBER • 7 G FAT • 2 G SATURATED FAT • 79 MG SODIUM

# WOODSON C. MERRELL, MD

*Chairman of the department of integrative medicine and executive director of the Continuum Center for Health and Healing at Beth Israel Medical Center in New York City; assistant clinical professor of medicine at Columbia University College of Physicians and Surgeons; and author of* The Source *and* The Arginine Solution.

F OR DR. MERRELL, A PERSON'S GOOD HEALTH COMES DOWN TO SIX fundamentals: eating properly, exercising, sleeping and resting, keeping a lid on stress, staying connected, and avoiding toxins in the environment. The most important one? "The one you're not doing," he says. He personally concentrates on his eating habits. "I have a very balanced diet, but I occasionally have to remind myself to stop eating when I'm still a bit hungry and to not eat between meals," he says. "I find that drinking water or tea helps tremendously."

**GET BENDY.** "I started doing yoga 45 years ago, and I highly recommend it for its physical and mental benefits. Qigong and tai chi are also wonderful meditative exercises. If you don't have access to classes, there are some great videos."

**CLEAN UP YOUR MEALS.** "The only acceptable packaging on foods is the rind or peel on fruits and vegetables. And don't forget to wash your produce—even those you buy frozen—to help remove pesticides."

**SOOTHE ACHES AND PAINS NATURALLY.** "Homeopathic remedies have almost no risk of side effects. I recommend topical Topricin for inflammation and sublingual arnica for muscle, joint, and tendon soreness and pain."

**DOUSE INFLAMMATION.** "The closer you can come to a vegan diet, the better it is for your body. Eat more plant-based colorful foods and less animal fats and

*(continued on page 250)*

# VEGAN CASSOULET

"TRADITIONALLY, THE FRENCH BAKED BEAN DISH CALLED A CASSOULET IS LOADED WITH MEATS OF ALL SORTS. BUT THE DENSITY AND FLAVORS OF BAKED TOFU MANAGE TO PROVIDE A GOOD VEGAN SUBSTITUTE."—**WOODSON C. MERRELL, MD**

**Serves 6**

2 packages (15 ounces each) extra-firm tofu

2 tablespoons fresh lemon juice

1 tablespoon extra-virgin olive oil

1 clove garlic, finely minced

2 tablespoons chopped fresh basil

2 teaspoons chopped fresh oregano

1 teaspoon chopped fresh rosemary

$\frac{1}{4}$ cup sunflower oil

1 medium onion, chopped

5 cloves garlic, minced

2 teaspoons dried thyme

1 bay leaf

4 cans (15.5 ounces each) navy beans, rinsed and drained

1 cup low-sodium vegetable broth

2 tablespoons chopped flat-leaf parsley

$\frac{1}{2}$ cup whole wheat panko or gluten-free bread crumbs

**1** Drain the tofu for 30 minutes. Preheat the oven to 375°F. In a small bowl, stir together the lemon juice, olive oil, garlic, basil, oregano, rosemary, and kosher salt to taste. Pat the tofu pieces dry and brush them all over with the herb mixture. Roast, flipping occasionally, until golden brown, 45 to 50 minutes.

**2** Heat the oven to 300°F. Warm the sunflower oil over medium heat in a large skillet. Add the onion and garlic, and cook until soft, about 5 minutes. Add the thyme, bay leaf, and salt and freshly ground black pepper, and cook for 3 minutes longer. Stir in the beans, broth, and tofu.

**3** Transfer the mixture to a 1-quart baking dish. Sprinkle the top with the parsley and $\frac{1}{4}$ cup of the bread crumbs. Bake for 45 minutes.

**4** Remove from the oven, stir the contents gently, and sprinkle with the remaining $\frac{1}{4}$ cup of bread crumbs. Bake for 30 minutes, or until the topping is crisp. Discard the bay leaf and serve.

NUTRITION PER SERVING: 442 CALORIES • 26 G PROTEIN • 41 G CARBS • 13 G FIBER • 20 G FAT • 2 G SATURATED FAT • 594 MG SODIUM

refined carbohydrates. And take some time to learn about herbs and spices. They're nature's gift to us when we need help reducing inflammation and oxidation."

GIVE YOURSELF A LIFT. "Fatigue is often a sign of dehydration. Drinking 12 ounces of water almost always helps you feel more alert. If you're still tired after that, brew a cup of green tea or have a piece of dark chocolate. Both are gentle energy boosters."

TAKE A BREATH BREAK. "Deep abdominal breathing—four or five slow inhales and exhales every hour or two—is the best stress reliever. No one needs to even know you're doing it."

HOLD ON TO YOUR DREAMS. "If you tend to wake up too early in the morning, try dream remembrance: As soon as you realize you are coming up to consciousness, focus on your dream, and very often you will fall right back into sleep."

GREET THE DAY GENTLY. "Meditate in the morning to start your day with a clear mind. Even if it's only for a couple of minutes, the intention makes a big difference. Thousands of studies attest to the power meditation and relaxation exercises can have on changing our minds, bodies, and spirits."

"THE CLOSER YOU CAN COME TO A VEGAN DIET, THE BETTER IT IS FOR YOUR BODY."

# LISA MUNCY-PIETRZAK, MD

*Internal medicine specialist at The Vitality Center in the Vail Mountain Lodge and Spa in Colorado, Diplomate of the American Board of Integrative Holistic Medicine, and contributing author to* Vail Valley Magazine.

"THINGS AREN'T WHAT THEY USED TO BE." THIS SAYING CAN apply to many things—the price of gas, TV sitcoms, and, according to Dr. Muncy-Pietrzak, the quality of our diets. "Unfortunately, what and how we eat today isn't nearly as nutritious as our grandparents' diets," she says. "Back then, more often than not, food came from local farms and was grown with natural fertilizers. Animals were free-range and grazed, rather than being penned in feed lots and given genetically modified corn, hormones, and antibiotics." As both an internal and holistic medicine specialist, Dr. Muncy-Pietrzak sees many patients who suffer from ailments that she says are connected to our declining diet, including heartburn, migraines, and arthritis. The remedy is to eat as close to nature as possible and to favor organic produce.

**THINK BEYOND THE WATER BOTTLE.** "It's true, staying hydrated helps your body work at peak efficiency, but you don't have to force yourself to guzzle eight 8-ounce glasses of water a day. Tea, soup, and even fruits and vegetables with a high water content all count."

**MAKE YOUR OWN VEGGIE CHIPS.** "I make it a priority to eat a variety of colorful foods—even at snack time. My kids and I love to munch on kale chips before dinner. They're so easy to make: Tear the leaves into bite-size pieces, brush them with a little olive oil, place them in a single layer on a baking sheet in a 300°F oven, and cook until they're crisp. Kale is loaded with vitamins, minerals, and isothiocyanates—substances that help prevent cancer."

**FIGHT FLU WITH FUNGI.** "Shiitake and maitake mushrooms contain beta-glucans, substances known as 'biological response modifiers' because of their ability to activate the immune system."

**POWER WALK WITH YOUR PUP.** "We have a beautiful Polish mountain sheepdog, and just his presence is so grounding and energizing. I find myself drawn into his joy and happiness. Being with him is an effortless stress reliever."

# MUNCY MORNING SMOOTHIE

"THIS SMOOTHIE PROVIDES SUPER ANTIOXIDANTS AND PROTEIN TO KICK-START MY MORNING ROUTINE. MACA IS AN ADAPTOGEN THAT HELPS SUPPORT MY ADRENAL SYSTEM. AND THE BENEFITS OF COCOA INCLUDE IMPROVED ARTERY FUNCTION."
—LISA MUNCY-PIETRZAK, MD

Serves 1

1 cup mixed berries

1 cup almond milk

2 tablespoons ground flaxseed

1 teaspoon chia seeds

1 teaspoon cocoa powder

½ teaspoon maca powder

2 ounces vegan protein powder

Combine the berries, almond milk, flaxseed, chia seeds, cocoa powder, maca powder, and protein powder in a blender. Blend until smooth and serve.

NUTRITION PER SERVING: 482 CALORIES • 53 G PROTEIN • 39 G CARBS • 9 G FIBER • 15 G FAT • 0 G SATURATED FAT • 1,069 MG SODIUM

# ANDREW WEIL, MD

*Director of the Arizona Center for Integrative Medicine at the University of Arizona in Tucson and author of numerous books, including* Spontaneous Happiness.

YOU MIGHT EXPECT SOMEONE LIKE DR. WEIL, WHO SPECIALIZES IN not just the body but also the mind, to have a complicated stay-healthy routine. But for the bestselling author, wellness comes down to three basic things: "Be physically active every day, spend time in the company of positive people, and, of course, follow a diet that's based on whole, not processed or refined, foods."

**GET HOOKED ON FISH.** "A piece of fresh fish brushed with olive oil and grilled, served with a green salad and broccoli tossed with lemon juice, garlic, and olive oil is a delicious and healthy meal. There's growing evidence for the power of anti-inflammatory foods like these to enhance both physical and emotional health. I only choose sustainable fish, such as sockeye salmon and sardines, that are low in mercury, PCBs, and other environmental contaminants."

**DON'T FIXATE ON "SUPERFOODS."** "There are so many great foods, you don't want to limit yourself. I love black Tuscan kale, brussels sprouts, broccoli, berries, olive oil, and dark chocolate."

**OPT FOR ORGANIC.** "I avoid fruits and vegetables on the Environmental Working Group's Dirty Dozen list, unless I can get organic versions. The fruits and veggies with the highest levels of pesticides are: apples, celery, strawberries, peaches, spinach, imported nectarines, imported grapes, bell peppers, potatoes, blueberries, lettuce, and kale and collard greens. So if you can't always go organic, at least choose organic when you buy these 12 foods."

**BUILD IMMUNITY NATURALLY.** "I take a daily mixed mushroom supplement for optimal immunity and astragalus root capsules when I travel to help protect against colds and flu."

**KNOW YOUR BODY.** "Be confident of your body's innate healing ability—it's your greatest health asset. I don't fight aging; I work to keep myself healthy as I grow older. I'm physically active every day, but I do what's right for me at this stage of my life: brisk walks with my Rhodesian ridgebacks twice a day, and daily swimming or cycling. That and a good night's sleep help me fight fatigue."

**BREATHE AWAY THE STRESS.** "This exercise calms your nervous system. Do it at least twice a day, and more often if something upsetting happens (do the exercise *before* you react) or if you are having trouble falling asleep. Place the tip of your tongue on the roof of your mouth behind your upper front teeth. Exhale through your mouth, making a "whoosh" sound. Inhale through your nose as you count to 4, hold your breath as you count to 7, and exhale with a whoosh through your mouth as you count to 8. Repeat this cycle 4 times."

# HASHED BRUSSELS SPROUTS

"AS A SIDE DISH, BRUSSELS SPROUTS MAKE A NICE CHANGE FROM BROCCOLI. THEY'RE BOTH MEMBERS OF THE CRUCIFEROUS PLANT FAMILY, SO THEY CONTAIN INDOLE-3-CARBINOL, SULFORAPHANE, AND ANTIOXIDANTS. IN COMBINATION, THESE COMPOUNDS ARE VERY LIKELY CANCER PROTECTIVE."—ANDREW WEIL, MD

Serves 4

1 pound brussels sprouts

2 tablespoons extra-virgin olive oil

1 medium onion, diced

1 teaspoon crushed red-pepper flakes, or to taste

1/4 teaspoon ground nutmeg, or to taste, preferably freshly grated

1/2 cup freshly grated Parmesan cheese

**1** Trim the ends off of the brussels sprouts and remove any discolored outer leaves. Cut or chop the sprouts into $\frac{1}{4}$-inch pieces. You should have about 4 cups.

**2** Warm the oil in a nonstick skillet over medium heat. Add the onion, red-pepper flakes, and a pinch of salt. Sauté, stirring frequently, until the onion is golden, 6 to 7 minutes. Add the chopped sprouts and sauté, stirring frequently, until the sprouts are bright green and crunchy-tender, about 5 minutes. Add the nutmeg and mix well.

**3** Turn off the heat, add the cheese, and mix well. Serve immediately.

NUTRITION PER SERVING: 165 CALORIES • 8 G PROTEIN • 13 G CARBS • 5 G FIBER • 10 G FAT • 3 G SATURATED FAT • 183 MG SODIUM

# W. CHRISTOPHER WINTER, MD

*President of Charlottesville Neurology and Sleep Medicine and medical director of the Martha Jefferson Hospital Sleep Medicine Center, both in Charlottesville, Virginia.*

Wherever the HAT AND WHEN YOU EAT AFFECTS HOW WELL YOU SLEEP, according to Dr. Winter. "I advise people to avoid late meals and snacking. This helps reduce the odds that you'll experience bloating, heartburn, and other digestive problems at night, allowing your digestive tract to rest a bit and ensuring peaceful slumber." A triathlete and consultant to professional sports teams, such as the Washington Capitals and the Oklahoma City Thunder, Dr. Winter has found that sleep has a big impact on performance. "I conducted a study that showed that pro baseball players who are sleepy don't stay in the league as long as players who are well rested. You're probably not a big-league pitcher, but I believe that these findings suggest that all of us could perform better in our own jobs if we made getting better sleep a priority."

**RETHINK MEAT.** "Growing up in southwest Virginia, eating steak and eggs for breakfast, a roast beef sandwich for lunch, and hamburgers for dinner (with green beans cooked with fatback until the 'green' was a distant memory) was considered 'light cuisine.' No one seemed to connect this kind of diet with the heart disease, hypertension, and high cholesterol that ran in my family. Now I tend to avoid red meat to keep my fat and cholesterol intake under control. I also feel strongly about the environmental impact of consuming a lot of red meat: Raising huge numbers of livestock places a large burden on our environment, and reducing the demand for red meat decreases that burden."

**SMASH STRESS.** "Hitting baseballs off a tee is incredibly relaxing and a great way to help my mind refocus. The batting tee can be a versatile fitness tool. While I'm working out the tension, I'm strengthening my core and improving my hand-eye coordination and focus."

**WAKE UP YOUR BREAKFAST.** "My perfect morning meal incorporates protein and complex carbs, not just because that combination keeps me from getting too hungry during the day, but also because it helps keep me alert. Protein helps your body make dopamine, a neurotransmitter that promotes wakefulness. Tyrosine, an amino acid found in yogurt, egg whites, and bananas, also triggers dopamine production in your brain."

**STRETCH IT OUT.** "As I approach my forties, I've come to the realization that strength and stamina don't mean much without flexibility, so I'm trying to incorporate more stretching into my workouts."

**EXPAND YOUR PALATE.** "I'm crazy for purple carrot juice. Purple carrots have more beta-carotene than orange ones, plus anthocyanins (which is what gives them their color). Both are powerful antioxidants that help protect against cell damage, and anthocyanins are good anti-inflammatory agents."

**CARBO-LOAD AT DINNER.** "Pasta, bread, and potatoes are high in tryptophan, an amino acid that's the precursor to serotonin and melatonin—both sleep-inducing neurotransmitters in your brain."

**KNOW WHEN TO BREAK THE RULES.** "Hunger can interfere with sleep, so if I'm *really* hungry at night, I'll go against my own advice to not eat before bed and have a small handful of almonds or hazelnuts. They're high in vitamin E—an important antioxidant—and sleep-inducing tryptophan."

# CHAI SMOOTHIE

"I'M NOT MUCH OF A COOK, BUT I LIKE TO EAT HEALTHFULLY. ANY MEAL THAT ONLY REQUIRES ME TO THROW A WHOLE BUNCH OF INGREDIENTS INTO MY BLENDER WORKS FOR ME! I TRY TO STAY AWAY FROM CAFFEINE, BUT SOMETIMES I CRAVE THE AROMA AND SPICE OF A GREAT CHAI LATTE, SO I CREATED MY OWN VERSION IN SMOOTHIE FORM. ONCE YOU MIX UP THE CHAI MIX, YOU'LL HAVE ENOUGH FOR 16 SMOOTHIES!"

—W. CHRISTOPHER WINTER, MD

**Serves 2**

## CHAI MIX

- 3 teaspoons ground ginger
- 2 teaspoons ground cinnamon
- 1 teaspoon ground cloves
- 1 teaspoon ground cardamom
- 1 teaspoon ground allspice
- 1/4 teaspoon ground white pepper
- 1/4 teaspoon ground anise

## SMOOTHIE

- 1/2 cup low-fat vanilla yogurt
- 2 bananas
- 1/2 cup ice cubes
- 1 cup almond milk
- 2 teaspoons unsweetened cocoa powder
- 1 teaspoon vanilla extract
- 4 tablespoons protein powder
- 1 tablespoon ground flaxseed
- 1 teaspoon chai mix
- Orange zest
- Agave syrup
- 2 cinnamon sticks (optional)

**1 Make the Chai Mix:** Mix together the ginger, cinnamon, cloves, cardamom, allspice, white pepper, and anise. Transfer to a glass jar with a tight-fitting lid.

**2 Make the Smoothie:** Place the yogurt, bananas, ice cubes, almond milk, cocoa powder, vanilla, protein powder, flaxseed, and chai mix in a blender. Add the orange zest and agave syrup to taste. Process until smooth, about 1 minute. Pour into 2 glasses and serve with cinnamon sticks, if using.

NUTRITION PER SERVING: 310 CALORIES • 16 G PROTEIN • 46 G CARBS • 7 G FIBER • 8 G FAT • 1 G SATURATED FAT • 207 MG SODIUM

# PAMELA YEE, MD

*Physician specializing in internal and holistic medicine at the Continuum Center for Health and Healing in New York City, and expert on nutrient-dense farming and local and sustainable food practices.*

FOR DR. YEE AND HER HUSBAND, GETTING ACCESS TO FRESH, locally grown food only requires a trip to their backyard. They own and manage Hook Mountain Growers, an organic microfarm in New York's Hudson Valley. "The way food is grown can affect its concentration of nutrients," Dr. Yee says. "I always want to be eating the healthiest foods possible." Knowing where food comes from and how it is produced is an important part of healthy eating, according to Dr. Yee. "My connection to the land and farming helps me be the best model and educator I can be for my patients."

**CHECK YOUR LIST.** "Instead of trying to keep mental track of the multiple 'to do' items swimming in my mind, I make a list every day and cross off the tasks as I accomplish them. This helps me let go of the worry and stress that comes with keeping track of my busy schedule and lets me just be in the moment."

**HEAL WITH HERBS.** "Washing your hands is crucial for preventing illness, but I also recommend taking herbs like astragalus and echinacea at the first sign of a cold or the flu. The earlier you take them, the more effective they will be."

**TAKE CONTROL OF CARBS.** "I mostly choose whole grains like quinoa and brown rice over bread and pasta to keep my weight in check. I don't exclude those other carbs. I just make sure to watch my portions and eat them only occasionally."

**KEEP IT REAL.** "I avoid the top genetically modified foods—soy, canola oil, and corn—unless they're labeled GMO-free. Some studies suggest that such scientifically altered foods are harmful to your health, although no one really knows—but they are certainly bad for the environment."

**GIVE IT 10 MINUTES.** "It's hard to keep yourself from reaching for a second helping when your food tastes and smells delicious. But chances are your belly is full and your brain just hasn't had time to realize it. I wait 10 to 15 minutes before refilling my plate, and most of the time, I decide I don't need to go back for more."

**GREEN YOUR PLATE.** "I even work leafy greens into my snacks. One of my favorites is collard green rolls. You put pureed cashews, grated carrots, smashed avocado, and whatever fresh herbs you like on a blanched collard leaf and roll it up. It's delicious and packed with nutrients and high in fiber, beneficial fats, and protein."

# WARM GREENS SAUTÉ

"GET YOUR TASTE BUDS USED TO STRONGER-FLAVORED GREENS, LIKE COLLARDS, IS BY MIXING THEM WITH MILDER-TASTING ONES, LIKE SPINACH."—**PAMELA YEE, MD**

**Serves 4**

1 tablespoon extra-virgin olive oil

4 cups mixed chopped greens
(such as collards, Swiss chard,
spinach, or kale)

1 teaspoon honey

2 tablespoons balsamic vinegar

1 teaspoon dried oregano

¼ teaspoon crushed
red-pepper flakes

**1** Warm the oil in a 10" nonstick skillet over medium-high heat. When the oil is hot, add the greens. Cover and cook, stirring occasionally, until the greens wilt, about 3 minutes.

**2** Remove the skillet from the heat. Stir in the honey, vinegar, oregano, red-pepper flakes, and ¼ teaspoon of salt. Toss well and serve.

NUTRITION PER SERVING: 54 CALORIES • 1 G PROTEIN • 5 G CARBS • 1 G FIBER • 4 G FAT •
<1 G SATURATED FAT • 155 MG SODIUM

# ALAN ARAGON, MS

*Los Angeles–based nutritionist, author of* Girth Control, *and consultant to the Los Angeles Lakers, Los Angeles Kings, and Anaheim Mighty Ducks.*

NUTRITIONIST ALAN ARAGON WILL NEVER TELL HIS CLIENTS THAT they can't eat something they crave. "I wouldn't label any food as taboo or off-limits. Why give any food that much power?" says Aragon. In fact, he believes that occasionally giving in to food temptation actually benefits your physical and mental health. "An all-or-nothing dietary approach isn't sustainable for most people in the long term. Cravings occur when you deprive yourself. Give yourself permission to 'spend' 10 to 20 percent of your daily calories on chocolate, ice cream, or whatever you desire."

MILK IT. "Some people claim that milk doesn't contribute to bone health, pointing to evidence in studies that tracked milk consumption. It's true that the results are evenly split—half of the studies show a protective effect, while the other half don't. But those studies were not randomized control trials, considered the gold standard of research studies. Virtually all randomized studies show milk's positive effect on bones. Calcium and protein—both plentiful in milk—work together to strengthen bones and help prevent osteoporosis, no doubt about it."

SNEAK IN VEGGIES. "I'm not one of those guys that gets excited at the thought of vegetables—but I do get excited at the thought of omelets. So I mix in spinach, mushrooms, and tomatoes, and I top it all with Parmesan cheese. I do eat vegetables when my wife prepares them, though. She can make any vegetable taste great."

**DITCH THE DIET MENTALITY.** "Stop reading all of the alarmist, whistle-blowing, nitpicky diet voodoo and get back to the basics: Eat a variety of mostly unrefined foods you love the taste of, and exercise regularly."

**DON'T UNDO YOUR WORKOUTS.** "Unless you're a competitive endurance athlete engaged in multiple training bouts per day, your focus should be on nailing your daily protein, carbohydrate, and fat targets. Translation: Don't think you have to eat extra food before or after exercise. If you do, you may be consuming the same number of calories you just burned off—or even more."

**BROWSE THE CEREAL AISLE.** "Cold cereal and milk is one of my favorite snacks. It's filling and healthy. Just be sure to pick a whole grain variety."

# MOCHA PROTEIN SHAKE

"ONE OF MY FAVORITE DAILY RITUALS IS MAKING THIS SHAKE. I LOVE THE TASTE OF IT; IT COMBINES TWO OF MY FAVORITE FLAVORS—COFFEE AND CHOCOLATE—BUT IT'S PACKED WITH NUTRITION. THE CALORIE COUNT MAKES THIS SHAKE A MEAL, NOT A SNACK, BUT IT IS LARGE ENOUGH TO SHARE."—ALAN ARAGON, MS

**Serves 2**

1½ cups black coffee (made in advance and cooled in the fridge)
1 large frozen banana (cut into bite-size chunks before freezing)
1 cup ice cubes
¼ cup walnuts
1 heaping tablespoon unsweetened cocoa powder
6 tablespoons chocolate protein powder

Put the coffee, banana, ice, walnuts, cocoa powder, and protein powder in a blender. Blend until smooth. Pour into 2 glasses and serve.

NUTRITION PER SERVING: 264 CALORIES • 24 G PROTEIN • 22 G CARBS • 4 G FIBER • 11 G FAT • 2 G SATURATED FAT • 58 MG SODIUM

# CHRISTINE AVANTI, CN

*Clinical and sports nutritionist, professional chef, co-host of Food Network's* Fat Chef, *and author of* Skinny Chicks Don't Eat Salads *and* Skinny Chicks Eat Real Food.

TEN YEARS AGO, NUTRITIONIST CHRISTINE AVANTI LOST 30 POUNDS and hasn't regained a single ounce. "Eating a combination of protein and carbs or fat and carbs every 4 hours keeps my blood sugar stable," she says. "I don't have the urge to overeat anymore because I'm no longer in constant 'starvation mode' from dieting. I love food and I love feeling free to eat anything, as opposed to being afraid that something will make me gain weight."

**BEWARE THE HEALTH HALO.** "The word 'salad' makes you think of a light, veggie-packed meal, but at restaurants, salads are often anything but. Between the cheese, croutons, candied nuts, and globs of dressing, you could be eating more than 1,000 calories. Before you order, consider the ingredients."

**EAT WITH YOUR HANDS.** "I don't measure portions. Instead, I use the palm of my hand as a guide to the right serving size for meat and fish and my fist as the right amount of grains or pasta per meal."

**NEVER GO HUNGRY.** "I eat every 4 hours and I recommend that my clients do the same. But that can be a lot of food prep! To make sure I always have something healthy at the ready, I shop for grab-and-go real foods every Sunday and do some cooking in advance. For instance, I'll hard-cook a dozen omega-3 organic eggs or roast a chicken, or I'll buy a rotisserie chicken."

**FIT IN FITNESS.** "The most effective thing about my exercise routine is that I make it happen—I do what I have time to do. I usually take three hot yoga and two body-sculpting classes each week. If I don't take a class, I do 45 minutes on the treadmill or elliptical, or I go for an hour-long walk or run with my dogs."

**COOK WITH COCONUT OIL.** "Coconut oil was once considered 'evil' because it's high in saturated fat, which raises cholesterol. However, it turns out that the type of saturated fat it contains isn't harmful to your heart—and it may help bust belly fat. Like butter, it's solid at room temperature, so it's great to use in vegan baked goods. It also adds a nutty flavor to vegetables when you sauté with it."

**HAVE A BACKUP PLAN.** "Because I eat often, I don't have the urge to overeat. But it can take your body a while to adjust to a new way of eating. To bust cravings, be sure you're drinking 16 cups of water a day; thirst is often mistaken for hunger. If you still get the urge, try having a cup of dessert-flavored tea—it's calorie-free."

# FARMERS' MARKET VEGGIE PASTA

"FORTUNATELY, MOST PREPARED PESTOS IN THE SUPERMARKETS' REFRIGERATED SECTIONS HAVE THE SAME INGREDIENTS AS HOMEMADE PESTO, SO THEY'RE STILL 'REAL' FOOD; JUST CHECK THE INGREDIENTS LIST."—CHRISTINE AVANTI, CN

**Serves 8**

1 pound asparagus, cut into 1" pieces

1 pound whole wheat penne

2 tablespoons extra-virgin olive oil

8 ounces water-packed or frozen artichoke hearts, thawed, cut into quarters

1 red onion, thinly sliced into rounds

1/4 cup vegetable stock or white wine

1/4 cup store-bought pesto

3/4 cup shredded part-skim mozzarella cheese

1 Bring a large pot of salted water to a boil. Add the asparagus and boil for 1 minute, until it turns bright green. Remove the asparagus with a slotted spoon and run it under cold water to stop the cooking.

**2** Bring the same pot of water back to a boil and add the penne. Cook according to package directions until al dente. Drain and set aside.

**3** Heat an extra-large skillet over medium-high heat and add the oil. Add the asparagus, artichoke hearts, and onion, and cook until the onion begins to caramelize, 5 to 7 minutes. Add the stock or wine and cook for 1 to 2 minutes, scraping up all the browned bits from the bottom of the pan. Reduce the heat and stir in the pesto until it is evenly distributed.

**4** Add the pasta and toss with tongs until the vegetables and pasta are well combined. Divide among 8 bowls and sprinkle with the cheese.

NUTRITION PER SERVING: 345 CALORIES • 14 G PROTEIN • 49 G CARBS • 8 G FIBER • 11 G FAT • 2 G SATURATED FAT • 170 MG SODIUM

# KERI GLASSMAN, MS, RD

*Founder and president of Keri Glassman, Nutritious Life nutrition practice in New York City and Nutritious Life Meals daily diet delivery program, and author of four books, including* The New You and Improved Diet.

KERI GLASSMAN HAD AN "ALL OR NOTHING" ATTITUDE TOWARD food in her teens and twenties. "I'd either live on grapefruit, turkey, and salads or go overboard on everything! " she says. "I definitely was an emotional eater and, *man,* can that be draining!" She worked at finding a healthy balance by concentrating on one meal at a time. If she thought she ate the "wrong" thing, she'd just vow to do better at her next meal. Today, she can say, "Bring on the chocolate chip cookies!" without worry. "I can now actually eat a couple of bites and feel satisfied."

ANSWER THE HUNGER CALL. "Learning to recognize when you are 'slightly hungry' and should eat and 'slightly satisfied' and should stop eating is critical to managing health and weight. I never let myself get too hungry, and I almost never eat until I'm stuffed, even if the food is healthy."

FIND YOUR FITNESS LEVEL. "I was a college athlete, and if I could, I 'd exercise every day. But as a working mother of two, my schedule doesn't always permit that. It's important to find a routine you can be consistent with given the demands of your life."

PACK IN THE PROTEIN. "What you should eat before and after your workout really depends on how long and how hard you exercise. For energy beforehand, I eat a small banana with 1 tablespoon of nut butter. Afterward, I make sure to replenish with a combination of protein, antioxidants, and a bit of whole grain. I work out in the morning, so breakfast is often eggs with oatmeal or quinoa. I try to mix some veggies in there, too—I love a good veggie scramble."

**BE A FRIEND TO A FARMER.** "Farmers' markets are popping up everywhere, more restaurants are incorporating organic and local foods into their menus, and grocery stores are expanding their health food aisles."

**FILL UP ON HEALTHY FAT.** "When I eat an adequate amount of healthy fat, I am much more satisfied all day and healthier overall as well. I love avocado because it's versatile—I add it to salads, blend it into smoothies, eat it plain, or mix it with veggies to make guacamole."

**EAT EMPOWERED!** "Food is supposed to be something we enjoy *and* something that fuels us and keeps us healthy. It's not one or the other. Feel good about putting the best foods you can in your body. Instead of thinking about what you can't have, think about what you *can* have."

# RASPBERRY-BALSAMIC GLAZED SALMON WITH ROASTED ASPARAGUS

"I'D EAT SALMON EVERY DAY IF I COULD. IT'S SO HEALTHY, BUT I ALSO JUST LOVE THE FLAVOR. AND I FEEL HEALTHY JUST WATCHING MY KIDS EAT IT."—KERI GLASSMAN, MS, RD

**Serves 4**

1 pound asparagus spears, tough ends trimmed

¼ cup extra-virgin olive oil

24 fresh raspberries

½ cup balsamic vinegar

4 teaspoons freshly squeezed orange juice

1 teaspoon orange zest

2 teaspoons honey

4 teaspoons red wine

1 pound skinless salmon fillet, preferably wild-caught (about ¾" thick)

1 Preheat the oven to 400°F. Layer the asparagus on a baking sheet, toss with the oil, and sprinkle with salt and freshly ground black pepper to taste. Roast in the oven for 15 minutes, turning the spears once.

2 Mash the raspberries and vinegar with a fork in a small bowl while the asparagus cooks. Stir in the orange juice, orange zest, honey, and wine until combined. Set aside.

3 Coat a large nonstick skillet with cooking spray and place it over medium heat. Cook the salmon until the fish is cooked through, turning once, for about 4 minutes per side. Transfer the salmon to a plate. Remove the skillet from the heat and carefully wipe away any liquid with a paper towel.

4 Return the skillet to medium heat and add the reserved raspberry mixture. Stirring constantly, cook until just thickened, about 2 minutes.

5 Cut the salmon into four even pieces and place each piece on a plate. Pour the sauce over the salmon and serve with the roasted asparagus on the side.

NUTRITION PER SERVING: 369 CALORIES • 26 G PROTEIN • 18 G CARBS • 3 G FIBER • 21 G FAT • 3 G SATURATED FAT • 540 MG SODIUM

# STEPHEN GULLO, PhD

*President of the Center for Health and Weight Sciences in New York City, former chair of the National Obesity and Weight Control Education Institute of the American Institute for Life-Threatening Illness at the Columbia University Medical Center, and author of two best-selling books,* Thin Tastes Better *and* The Thin Commandments Diet.

FOR MORE THAN 30 YEARS, DR. GULLO HAS HELPED THOUSANDS OF patients lose weight and keep it off. One of the most common misconceptions he hears is that you can enjoy all foods in moderation. "For many people, food is a compulsion, and 'all foods in moderation' is a more idealistic than a realistic statement of human behavior," he says. "In matters of pleasure and convenience human beings are not given to moderation, but to excess. I teach my patients to ask themselves, 'Does this food satisfy or stimulate?' Food must be satisfying and taste great without stimulating overeating." Similarly he reminds his patients that exercise is wonderful for weight maintenance, but not for weight loss. "Exercise will give you fitness, but it will never save you from fatness," he says. "The most important exercise of all isn't done at a gym: It's the exercise of good judgment with your food choices. Changing your eating habits is the most effective way to lose weight."

EXPLORE YOUR FOOD HISTORY. "Just as we all have unique and defining characteristics that remain with us throughout life, such as fingerprints, so too do we have an individual eating print—the sum of foods, behaviors, situations, and moods that cause us to lose control of our eating. There are no good or bad foods; there are only good or bad histories with foods. If you study the foods, places, and times of day that trip you up, it's easy to see definite, predictable patterns. Those who honor their food histories keep weight off. Those who violate their food histories gain back the weight again and again."

SKIP THE DESSERT MENU. "You'll always struggle with weight control if you react to cravings and give in to a food you have a long history of abusing. If you're like me and you have a strong genetic preference for sweets, it's best to avoid temptation. But I never tell myself I can't have my favorite foods; that mind-set only makes me want them more. Instead I say, 'This food doesn't work for me.' Too many of us romanticize sweets, calling them goodies or treats. But they're simply high-calorie, fattening foods that taste good."

TAKE THE STAIRS. "It can be hard for me to squeeze in exercise 3 or 4 days a week. I've countered this to some extent by walking up nine flights of stairs to my top-floor apartment instead of taking the elevator, and I walk wherever I can. For total body shaping, I like 'slow burn' exercise—lifting and lowering weights very slowly—which studies have shown gives you a great workout in just a single ½-hour session a week."

SHOP SMARTER. "Remember, thin starts in the supermarket! Before you put a food in your shopping cart, ask, 'What's my history with this food?' If it's something that stimulates rather than satisfies your appetite, don't buy it. More than 75 percent of my female patients and 50 percent of my male patients wouldn't need my services if they just stopped buying certain foods. And don't feed yourself that great lie 'I'm buying it for someone else.' That person won't have to wear it. You will."

PHONE A FRIEND. "Reaching out to someone with whom you can share your stress, even if you don't tell that person why you're calling, diverts your mind and gets you past an impulse to eat. Stress eating is about immediacy; it's about nibbling. Accordingly, it almost always involves bite-size foods such as candies or cookies. (After treating more than 15,000 patients, I've never had one turn to baked chicken or lasagna when they're stressed!) Distractions help, but prevention is even better. If you're prone to stress eating, keep those foods out of the house."

# CAJUN-STYLE GRILLED SHRIMP

"SHRIMP IS MY FAVORITE HEALTHY MEAL. IT'S CHEWY. YOU CAN HAVE A GENEROUS
AMOUNT FOR RELATIVELY FEW CALORIES. DID YOU EVER MEET ANYONE WHO
GOT FAT FROM EATING SHRIMP?"—STEPHEN GULLO, PhD

**Serves 4**

1¾ teaspoons light brown sugar

1½ teaspoons oregano

¾ teaspoon thyme

¼ teaspoon ground red pepper

1½ pounds large shrimp, peeled and deveined

2 teaspoons vegetable oil

⅓ cup ketchup

2 tablespoons + 2 teaspoons red wine vinegar

½ teaspoon ground ginger

2 cups frozen corn kernels, thawed

2 scallions, thinly sliced

1 Combine 1 teaspoon of the brown sugar, the oregano, thyme, red pepper, ¼ teaspoon of salt, and ¼ teaspoon of freshly ground black pepper in a medium bowl. Add the shrimp and oil, tossing to coat. Cover and refrigerate for 30 minutes.

2 Combine the ketchup, vinegar, ginger, and the remaining ¾ teaspoon of the brown sugar in a medium bowl. Stir in the corn and scallions.

3 Preheat the broiler. Broil the shrimp 6 inches from the heat, turning once, until opaque throughout, about 4 minutes total. Toss the hot shrimp with the corn mixture and serve.

NUTRITION PER SERVING: 285 CALORIES • 33 G PROTEIN • 25 G CARBS • 1 G FIBER • 6 G FAT •
1 G SATURATED FAT • 443 MG SODIUM

# MELINA B. JAMPOLIS, MD

*Internist, certified physician nutrition specialist, author of* The Calendar Diet, *and the diet and fitness expert for CNNhealth.com.*

A KEY LESSON DR. JAMPOLIS LEARNED FROM HER NUTRITION training: "Staying lean is all about trade-offs, not perfection." While consistency in both your diet and exercise routines is important, an all-or-nothing attitude can backfire—you might think that if you can't do it flawlessly, you shouldn't do it at all. "You have to pay attention to the choices you make," she says. "For instance, if I'm going out for dinner, I decide ahead of time whether I'm going to have a glass of wine or dessert (but not both). And when it comes to chocolate chip cookies—my weakness—I have a rule: If they aren't fantastic, I don't bother!"

TAP INTO PLANT POWER. "I'm amazed at all the research demonstrating the health benefits of plant-based nutrients—they can prevent and sometimes even cure disease. I eat a lot of fresh, brightly colored, seasonal produce and flavorful spices, and I encourage my patients to do the same."

FORGET ABOUT FAT-FREE. "During my residency, I lived on fat-free packaged snacks, starches, and sweets—think bagels with fat-free cream cheese, pasta with fat-free marinara sauce, and fat-free candy. I was hungry, I had zero energy most of the time, and I weighed 20 pounds more than I do today. Now my diet is made up of foods that supply healthful fats, low-glycemic carbs, and lean, satiating protein."

DON'T DENY YOUR CRAVINGS. "I have a drawer full of partially eaten candy

*(continued on page 276)*

# BLACK BEAN SOUP WITH AVOCADO CRÈME

*"SOUP IS A HIGH-VOLUME FOOD—MEANING SOMETHING THAT'S FILLING, BUT LOW IN CALORIES. THIS ONE FROM MY BOOK THE CALENDAR DIET, IS NUTRIENT DENSE, CONTAINING FIBER, PLANT-BASED PROTEIN, ANTIOXIDANT-RICH SPICES LIKE CUMIN, AND METABOLISM-BOOSTING CHILI POWDER."—MELINA B. JAMPOLIS, MD*

**Serves 2**

2 teaspoons extra-virgin olive oil

1/2 cup chopped onion

1 clove garlic, minced

1 can (15.5 ounces) no-salt-added black beans, rinsed and drained

1 cup chopped canned tomatoes

2 cups low-sodium vegetable or chicken broth

1/2 teaspoon ground cumin

1/4–1/2 teaspoon chili powder

1/4 cup 0% Greek yogurt

1/4 avocado

1/2 teaspoon lime zest

1 teaspoon fresh lime juice

1 Warm the oil in a large pot over medium-low heat. Add the onion and sauté for 2 minutes. Add the garlic and sauté for 1 additional minute.

2 Add the beans, tomatoes, broth, cumin, chili powder, 1/4 teaspoon of salt and freshly ground black pepper. Bring to a boil and reduce heat to low. Simmer uncovered for 20 minutes. Remove from heat and let soup cool to lukewarm.

3 Put the yogurt, avocado, lime zest, and lime juice in a blender. Puree until smooth. Set aside.

4 Transfer soup to a blender. Blend until smooth.

5 Reheat the soup. Divide between 2 bowls. Top each bowl with half of the avocado crème.

NUTRITION PER SERVING: 268 CALORIES • 12 G PROTEIN • 37 G CARBS • 10 G FIBER • 8 G FAT • 1 G SATURATED FAT • 754 MG SODIUM

in bags. I've discovered that if I eat what I really want, it helps me feel satisfied with a small portion. If you have a strong craving and don't give in to it, you often eat much more than you would if you had just a few bites of what you wanted in the first place. For instance, I love milk chocolate—even though I know dark is healthier—so I buy portion-controlled servings. Then I have just one, rather than having a bunch of the 'healthy' dark stuff before finally giving in to my craving and having what I wanted from the start."

FIT FITNESS IN. "I do yoga and walk or jog on a treadmill, but as a busy mom, doctor, and TV personality, I need a flexible workout schedule that lets me squeeze in exercise whenever and wherever I can. I keep a set of 8-pound weights in the bathroom so I can do arm exercises while my son is taking a bath. I'll put on loud music and dance around the house with my son. On the weekends, my family and I go hiking. You can burn just as many calories outside of the gym as you do in the gym."

ACTIVATE YOUR DAY. "Formal exercise is important, but research shows that little movements matter, too. Thanks to mechanization—dishwashers, cars, escalators—we burn 120 fewer calories a day than we did a few generations ago. TV and computers don't help, either. So take the stairs, stand up when you're on the phone, and get off the bus two stops early every day."

FAT-PROOF YOUR ENVIRONMENT. "Eating off smaller plates and bowls and drinking out of tall, thin glasses gives you built-in portion control. When you're making dinner, cook extra vegetables and lean protein so you have healthy leftovers to pack for lunch or throw together for another dinner. Keep a measuring cup near your cereal box, or measure out $^1/_4$-cup servings of nuts and pack them in baggies to take along for a quick, healthy snack. All of these steps can make a big difference in your calorie intake."

# DAVID KATZ, MD

*Director of the Prevention Research Center at Yale University, author of* The Flavor-Full Diet, *and principal inventor of the NuVal System.*

D R. KATZ'S MOTTO IS: LOVE FOOD THAT LOVES YOU BACK. "WHEN you develop an optimal diet and sustain it, your taste buds quickly acclimate to less salt, less sugar, and more healthful foods," he says. Dr. Katz says his wife Catherine's love of food and cooking helped him confirm that a healthy diet and an enjoyable one need not be mutually exclusive. "Our diets are optimal for health, but they are also a daily source of pleasure. It's a nice combination."

IMAGINE YOUR FOOD AS PART OF YOUR BODY. "Don't let what you put in your body be arbitrary, haphazard, or dictated by circumstances or the choices of others. I never eat a food I don't want my cells, hormones, and enzymes to be built out of. That means no soda, no junk food, no deli meats, and no fast food."

RETHINK CRAVINGS. "If your diet is poor, cravings are not a reliable indicator of what your body needs, but if your diet is close to nature, cravings are much more in sync with biology and much more trustworthy. If your diet is very 'good,' you don't tend to yearn for foods that are 'bad.'"

EAT CHOCOLATE. "Dark chocolate is antioxidant rich. I eat it when I want it—in moderation, of course. One of my favorite chocolate treats is my wife's Almond-Oat–Dark Chocolate Cookies. Just combine 2 cups of rolled oats, 2 cups of almond meal, $^1/_2$ cup of canola oil, $^1/_2$ cup of agave syrup, 1 teaspoon of vanilla

*(continued on page 280)*

# QUINOA SALAD WITH ALMONDS AND GREEN BEANS

"QUINOA COOKS MORE QUICKLY THAN BROWN RICE, AND IT HAS MORE PROTEIN AND FIBER."—DAVID KATZ, MD

**Serves 4**

²/₃ cup quinoa

1¹/₃ cups water or low-sodium chicken broth

6 cups (about 20 ounces) frozen French-cut green beans

4 teaspoons Dijon mustard

2 tablespoons balsamic vinegar

2 tablespoons extra-virgin olive oil

2 tablespoons crumbled feta cheese

2 medium red onions, thinly sliced

¹/₃ cup toasted sliced almonds

1 Place the quinoa and water or broth in a medium saucepan and bring to a boil over high heat. Reduce the heat to low, cover, and simmer until all of the liquid is absorbed, about 15 minutes. Let stand, covered.

2 Bring 2 cups of water to a boil in another medium saucepan over medium heat. Add the green beans and cook for 2 minutes. Drain and set aside.

3 Whisk together the mustard, vinegar, oil, a pinch of salt, and freshly ground black pepper to taste in a large bowl. Add the green beans and toss to coat.

4 Fluff the quinoa with a fork. Add the cheese, onions, almonds, and quinoa to the bowl with the beans and toss gently to combine. Divide into 4 bowls and serve.

NUTRITION PER SERVING (2½ CUPS): 348 CALORIES • 11 G PROTEIN • 45 G CARBS • 10 G FIBER • 16 G FAT • 2 G SATURATED FAT • 171 MG SODIUM

extract, and $1\frac{1}{2}$ cups of bittersweet chocolate chips. Drop by the rounded table-spoon on a parchment-lined baking sheet and bake in a 350°F oven for 9 minutes."

FOLLOW A SMART-FAT DIET. "After reviewing the evidence on the health effects of low-fat diets, some years ago I went from a very low-fat diet to a diet that's still relatively low in fat, but with more emphasis on healthy oils—nuts, seeds, olive oil, and avocados."

TRADE UP YOUR GROCERIES. "I developed the NuVal nutritional profiling system (www.nuval.com) to help people make healthier choices at the supermarket. Food scores are displayed on the shelf tags, allowing you to compare nutrition the way you do price. For instance, a fresh apple scores a healthy 96, while applesauce scores only a 4."

## "I NEVER EAT A FOOD I DON'T WANT MY CELLS, HORMONES, AND ENZYMES TO BE BUILT OUT OF."

# TRAVIS STORK, MD

*Emergency medicine physician, host of TV's* The Doctors, *and the author of* The Lean Belly Prescription.

"WE LIVE IN A DAY AND AGE WHERE PEOPLE THINK TAKING A pill can make them healthy. But most of us should be getting our vitamins and other nutrients from whole foods," says Dr. Stork. "Spend your money on nature's supplement: good food. It's the symphony that whole foods play in our bodies that gives us just the right balance of the nutrients we need." Dr. Stork grew up in the Midwest, where heaping portions of fattening foods were the norm, but he changed his eating habits in college. "I've spent a lot of time learning about food, tweaking my diet so that I could enjoy my food and my life more," he says. "You don't have to sacrifice taste to eat healthy, you just have to choose foods that you love that actually *are* healthy."

EAT AS IF YOUR LIFE DEPENDS ON IT. "As an ER doctor, I too often see the results of a lifetime of bad food choices. But just as you can cause trouble with a collection of seemingly inconsequential choices, you can immediately see benefits when you make changes. My wife, Charlotte, is an amazing 'healthy' cook. She's taught me how to incorporate ever-increasing amounts of veggies into our meals without sacrificing taste. The really good news is that my parents are now eating the way Charlotte and I do, and they seem younger and more vigorous than ever. It's never too late to improve your diet and feel better at the same time."

PUT YOUR MIND IN YOUR MEALS. "I've seen plenty of studies that show

*(continued on page 284)*

# RIGATONI WITH TURKEY AND VEGETABLE BOLOGNESE

"I LOVE TO EAT. FOR ME A GOOD MEAL IS HEARTY AND HEALTHY!"—TRAVIS STORK, MD

**Serves 8**

2 tablespoons extra-virgin olive oil

1 medium onion, chopped

3 large cloves garlic, minced

8 ounces chopped white or portobello mushrooms

2 medium carrots, finely chopped

1 red bell pepper, chopped

1/2 cup chopped celery

1 medium zucchini, finely chopped

1 pound ground turkey

1 teaspoon dried basil

1 teaspoon dried oregano

1/4 teaspoon crushed red-pepper flakes

6 cups jarred low-sodium pasta sauce

1 pound whole wheat rigatoni (or other pasta)

1/4 cup grated Parmesan cheese

1 Warm the oil in a large, deep skillet over medium heat. Add the onion and garlic and cook, stirring, until the onion is translucent, about 3 minutes. Add the mushrooms, carrots, bell pepper, celery, and zucchini. Cook until the vegetables are tender, about 10 minutes.

2 Add the turkey, basil, oregano, red-pepper flakes, 1/2 teaspoon of salt, and 1/4 teaspoon of freshly ground black pepper. Cook, breaking up the lumps of turkey, until it's no longer pink, about 5 minutes. Stir in the sauce, reduce the heat and simmer gently, stirring occasionally, 15 to 20 minutes. Meanwhile, prepare the pasta according to package directions.

3 Drain the pasta and add it to the sauce. Stir to combine, and season to taste with salt and black pepper. Serve with the cheese.

NUTRITION PER SERVING (ABOUT 2 CUPS): 421 CALORIES • 22 G PROTEIN • 60 G CARBS • 9 G FIBER • 11 G FAT • 2 G SATURATED FAT • 261 MG SODIUM

how distracted eaters make poor choices, both with the type and the quantity of food they eat. People who are overstressed often tend to reach for food to comfort or distract themselves, and that can lead to weight gain and even more stress. If you pay attention to food—that means no eating in front of the TV!—and notice how you feel after a good versus a bad meal, you will eventually crowd out the negatives: fast food, sweet drinks, junk food. "

BECOME A FAN OF FARMERS' MARKETS. "The closer the food you eat is to the way nature intended it to be, the better it will be for you. If you can ditch the supermarket entirely and shop at farmers' markets, you'll never suffer the consequences of eating overprocessed foods. That may not be practical, though, so the second best step is to shop the edges of the store—the produce section, dairy aisle, and meat and seafood counters. (Choose lean cuts of meat.) If a food you're considering at the grocery store has more than five ingredients, think about putting it back. An apple has only one ingredient: apple."

MAKE BURNING CALORIES FUN. "Before I went to medical school, I worked in the consulting industry. After saving money to buy a bike, I decided to use it to commute to work. It cleared my mind like nothing else could, both at the start and the end of the day. I still ride to work every day, and the mental health benefits are at least as important as the physical health benefits. I spend as much time as possible outdoors being active in nature. When I'm out riding my mountain bike, it's not about fitness, it's about living. The combination of fresh air and steep inclines makes for a great workout, but more importantly, it always inspires me."

KEEP YOUR FRIENDS CLOSE. "Being truly healthy means being mentally healthy. A key to that: Stay connected to the people you love, and meet new people by volunteering or doing other worthwhile things in your community. As you grow older, the quality of your friendships will keep your mind sharp and your emotional health high."

# TANYA ZUCKERBROT, MS, RD

*Registered dietitian in private practice, founder and CEO of The F-Factor Diet, and author of* The F-Factor Diet *and* The Miracle Carb Diet.

ONE OF THE FIRST HEALTH EXPERTS TO RECOGNIZE THE CONnection between fiber and improved health and weight loss, Zuckerbrot has helped thousands of people slim down without deprivation. She knows her methods work because she eats exactly the same kind of diet she recommends for her clients and readers. Even though she lives in the "bagel capital of the world"—New York City—Zuckerbrot rarely indulges in this local specialty. "Just one bagel has 560 calories and very little fiber—it's the carbohydrate equivalent of seven slices of white bread," she says. "But because New York bagels truly are the best, I do have one occasionally. I always choose whole wheat to get a fiber boost, and I scoop out the insides, saving the carb equivalent of three slices of bread."

TRY THIS RECIPE FOR RELAXATION. "There's scientific evidence suggesting that lavender may calm the nervous system and improve sleep quality, and that sea salt helps relax muscles. There's no need to buy fancy salts; I make my own. Just mix 2 cups of sea salt and $^1\!/_2$ teaspoon of pure essential lavender oil in a bowl, then transfer the mixture to a glass jar with a tight-fitting lid. Use $^1\!/_4$ cup per bath."

RETHINK FIBER. "A lot of people think fiber equals brown and boring, but in reality, it's found in all plant foods—fruits, vegetables, whole grains, beans, and nuts. Because fiber is indigestible, it has zero calories. High-fiber foods swell in your stomach and take longer to digest, leaving you feeling fuller, longer. Fiber serves as nature's detox by pulling toxins, cholesterol, and estrogen out of your body, lowering your risk for colon cancer, breast cancer, and cardiovascular disease. And the most exciting news: A groundbreaking 10-year study found that people who ate a high-fiber diet lived the longest."

**DECODE YOUR EATING HABITS.** "Keeping a food diary significantly increases your odds of weight-loss success. Journaling makes you accountable for every bite and sip—and on average, every mouthful equals 25 calories. Four extra bites a day can lead to 10 extra pounds in a year. When you write down what you eat, you become more aware of your eating habits and patterns, so you can correct them. For instance, do you tend to overeat at night? You might discover that it's more likely to happen when you skip lunch."

**BE PICKY ABOUT PACKAGED.** "Our grocery store shelves are chock-full of processed foods, and most of them put convenience ahead of nutrition. But there is a place for packaged foods, and more manufacturers are bringing nutritious products to the market. My line of F-Factor cereals and other products is just one example."

**TOAST TO YOUR HEALTH.** "Moderate drinkers not only tend to have better health and live longer, they are 30 percent less likely to gain weight over time than those who abstain from alcohol. Wine or spirits (such as vodka, tequila, and scotch) served on the rocks are your best choices; they typically contain 80 to 100 calories. Mojitos, margaritas, and other cocktails made with sugary mixes can easily contain 200 to 400 calories each."

**STRENGTHEN YOUR METABOLISM.** "My workouts used to be all about cardio, but there's strong evidence that strength training is far more effective for weight control. Adding muscle boosts metabolism better and for longer than cardio does, and it provides a host of anti-aging benefits. By preserving muscle, I don't have to eat less as I get older just to keep my weight steady. Plus strength training promotes bone health, flexibility, and more."

# GRANDMA CLAIRE'S CHICKEN SOUP

"MY GRANDMOTHER WOULD SPEND HOURS MAKING THIS SOUP, SIMMERING A WHOLE CHICKEN, SKIN AND ALL. I CUT DOWN ON THE TIME (AND THE CALORIES) BY USING BONELESS, SKINLESS CHICKEN TENDERS. IT'S WARM, FLAVORFUL, AND SO AROMATIC. AND IT'S TRULY FILLING, TOO, BECAUSE IT HAS LOTS OF VOLUME AND THE COMBINATION OF PROTEIN FROM THE CHICKEN AND FIBER FROM THE VEGGIES DIGESTS SLOWLY."—TANYA ZUKERBROT, MS, RD

**Serves 8**

8 whole black peppercorns

2 bay leaves

3 sprigs fresh dill

3 sprigs fresh flat-leaf parsley

1 pound boneless, skinless chicken tenders

4 carrots, peeled, cut into halves

2 turnips, peeled, cut into halves

1 onion, chopped

4 ribs celery, cut into halves

4 cups low-sodium chicken broth

1 Wrap the peppercorns, bay leaves, dill, and parsley in a piece of cheesecloth to form a pouch and tie it closed with kitchen twine. Place the chicken, carrots, turnips, onion, and celery in a large pot. Add 4 cups of water and the chicken broth.

2 Bring to a boil over high heat. Reduce the heat to low and simmer, uncovered, for 1 hour. Check occasionally, skimming and discarding any fat that rises to the top of the soup.

3 Discard the cheesecloth and herbs. Carefully remove the chicken tenders, carrots, turnips, and celery, and place them on a cutting board to cool. Once they're cool enough to handle, shred the chicken and cut the vegetables into bite-size chunks. Put the chicken and vegetables back in the pot, reheat the soup, and serve.

NUTRITION PER SERVING (2 CUPS): 121 CALORIES • 20 G PROTEIN • 10 G CARBS • 3 G FIBER • <1 G FAT • 0 G SATURATED FAT • 165 MG SODIUM

# SUSAN BOWERMAN, MS, RD

*Assistant director of the UCLA Center for Human Nutrition, consultant to Herbalife International, and coauthor of* What Color Is Your Diet?

RED, ORANGE, BLUE, GREEN: BOWERMAN MAKES SURE SHE SAMPLES something from every color of the dietary rainbow on a daily basis—and many of her produce picks come from her own garden. "My husband and I have always found a way to grow some of our own food. Even when we lived in a tiny apartment, we had a patio garden," she says. "We have a bigger plot today, and I eat more fresh produce than ever." Having a connection to the way food is grown gives you a true appreciation for local, seasonal fruits and vegetables. "When you see the same produce in the super-market all year round, it's easy to lose track of the seasons," she says. "But when you garden or visit the farmers' market regularly, you're much more appreciative of the abundance of fresh greens in early spring or those first stone fruit in early summer."

**CHANNEL YOUR INNER ADELE.** "If no one is home, I love to sing and play the piano. I wouldn't want anyone to ever hear me—I have a terrible voice and I 'play at' the piano more than I actually 'play' it—but I do find that pretending to be a diva for 15 minutes really does take the stress away."

**DON'T SELL YOURSELF SHORT.** "Nothing would make me happier than if more of my patients spent their energy trying to achieve better health, rather than focusing on all of the reasons and excuses why they can't eat well or exercise. At the same time, I've had so many patients who have made incredible strides toward better health—

often in the face of really adverse circumstances. I know if they can do it, anyone can."

**BE A PASTA PURIST.** "I'm not a fan of whole grain pasta. It just doesn't have the taste and texture that I love in authentic Italian pasta dishes. So I buy good-quality imported pasta and eat it occasionally, without any guilt. I also can't resist crusty sourdough bread—but it has to be really exceptional, usually fresh from a bakery, in order for me to splurge."

**GET CREATIVE ABOUT EXERCISE.** "I *have* to read the newspaper while I have my breakfast, so I decided to cancel my newspaper delivery service and walk to the newsstand every morning. I've turned my quest for the paper into a 1-hour walk every single day. Having a goal and a reward keeps me motivated."

**POWER UP WITH PROTEIN.** "When I'm in a rush in the morning, I make a protein shake with fat-free milk, vanilla- or chocolate-flavored protein powder, and frozen fruit. I mix up the type of fruit I use so I never get bored. I like the fact that I'm getting a serving of dairy, a serving of fruit, and about 20 grams of protein in my glass."

**PACK A SNACK.** "When I remember to include something in my brown-bag lunch to nibble on midafternoon—like a Greek yogurt, or a piece of fruit and a low-fat string cheese—I have more energy. Plus I'm not starving when I get home at night, so I don't snack on all the wrong stuff before dinner!"

**PERK UP YOUR SALAD.** "You'll find a big bowl of leafy greens at my dinner table nearly every night. It's a tradition my mother started and I continue. Her secret ingredient for a better-tasting salad is adding a big handful of chopped parsley. I dress the greens simply with a homemade dressing of olive oil, balsamic vinegar or lemon, some grainy mustard, and salt and pepper."

**FIND PLEASURE ON YOUR PLATE.** "Even though as a dietitian I spend a lot of time counseling people on what they should and shouldn't eat, I always emphasize that eating is meant to be enjoyable. When we spend too much time focusing on nutrients and move too far away from appreciating the actual food, we lose the forest for the trees."

# VEGETARIAN SOUP WITH SHIRATAKI NOODLES

"THIS RECIPE IS VERY VERSATILE. IF YOU DON'T HAVE THE FRESH SHIRATAKI (YAM) NOODLES AVAILABLE, YOU CAN USE DRIED BUCKWHEAT (SOBA) NOODLES. YOU CAN SWAP THE VEGETABLE BROTH FOR CHICKEN OR BEEF, YOU CAN TOSS IN SOME SHRIMP OR LEFTOVER DICED CHICKEN, OR YOU CAN ADD OTHER VEGETABLES."

—SUSAN BOWERMAN, MS, RD

Serves 4

1 cup boiling water

10 dried shiitake mushrooms

3 cans (14½ ounces each) low-sodium vegetable broth

1 package extra-firm tofu, cut into ½" cubes

1 package (10 ounces) frozen shelled edamame

2 packages (8 ounces each) shirataki noodles

1 bag (6 ounces) prewashed baby spinach leaves

Seasoned rice vinegar

Ground white pepper

Toasted sesame oil

1 Pour boiling water over the shiitake mushrooms. Let them stand until the mushroom caps are tender, about 15 minutes.

2 Remove the mushrooms and reserve the soaking liquid. Slice the caps into strips, discarding any tough stems.

3 Pour the broth, mushrooms, and their soaking liquid into a medium-size stockpot and bring to a boil over high heat. Reduce the heat to low and simmer for 10 minutes to let the flavors blend. Add the tofu and edamame and stir gently. Cook until the tofu and edamame are heated through, 5 to 7 minutes. Turn off the heat.

4 Add the noodles and fresh spinach, cover the stockpot, and allow the heat of the soup to wilt the spinach and cook the noodles. Check to make sure all the ingredients are hot, then add rice vinegar and white pepper to taste. Ladle into 4 bowls, drizzle a few drops of sesame oil on top of each bowl, and serve.

NUTRITION PER SERVING (ABOUT 2 CUPS): 242 CALORIES • 19 G PROTEIN • 28 G CARBS • 12 G FIBER • 7 G FAT • <1 G SATURATED FAT • 289 MG SODIUM

# TED EPPERLY, MD

*Family physician, program director and chief executive officer of the Family Medicine Residency of Idaho (FMRI) in Boise, immediate past board chair and past president of the American Academy of Family Physicians, and author of* Fractured: America's Broken Health Care System and What We Must Do to Heal It.

FINDING A WAY TO KEEP CALORIES IN CHECK WITHOUT GOING hungry—that's the toughest thing about trying to lose weight. But Dr. Epperly points to two easy moves that can have a big impact. "Drink water. Most people are relatively dehydrated. Water fills you up, acts as a natural lubricant, and has zero calories—compared to 122 in 5 ounces of white wine and 150 in 12 ounces of soda," he says. His next piece of advice is to cut back on high-fat foods. "Some good fats are healthy, but in moderation. Remember that fat contains 9 calories per gram—more than twice as much as protein or carbohydrates." Give up one soda a day and have one handful of nuts instead of two, and you'll slash 320 calories from your diet— enough to help you drop nearly 3 pounds in a month with practically no effort.

PRACTICE YOUR ABCs. "I like to eat, so I tend to overdo it, especially with the wrong things, such as chips. That's why I've established my ABC regimen: Eat apples, bananas, and carrots. I find that reaching for healthy snacks when you're hungry or stressed pays great health dividends. The increased fiber and low calorie count helps you maintain your weight and feel better mentally, as well as physically. You feel good about yourself when you do something good for yourself."

BRUSH AWAY CRAVINGS. "Brush your teeth immediately after dinner. This sends the message that you're not going to eat anything more for the rest of the evening."

*(continued on page 294)*

# NORTH WOODS BEAN SOUP

"SOUP IS NUTRITIOUS, RELATIVELY LOW IN CALORIES, AND VERY FILLING. MY WIFE MAKES A VARIETY OF SOUPS AND I LOVE THEM ALL. THIS ONE IS PACKED WITH FIBER AND PROTEIN AND IS VERY TASTY."—**TED EPPERLY, MD**

**Serves 4**

1 cup baby carrots, halved lengthwise

1 cup chopped onion

2 garlic cloves, minced

5 ounces fresh turkey kielbasa, halved lengthwise and cut
    into $1/2$" pieces

4 cups low-sodium chicken broth

$1/2$ teaspoon dried Italian seasoning

2 cans (15.8 ounces each) organic great Northern beans,
    rinsed and drained

6 ounces fresh baby spinach

**1** Coat a large saucepan with cooking spray and warm over medium-high heat. Add the carrots, onion, garlic, and kielbasa. Sauté, stirring occasionally, until the vegetables soften, about 3 minutes. Reduce the heat to medium and cook for 5 minutes more. Add the broth, Italian seasoning, and beans. Bring to a boil, reduce heat to low, and simmer for 5 minutes more.

**2** Place 2 cups of the soup in a food processor or blender, and process or blend until smooth. (Be careful when blending hot liquids.) Return the pureed soup to the pan. Simmer for an additional 5 minutes. Add the spinach, stirring until it wilts, about 30 seconds. Ladle into 4 bowls and serve.

NUTRITION PER SERVING (ABOUT 2 CUPS): 235 CALORIES • 14 G PROTEIN • 36 G CARBS • 12 G FIBER • 4 G FAT • 1 G SATURATED FAT • 901 MG SODIUM

**SET AN INTENTION FOR THE DAY.** "Someone once told me that what you do in the first hour of every day is like a rudder on your ship of life, as it will steer you in the direction you will take. I exercise first thing in the morning to remind myself of my commitment to my own health. If I were to try to work out later in the day, I'd get so busy and overwhelmed with other things."

**LOSE YOUR BELLY, BUILD YOUR BRAIN.** "Taking in more than 2,600 calories a day can lead to mild cognitive impairment and memory loss. Studies indicate that eating less than that has a beneficial effect on your memory."

**EXERCISE MORE!** "If I were limited to giving just one piece of health advice, this would be it. The benefits of exercise are increasingly apparent. Exercise actually increases your immune system's capacity, which will help you fight off colds and flu. It helps you reduce stress, improve focus, and keep your body young. And of course, it protects your heart and helps keep you lean."

**STRIVE TO BE HAPPY.** "An optimistic outlook, the ability to see humor in life (and in yourself), and having a passion—these three things help you lead the kind of life that brings you joy and satisfaction."

**FIND A FURRY FRIEND.** "Pets light up your life and remind you that there is something more important than the issues you face on a day-to-day basis. When you have a pet, you always have a loving friend at home waiting for you."

"SOME GOOD FATS ARE HEALTHY, BUT IN MODERATION. REMEMBER THAT FAT CONTAINS 9 CALORIES PER GRAM—MORE THAN TWICE AS MUCH AS PROTEIN OR CARBOHYDRATES."

# SALLY KUZEMCHAK, MS, RD

*Co-author of* Flat Belly Diet! Family Cookbook *and a blogger for Real Mom Nutrition (www.realmomnutrition.com).*

AS A RECOVERING "PICKY EATER," KUZEMCHAK KNOWS firsthand how tough it can be to break old diet habits. "I grew up on plain, buttered noodles because I refused to eat so many other foods," she says. "Salmon, asparagus, and lentils are some of my favorites today, but I was in my twenties or thirties before I'd even tried them." Having children inspired her to make even more of an effort to expand her palate. "I want to be a good example for my kids—and I want them to become adults who will happily eat most any food."

**TRY A SUGAR CLEANSE.** "We're learning so much about the adverse effects of foods with added sugar. You hear a lot about the possible health problems associated with added fructose in processed foods, but that's not the only concern. Sugar may mimic addictive substances and cause chemical changes in your brain that leave you wanting more. I recently challenged myself and the readers of my blog to give up added sugar for 2 weeks. I was shocked to find that my cravings diminished in just 2 days—and I felt fantastic."

**CARVE OUT COUPLE TIME.** "My husband and I meet on our couch every night after the kids are in bed. We discuss our days, brainstorm ideas for each other, and talk through problems. Issues that seemed huge often feel quite small after we're done talking."

**WORK OUT ON YOUR OWN TERMS.** "With two small kids, I don't have the time to get to the gym—or the budget to afford it. I've stocked a small library of workout DVDs, plus hand weights, a resistance band, and a yoga mat. There are some days I don't get around to exercising until 9 p.m., after the kids are in bed. But it works for me right now, and that's the most important thing."

**FACE YOUR FOOD FEARS.** "Even now, I sometimes have to push myself to try new things. I've been learning to cook more with beans and lentils. Their texture bothers me, though, so I puree or mash them up—for instance, in hummus, lentil meatloaf, or pureed lentil soup. I put mashed black beans in burritos—and even in brownies! I also purposely try new foods in front of my kids. It forces me to be brave!"

**TRAVEL FOR TREATS.** "My family loves ice cream, but instead of keeping it in the freezer, we'll go out for some occasionally. If whatever tempts you isn't right there in your kitchen, you won't fall into the trap of eating it mindlessly."

**BEFRIEND YOUR LOCAL FARMER.** "I buy shares in a local grass-fed cow and get my chicken and pork from local farms, too. The meat is higher in quality, but it's pricier than what you find at the grocery store. So we just eat it less often."

**HAVE A FRUIT CHASER.** "If I want something sugary, I have a small portion, then follow it up with a piece of fruit. I find that the sweetness of the fruit is all it takes to break the cycle of wanting more sugar."

**COOK FOR YOURSELF.** "When I'm home alone, it's tempting to grab a bowl of cereal or a string cheese and some crackers instead of eating a proper lunch. But when I take the time to prepare a nice big salad or reheat some leftover soup, I feel much better and end up eating a more balanced meal."

# TURKISH WEDDING SOUP

"THIS HEARTY MEATLESS SOUP IS GOOD FOR YOU AND THE PLANET—AND IT'S
ECONOMICAL (ONE BAG OF LENTILS WILL MAKE MANY BATCHES OF THIS SOUP). I
USUALLY SERVE IT WITH SOME HOMEMADE ROLLS AND A GREEN SALAD."
—SALLY KUZEMCHAK, MS, RD

**Serves 4**

4 tablespoons extra-virgin olive oil

2 onions, finely chopped

1 teaspoon paprika

1 cup red lentils

½ cup bulgur

2 tablespoons tomato paste

8 cups low-sodium vegetable stock

⅛ teaspoon ground red pepper

1 lemon, cut into quarters

**1** Place a pot over high heat and add the oil. When the oil is just smoking, add the onions and cook until they are translucent, about 5 minutes. Add the paprika, lentils, bulgur, and tomato paste. Stir to combine.

**2** Add the stock and red pepper and cook until the lentils are soft, about 1 hour. Ladle into 4 bowls and squeeze a lemon wedge into each bowl of soup before serving.

NUTRITION PER SERVING (SIZE 2½ CUPS): 425 CALORIES • 16 G PROTEIN • 58 G CARBS • 12 G FIBER •
15 G FAT • 2 G SATURATED FAT • 506 MG SODIUM

# STEVEN LAMM, MD

*Internist, faculty member at the New York University School of Medicine in New York City, and author of* No Guts, No Glory.

YOU CAN COUNT YOUR BLESSINGS, BUT YOU DON'T ALWAYS HAVE TO count your calories. "Most of us are too preoccupied with calories and fail to understand that the reason we eat is to get nutrition for our bodies," says Dr. Lamm. To make sure he doesn't consume more than he burns off, he mostly sticks to three squares a day and he never eats snack foods like chips or popcorn. So what does he do when he gets hungry in between meals? He grabs a piece of fruit. "I appreciate that I have an opportunity to ingest only a certain number of calories, so I make them count by considering nutrients as well as taste."

**PLAN FOR THE ROAD.** "Often, the foods that you're comfortable eating aren't available when you're traveling. At hotels I can usually get an egg white omelet or a high-fiber cereal for breakfast, and there's usually turkey, chicken, or tuna salad for lunch. Dinner is tougher because I'm often invited out for business and don't choose the restaurant, but I try to order the healthiest thing on the menu—for instance, I'll choose fish or chicken at a steakhouse."

**DON'T FEED YOUR ADDICTION.** "Carbs have an almost cocainelike effect, changing your brain chemistry to make you keep eating. Our bodies are capable of ingesting very large quantities of carbs, so I always order the vegetable side dish rather than the french fries and to ask the waiter to remove the bread basket."

REPLACE RICE. "Buckwheat (kasha) isn't a grain, but a fruit seed that is related to rhubarb and sorrel, so it's a suitable replacement for people who are sensitive to wheat, and it's significantly higher in protein than brown rice. Eating buckwheat can lower your risk of developing high cholesterol and high blood pressure. It's rich in flavonoids, which protect against disease by extending the action of vitamin C and acting as antioxidants. Other benefits of buckwheat include better blood sugar control and a lowered risk of diabetes. Try using buckwheat flour instead of all-purpose flour when you make pancakes."

STOP STARVING YOURSELF. "Many people think that if they skip breakfast or lunch, they're entitled to eat whatever they want later on. In reality, the thinnest people are the ones who eat small portions all day long. When you deprive yourself of food, your metabolism changes, your hormone production changes, and your body goes into starvation mode—making it harder for you to lose weight."

REIN IN STRESS WITH A ROPE. "Jumping rope is a big part of my workout routine and a great way to relax. I try to get in at least 500 to 700 jumps during a 25-minute workout. I'll alternate weight training with 25 jumps at a time. I also suggest jumping rope to my patients—even if they have to do it without a rope. You can work yourself up to 300 to 500 jumps per day. But make sure you're on your toes, not pounding your knees or hips."

## "THE THINNEST PEOPLE ARE THE ONES WHO EAT SMALL PORTIONS ALL DAY LONG."

# MEXICAN WRAP

"YOU CAN MAKE THIS QUICKLY, AND IT'S EASY TO PACK AND TAKE TO WORK FOR LUNCH. THE OLIVE OIL AND AVOCADO PROVIDE HEALTHY FATS, AND THE FIBER IN THE VEGETABLES, BEANS, AND WHOLE GRAIN WRAP KEEP YOU FULL."

—STEVEN LAMM, MD

**Serves 2**

1 tablespoon extra-virgin olive oil

1 medium yellow onion, chopped

1 medium red bell pepper, chopped

1 can (16 ounces) fat-free refried beans

2 whole grain, flourless wraps (8-inch diameter)

¼ medium avocado, cut into 4 thin slices

4 tablespoons shredded low-fat Cheddar cheese

Salsa

1 Place a large skillet over high heat. Add the oil, onion, and pepper. Sauté, stirring, until the onions are translucent and the pepper is soft, about 7 minutes.

2 Reduce the heat to medium and add the beans. Stir until the beans are heated through, about 1 minute.

3 Divide the mixture evenly between the two wraps, placing it in the center. Top each with 2 avocado slices, 2 tablespoons of cheese, and salsa, and fold in the bottom and sides of the wrap. Roll up and serve.

NUTRITION PER SERVING: 416 CALORIES • 19 G PROTEIN • 57 G CARBS • 16 G FIBER • 12 G FAT • 2 G SATURATED FAT • 1,233 MG SODIUM

# MARYANNE LEGATO, MD

*Professor of clinical medicine at Columbia University College of Physicians & Surgeons. Specialist in gender-specific medicine and author of eight books, including* Why Men Never Remember and Women Never Forget.

THE FIRST MEAL OF THE DAY IS THE MOST IMPORTANT, ACCORDING to Dr. Legato. But while she advises her patients to eat breakfast every day, she also emphasizes eating small meals more often rather than large meals less frequently. And if you have a health condition that can be helped with diet or weight loss, get professional advice. "Although people often tell me, 'I know everything the dietitian will tell me,' they don't. Consult with a nutritionist; he or she can help plan out the best diet program for you."

PARK THE CAR. "I walk everywhere I can. It keeps my weight stable and allows me to indulge in an occasional dessert."

TAKE A RISK. "I set up a private practice, so I run my own business. Working for an institution would not be as much fun as being my own boss. It's riskier, but it's much more rewarding in every way."

STAY YOUNG. "Nothing ages you like boredom and self-involvement. Loving life and the people in it keeps me young. Physical contact and frequent exchanges with the people you love are life-giving and health-preserving."

DON'T TAKE THE EASY WAY OUT. "Many patients would rather take a pill than pass up that forbidden dessert. I encourage everyone to practice more self-discipline and stop relying on pharmaceuticals to fix their dietary mistakes."

**ALLOW YOURSELF TO INDULGE.** "My biggest eating challenge is restricting myself to optimal choices in a wonderful restaurant. How do I overcome it? I don't! I make up for it by limiting dining out to twice per week and by eating carefully for the rest of the week."

# BERRY-CHERRY OATMEAL

"I LOVE OATMEAL WITH BLUEBERRIES IN THE MORNING. IT'S A TASTY, NUTRITIOUS, AND LOW-CALORIE BREAKFAST."—MARYANNE LEGATO, MD

Serves 2

2 cups 1% or 2% milk

2 tablespoons brown sugar

1 cup old-fashioned oats

¼ cup dried tart cherries

¼ teaspoon ground cinnamon

½ teaspoon vanilla extract

½ cup fresh blueberries

1 Combine the milk with the sugar and ⅛ teaspoon of salt in a small saucepan. Bring to a boil over medium-high heat. Stir in the oats and cherries.

2 Reduce the heat to medium and simmer, stirring occasionally, until the mixture has thickened and the oats are cooked, 5 to 6 minutes. Remove from the heat and stir in the cinnamon, vanilla, and blueberries. Serve.

NUTRITION PER SERVING: 375 CALORIES • 16 G PROTEIN • 66 G CARBS • 9 G FIBER • 5 G FAT • 2 G SATURATED FAT • 256 MG SODIUM

# MARY JANE MINKIN, MD

*Clinical professor of obstetrics, gynecology, and reproductive sciences at Yale School of Medicine and author of* A Woman's Guide to Menopause and Perimenopause *and* A Woman's Guide to Sexual Health.

D R. MINKIN DIDN'T DISCOVER EXERCISE UNTIL SHE STARTED medical school, but now it's a major part of her daily routine. "I've found out how much good health habits help," she says. After a year of regular strength training, her HDL (good cholesterol) went up 10 points and her fasting blood sugar came down 15 points. "Strength training, vigorous aerobic activity, and good nutrition are better than any medications you could take."

**DITCH THE DIET MENTALITY.** "I hate to use the word 'diet.' If you're trying to lose weight, pick any reasonable plan that cuts calories, and make sure it's something you can stick with."

**SET AN EXAMPLE.** "When I can make suggestions for my patients based on personal choices and experiences, it really hits home. Who wants health advice from an obese physician or one who smokes?"

**QUIT MAKING EXCUSES.** "If you haven't learned about good health until you've developed significant arthritic problems such as bad knees, and you now think you can't exercise—you're wrong! Find the nearest Y with a warm water pool and start doing water aerobics. This will help you lose weight, while protecting your joints at the same time. The worst thing for your arthritis would be to let yourself become obese and put even more stress on your joints."

**QUESTION YOUR ROUTINE.** "I teach my residents and medical students to take an exercise history on patients. This means not just asking if someone exercises, but asking specifically what he or she does for exercise, how long they do it for, and at what intensity. Often, the exercise patients are doing is a good start, but it is rarely enough. For example, if you're only walking 1 mile twice a week, I encourage you to gradually increase your walking to 15 to 20 miles per week."

**FEED INTO YOUR FAVORITE FOOD.** "I love french fries. To limit my intake, I eat a few when I'm out to dinner—but only if they're really good ones!"

> "STRENGTH TRAINING, VIGOROUS AEROBIC ACTIVITY, AND GOOD NUTRITION ARE BETTER THAN ANY MEDICATIONS YOU COULD TAKE."

# STEAMED SOLE
# WITH CREAMY DILL SAUCE

"THIS IS A LIGHT MEAL THAT IS FLAVORFUL AND PACKED WITH NUTRIENTS."

—MARY JANE MINKIN, MD

**Serves 4**

¼ cup 1% cottage cheese

¼ cup fat-free plain yogurt

2 teaspoons Dijon mustard

1 teaspoon fresh lemon juice

1 teaspoon minced shallots

⅛ teaspoon reduced-sodium
   soy sauce

1 tablespoon minced fresh dill

4 (4-ounce) sole fillets

1 red bell pepper, thinly sliced

1 rib celery, thinly sliced
   on the diagonal

1 carrot, halved lengthwise and
   thinly sliced on the diagonal

¾ cup green beans, split
   lengthwise and halved

1 tablespoon fresh lemon juice

2 teaspoons extra-virgin olive oil

2 teaspoons minced fresh dill

1 teaspoon minced onion

⅛ teaspoon reduced-sodium
   soy sauce

1 Put the cottage cheese, yogurt, mustard, lemon juice, shallots, and soy sauce in a blender or food processor. Blend or process until smooth. Transfer the sauce to a small bowl and stir in the dill. Cover and refrigerate until ready to serve.

2 Bring about 1 inch of water to a boil in a large saucepan. Place the fish in a steamer basket and add it to the saucepan. Cover and steam for 3 to 4 minutes.

3 Add the pepper, celery, carrot, and beans to the steamer basket. Cover and steam until the vegetables are tender and the fish flakes easily with a fork, 3 to 5 minutes. Set aside.

4 In a large bowl, combine the lemon juice, oil, dill, onion, and soy sauce. Using a spoon or metal spatula, transfer the cooked vegetables to the bowl. Toss to coat.

5 Divide the vegetables among 4 dinner plates, forming them into nests. Place a piece of fish in each nest. Top each piece with the dill sauce and serve.

NUTRITION PER SERVING: 168 CALORIES • 25 G PROTEIN • 8 G CARBS • 2 G FIBER • 4 G FAT •
<1 G SATURATED FAT • 249 MG SODIUM

# MARK A. MOYAD, MD

*Jenkins/Pokempner director of complementary and alternative medicine at the University of Michigan Medical Center in Ann Arbor and president of the Promoting Wellness Foundation.*

DR. MOYAD IS ARGUABLY THE WORLD'S LEADING MEDICAL EXPERT ON dietary supplements, but he's not quick to recommend them to everyone. "So many times, we give supplements or prescription drugs credit for what we are really doing for ourselves through healthy habits," he says. He points to government-sponsored research that found that following just seven lifestyle habits (not smoking; maintaining a healthy weight, cholesterol, blood pressure, and blood glucose levels; exercising daily; and following a moderately healthy diet) not only can reduce your risk of heart disease to close to zero, but it also protects against almost every other major medical condition or disease. "Think about this: Your tax dollars have helped to figure out the greatest anti-aging secrets ever discovered, but only 1 to 2 percent of Americans take advantage of all of them," he says. "Wow! Where is *that* television commercial?"

DIVERSIFY. "I run, swim, Spin, walk, ski, or bike outside. Mixing up what exercise I do keeps me interested. Making it a social event helps, too, so once a year I try to complete a marathon, triathlon, or other fitness event for charity. This is a combination selfish and selfless act: It keeps me motivated and healthy, and it gives back to the community."

SEE THE BIG PICTURE. "Too many people stress about the medical minutiae, or what I call 'distractions'—such as high-fructose corn syrup, artificial sweeteners, wondering whether an egg is good or bad for them, wondering whether they need alkaline water. These 'distractions' may get headlines, but we only have so much time to pay attention to our health. Focus on conquering the big seven, then move on to the 'distractions' if you have time—but who does? Personally, I'll be trying to conquer the big seven for the rest of my life."

SOOTHE A COUGH SWEETLY. "Try a teaspoon of dark honey, like buckwheat, for coughs and colds. Studies show that it's a great antimicrobial agent, plus it's cheap, simple, and works for everyone over the age of 2."

GET A BUZZ. "I tell people not to be scared of 1,3,7-trimethylxanthine (also known as caffeine) in moderation because it turns out that this is a healthy compound that not only prevents fatigue but also numerous other medical conditions. In addition, evidence shows that lifting weights just twice a week is one of the best and most fabulous things you can do to improve your energy levels. (And you thought it was just for building muscles and burning belly fat!)"

DITCH THE DOWNERS. "I surrounded myself with only positive people and things—my wife, my kids, my dog, friends, other family, co-workers, and church. This isn't to say that I (or my friends) do not have down days, but in the end, you only have one of two ways to be in this life—mostly positive or mostly negative. If you choose the latter, life gets lonely quickly."

GET A SPIRITUAL HEALTH CHECKUP. "Doctors should do spiritual health screenings as part of annual physicals, but if yours doesn't, do one yourself. In the past 12 months, have you volunteered, donated blood, signed up for the bone marrow registry or for organ donation, or raised money for a cause? There's evidence that the more you give, the more you get back in health benefits! I started PromotingWellness.org when another doctor asked me what I was doing for other people in Haiti, New Orleans, or even my hometown. I never in my wildest, craziest dreams believed that I could start a foundation that could help others, and it came from being asked about the status of my own spiritual health."

# KALE-CHERRY SALAD WITH LEMON VINAIGRETTE

"MY WIFE, MIA, CREATED THIS PERFECT SALAD. IT'S HIGH IN FIBER, HEALTHY FATS, VITAMINS, MINERALS, AND EVEN ELECTROLYTES, SUCH AS POTASSIUM. PLUS IT'S LOW IN CALORIES, AND IT'S YUMMY!"—MARK A. MOYAD, MD

**Serves 4**

- 1 teaspoon Dijon mustard
- 1½ teaspoons finely grated lemon zest
- 2 tablespoons freshly squeezed lemon juice
- 6 tablespoons extra-virgin olive oil
- 4 cups chopped young kale
- ½ cup dried tart cherries
- ¼ cup toasted pine nuts

1 Whisk together the mustard, lemon zest, lemon juice, oil and salt and freshly ground black pepper to taste in a large salad bowl. Set aside.

2 Chop the kale coarsely. Place the kale in the bowl with the dressing and, using clean hands, toss gently to coat the leaves. Add the cherries and pine nuts and toss gently again. Divide the salad among 4 plates and serve.

NUTRITION PER SERVING (1½ CUPS): 331 CALORIES • 3 G PROTEIN • 20 G CARBS • 6 G FIBER • 27 G FAT • 3 G SATURATED FAT • 55 MG SODIUM

# ROSHINI RAJ, MD

*Gastroenterologist and internist, attending physician and assistant professor of medicine at NYU Langone Medical Center/Tisch Hospital in New York City, and author of* What the Yuck?!

SLIM DOESN'T ALWAYS EQUAL HEALTHY, AS DR. RAJ CAN ATTEST. "I've always been naturally thin, but I never used to put any thought into my diet," she says. "I ate a lot of processed foods and not enough fruits and vegetables." When she hit 30, she began to understand the harm a nutrient-poor diet could be doing to her body, and she changed her ways. "As a gastroenterologist, I'm very aware of the risk of colon cancer. Studies show that a diet rich in animal fats and low in fruits and vegetables increases your cancer odds," she says. She pumped up her produce intake and gave up processed meats, like hot dogs. "They're high in nitrites, which are linked to gastric cancers."

UNRAVEL A MYSTERY. "No matter how tired, cranky, or stressed I am, I make sure to read for at least 15 minutes before going to sleep to help me unwind and decompress. I love British historical mystery novels. I get sucked into another world, and I forget the worries of the day."

DON'T JUST SIT THERE! "A lot of my patients think they're too busy to exercise, but incorporating just 20 minutes of movement into your day can make a difference to your risk of heart disease, cancer, dementia, and depression, among many other illnesses. You don't have to do it all at once. Take the stairs instead of the elevator, or walk outside to get lunch rather than ordering in."

**END ON A SWEET NOTE.** "For me, a meal isn't complete without dessert, but I can't have cookies and cake every night! Instead, I eat a handful of golden raisins after dinner—they contain fiber and antioxidants, have zero fat, and satisfy my sweet tooth. I save the chocolate mousse for special occasions."

**BE GOOD ABOUT BREAKFAST.** "Every day I have the same breakfast: low-fat granola with blueberries, strawberries, blackberries, raspberries, and fat-free plain yogurt. This mixture is delicious and filling, and I feel great about the antioxidants, fiber, calcium, and protein I'm getting. Frozen fruit has the same nutritional value as fresh, so I buy a bag of mixed frozen berries and keep them in the fridge. That way they're soft and ready to eat when I want them."

**PUT OUT THE FIRE.** "Foods that are low in fat and high in fiber, like oatmeal, beans, and whole grain breads and pastas, help prevent heartburn. Fatty foods, caffeine, alcohol, tomato sauce, peppermint, chocolate, and citrus fruits, on the other hand, can trigger it."

**BEAT THE BLOAT.** "Ginger can help with many stomach symptoms, including bloating and nausea. Eating papaya, pineapple, and asparagus can also help."

**BREAK THE STRESS-BELLY LINK.** "The mind-gut connection is very strong and can be tough to manage. One strategy is deep breathing combined with thought blocking, a technique where you visualize a stop sign and use it to stop a negative or stressful thought pattern that you're stuck in."

# ROASTED WINTER VEGETABLES

"AS A GASTROENTEROLOGIST, I KNOW HOW IMPORTANT FIBER, VEGETABLES, AND FRUIT ARE IN PROTECTING AGAINST COLON CANCER. ROASTING VEGETABLES BRINGS OUT THEIR SWEETNESS, SO YOU EAT MORE OF THEM."—**ROSHINI RAJ, MD**

**Serves 4**

1 pound winter squash, such as butternut or acorn, peeled and cut into 1" cubes

1/2 pound brussels sprouts (about 12), quartered

3 large carrots, peeled and cut into 1/4" diagonal slices

1 red onion, chopped

3 tablespoons extra-virgin olive oil

2 tablespoons chopped fresh flat-leaf parsley

1 1/2 tablespoons white wine vinegar

**1** Preheat the oven to 450°F.

**2** Toss the squash, brussels sprouts, carrots, and onion with 2 tablespoons of the oil and 1/4 teaspoon of salt in a large bowl. Spread the vegetables in a single layer on a baking sheet (use two sheets, if necessary) and roast, stirring once or twice, until they're browned and tender, about 30 minutes.

**3** Transfer the vegetables to a bowl. Toss with the parsley, vinegar, the remaining 1 tablespoon of oil, and 1/4 teaspoon of salt and freshly ground black pepper to taste. Serve warm or at room temperature.

NUTRITION PER SERVING: 189 CALORIES • 4 G PROTEIN • 24 G CARBS • 6 G FIBER • 11 G FAT • 2 G SATURATED FAT • 177 MG SODIUM

# MARIE SAVARD, MD

*Internist in private practice in Philadelphia and author of four books, including* Ask Dr. Marie.

D R. SAVARD RECOMMENDS A MAGIC PILL TO ALL OF HER PATIENTS: She calls it the "lifestyle pill." "We now know that people who follow a prudent diet, drink small amounts of alcohol, exercise regularly, and maintain a healthy weight reduce their risk of cardiovascular disease by 80 percent and cut their odds of some cancers by half or more," she says. Fortunately, it's not such a tough pill to swallow. Dr. Savard points out that a few simple adjustments to your routine can make a big difference. "I keep 8- to 10-pound hand weights in my kitchen and do upper-body exercises when I'm waiting for water to boil. I'll do squats when I'm brushing my teeth or situps while I'm watching TV. Slipping in something whenever I can feels natural to me."

PRIORITIZE FIBER. "Eating fiber means you're eating unprocessed plants—vegetables, whole grains, and fruit. If a food is naturally high in fiber, it hasn't been processed, and as a result, it's rich in nutrients and phytochemicals. I always check food labels for the fiber content and expect crackers, bread, and cereals to have at least 2 grams per serving. If they don't, I move on to another brand."

WEAR COMFY SHOES. "I always have my walking shoes with me so I can slip them on and go for a walk. I firmly believe that daily activity is more important and sustaining than having a regular gym membership. I walk everywhere I can, and I take the stairs—sometimes running up them or taking them two at a time."

**KICK YOUR DIET SODA HABIT.** "There's something about the intense sweetness of artificial sweeteners in diet sodas, yogurts, and other foods that triggers changes in the hormonal balance in your digestive system and metabolism. There's evidence that artificial sweeteners raise the risk of metabolic syndrome and heart disease. They stimulate your sweet taste buds 500 times more than sugar does."

**THINK AWAY TEMPTATION.** "I love licorice and gummy candy, but they're full of sugar and empty calories. I have no thermostat, so to speak, that helps me gauge when I've had enough. I can—and I have—eaten a whole big bag of Twizzlers. This leaves me feeling a little sick and jittery (not to mention guilty). So when I get the urge to eat them, I visualize how I'll feel afterward, and I imagine my insulin levels surging and then plummeting. It's enough to keep my hands out of the candy jar."

**SNACK LIKE A KID.** "One of my favorite after-school treats as a child was celery sticks filled with natural peanut butter—and it's a healthy, filling option that I love to this day. Another good snack choice: microwave popcorn and a big glass of water. Popcorn is a fiber-rich whole grain. I avoid butter versions because the chemicals used to flavor the popcorn may damage your lungs if you inhale them frequently."

**REPLACE YOUR SCALE WITH A MEASURING TAPE.** "Excess weight is more of a health risk for people with an apple shape than those with a pear shape. Losing just 2 inches from your waist can have a big positive impact. I judge my weight by how my clothes fit. When my pants get tight, I commit to quickly losing a few pounds by cutting out alcohol or whatever I think contributed to the gain."

# HEALTHY GRANOLA

"HOMEMADE GRANOLA TASTES BETTER THAN STORE-BOUGHT, AND IT'S BETTER FOR YOU. EAT IT WITH YOGURT AND FRUIT FOR BREAKFAST. IT KEEPS WELL IN THE FREEZER, SO I ALWAYS MAKE A BIG BATCH." —MARIE SAVARD, MD

**Makes 8 cups**

4 cups rolled oats

1 cup ground golden flaxseed

¼ cup ground wheat bran

¼ cup pumpkin seeds

¼ cup sunflower seeds

¼ cup sesame seeds

½ cup slivered or sliced
    almonds, pecans, or walnuts,
    or a combination

⅓ cup canola oil

⅓ cup natural peanut butter

¼ cup honey

2–3 teaspoons ground cinnamon

1 cup dried fruit (raisins, cherries,
    blueberries, figs, dates,
    apricots, or a combination)

1 Preheat the oven to 325°F. Combine the oats, flaxseed, wheat bran, pumpkin seeds, sunflower seeds, sesame seeds, and nuts in a large bowl.

2 Place the oil, peanut butter, honey, cinnamon, and a splash of water into a 2-cup glass measuring cup and heat at 50 percent power in the microwave for about 2 minutes. Stir to blend the ingredients. (The peanut butter will stay lumpy.)

3 Stir the wet ingredients into the dry ingredients. Spread the mixture evenly across one or two baking sheets with sides. Bake, stirring once or twice until golden, 20 to 30 minutes.

4 Cool completely and toss with dried fruit. Place in resealable plastic bags and store in the freezer.

NUTRITION PER SERVING (¼ CUP): 148 CALORIES • 4 G PROTEIN • 15 G CARBS • 4 G FIBER • 8 G FAT • 1 G SATURATED FAT • 14 MG SODIUM

# JACOB TEITELBAUM, MD

*Medical director of the Fibromyalgia and Fatigue Centers and Optimized Health and Wellness, developer of the iPhone App "Cures A–Z," and author of* Beat Sugar Addiction Now, Beat Sugar Addiction Now Cookbook, *and* Real Cause, Real Cure.

FOR MORE THAN 30 YEARS, DR. TEITELBAUM—A FORMER SUGAR addict himself—has been showing patients how a "sugar detox" can help alleviate a number of chronic health problems. "Sugar addiction is the canary in the coal mine. It usually points to a larger problem that is also dragging you down," he says. He suggests keeping track of how much sugar you eat, noting how you feel, and then cutting back on sugar to see if you notice a difference. "Tune in to your body to see what, over time, leaves you feeling the best," he says. "Though physicians and other health practitioners can guide you toward a healthy lifestyle, at the end of the day, it is your own intuitive sense of yourself that can guide you best."

CAN THE ENERGY DRINKS. "The basic ingredients in most energy drinks are sugar and caffeine. When this mixture of empty calories hits your system and your blood sugar rises, you get an immediate energy boost. Unfortunately, 1 to 3 hours later you feel even more fatigued than you did before, and you also crave more sugar."

SWEETEN WITH STEVIA. "This excellent sugar substitute is safe, healthy, and natural. More and more products are being made with it."

SAVE SUGAR FOR DESSERT. "Food manufacturers dump about 140 pounds of sugar per person into our diets each year. It's in all sorts of products you don't expect to be sweet, like whole wheat bread, ketchup, and spaghetti sauce. Make a conscious effort to keep sugar as a treat. Dark chocolate is a good choice—there are about 4 grams (or 1 teaspoon) of sugar in 1 ounce of dark chocolate, compared to 13 grams in the same quantity of milk chocolate. And when you decide to have something sweet, savor it. Eighty percent of the pleasure comes from the first two bites—if you're paying attention to the flavor, you might feel satisfied just with that."

LOWER CHOLESTEROL NATURALLY. "Have a low-sugar oat cereal for breakfast topped with berries, bananas, and cinnamon. The soluble fiber in the oats helps control cholesterol; the berries also have fiber, plus antioxidants; the bananas have blood pressure–lowering potassium; and the cinnamon helps keep blood sugar levels even."

PASS THE TURKEY. "A high-protein bedtime snack will keep your blood sugar stable while you sleep. A few ounces of turkey is a good option—it balances your blood sugar and contains tryptophan, which may also improve your sleep."

BANISH THE BLOAT. "Peppermint oil can alleviate intestinal pain, gas, and bloating, especially in people who have irritable bowel syndrome. Choose an enteric-coated supplement; that way, the oil is released in your bowel, where it can be beneficial, instead of in your stomach, where it won't do any good."

> "THOUGH PHYSICIANS AND OTHER HEALTH PRACTITIONERS CAN GUIDE YOU TOWARD A HEALTHY LIFESTYLE, AT THE END OF THE DAY, IT IS YOUR OWN INTUITIVE SENSE OF YOURSELF THAT CAN GUIDE YOU BEST."

# REFRESHING RHUBARB
# AND STRAWBERRY PUDDING

"THIS DESSERT FROM MY BOOK *BEAT SUGAR ADDICTION NOW* IS ELEGANT AND FEELS
INDULGENT BUT IT IS COMPLETELY FREE OF ADDED SUGAR."
—JACOB TEITELBAUM, MD

**Serves 4**

4 cups sliced strawberries + additional for garnish

2 cups diced rhubarb

3 tablespoons maple syrup, or to taste

1 teaspoon lemon zest

2 tablespoons agar-agar flakes

1 tablespoon kudzu,* diluted in 2 tablespoons cold water

1 cup plain yogurt

1/2 cup almonds, chopped

1/4 cup walnuts, chopped

1 Combine strawberries, rhubarb, maple syrup, and lemon zest in a saucepan and bring to a boil.

2 Sprinkle in agar-agar flakes and simmer until all flakes are dissolved, about 7 to 10 minutes. Add dissolved kudzu and stir until mixture thickens.

3 Transfer to a bowl or individual cups and refrigerate until set. Serve with yogurt and chopped nuts and garnish with strawberry slices and a sprig of mint, if desired.

NUTRITION PER SERVING: 267 CALORIES • 9 G PROTEIN • 35 G CARBS • 6 G FIBER • 12 G FAT • 1 G SATURATED FAT • 49 MG SODIUM

*Kudzu is a thickener and is available in well-stocked supermarkets.
If you can't find it, substitute corn or rice starch.

# LYNNE KENNEY, PsyD

*Pediatric psychologist in Arizona, creator of The Family Coach method, and author of the book of the same name.*

AS A PROUD MOTHER OF TWO AND AN EXPERT IN CHILDREN'S health, Dr. Kenney is understandably concerned with the way families eat. You'll only find real, whole foods in her shopping cart and on her dinner table. "At the grocery store, I keep this motto in mind: 'If it doesn't rot or sprout, do without,'" she says. But if you can't always get that close to nature, she recommends making sure the boxed, bagged, or canned foods you buy don't have more than five ingredients on the label.

**AVOID SUGAR, AVOID THE SNIFFLES.** "Start taking vitamin C in September, and then don't eat too much Halloween candy. Sugar suppresses your immune system—something you don't want as you enter cold and flu season."

**REPEAT AND RELAX.** "One of my favorite stress busters is cleaning stalls on my horse ranch. It's repetitive and any repetitive movement—chopping vegetables, rocking, raking—can be calming. A warm soak with lavender bath salts always works, too."

**GET OUT OF THE GYM RUT.** "I meet with a trainer and lift weights 3 days a week, walk 4 days a week, and ride horses and play sports whenever I have the time. I like to play and live to be fit, so even though I have a gym membership, I hardly ever go. I'd rather clean those previously mentioned horse stalls for exercise."

CONNECT OFFLINE. "Four years ago I learned more about mindfulness and became determined to be present in the moment. Being really 'there' when I talk with clients, cook with my kids, or have coffee with my husband has improved the quality of all of our lives."

DO WHAT YOU LOVE. "Being creative and having fun keeps me sharp. When you love what you do, you live with gusto."

SWITCH OUT SALT. "I like to snack on salty foods late at night, but eating them is not only bad for my health, it also disturbs my sleep. So I always keep carrots and frozen cherries on hand; I get the crunch without the sodium."

ACT YOUR AGE. "I try to embrace being 50. No one can remain 30 forever. We need to love where we are."

"AT THE GROCERY STORE, I KEEP THIS MOTTO IN MIND: IF IT DOESN'T ROT OR SPROUT, DO WITHOUT."

# DR. LYNNE'S BAKED MEATBALLS

"I ALWAYS MAKE SURE TO HAVE PROTEIN FOR BREAKFAST, SO WHETHER WE HAD A STIR-FRY OR MEATBALLS THE NIGHT BEFORE, I ENCOURAGE EVERYONE IN MY FAMILY TO TAKE A BITE OF THE LEFTOVERS IN THE MORNING. PROTEIN HOLDS THE KIDS OVER IN SCHOOL MUCH BETTER THAN CEREAL DOES. I USE CRUSTY OLIVE BREAD TO BIND THESE MEATBALLS, BUT ANY BREAD YOU LIKE WILL DO." —LYNN KENNEY, PsyD

**Makes 42 meatballs**

3/4 pound ground organic turkey

3/4 pound lean ground organic beef

2 slices bread soaked in 1/3 cup milk then squeezed

1/4 cup marinara sauce

1 teaspoon Worcestershire sauce

1 teaspoon dried oregano or mixed Italian herbs

1 teaspoon minced garlic

1/4 cup grated Parmesan cheese

2 eggs, beaten

3–4 tablespoons grated onion

1 Preheat the oven to 350°F. Combine the turkey, beef, bread, marinara sauce, Worcestershire sauce, oregano or herbs, garlic, cheese, eggs, and onion in a large bowl. Add 1/2 teaspoon of salt and freshly ground black pepper. Mix together well.

2 Form tablespoon-size meatballs and place on 2 baking sheets. Bake, switching racks about halfway through, until done, about 25 minutes.

3 Serve the meatballs with any sauce—tomato, pesto, or curry—alone or over noodles or rice.

NUTRITION PER SERVING (7 MEATBALLS): 233 CALORIES • 27 G PROTEIN • 6 G CARBS • 1 G FIBER • 11 G FAT • 4 G SATURATED FAT • 293 MG SODIUM

# GWENN S. O'KEEFFE, MD

*Pediatrician, health journalist, CEO of Pediatrics Now (www.pediatricsnow.com), and author of* CyberSafe.

WHEN IT COMES TO LIVING A HEALTHY LIFESTYLE, DR. O'KEEFFE tries to lead by example, whether she's at home with her teenage daughters or working with her patients. "If everyone moved a bit more and ate a bit less, we'd have a much healthier country of parents and kids," says Dr. O'Keeffe. "Doctors can really help people take charge of their weight, but many patients don't even bring up the subject because they feel guilty for not being successful at weight control so far." She cautions against focusing too much on the scale, though. "You can be doing everything right and sometimes it will still climb a bit," she says. "I try to show my daughters that it's not the end of the world. If you tweak how you eat and how you move, it all comes out okay."

LEAVE A FEW BITES BEHIND. "I was raised with a bit of a 'clean plate' mentality, which no doubt contributed to my on-and-off weight struggles before my youngest daughter was born. Since then, I've learned to reduce my portions and eat smaller meals more frequently. I rarely go to restaurants, but when I do I cut my meal in half because the portions are so big."

SHAPE UP, DIGITALLY. "As a cybersafety expert, I've come across many apps that help families use technology to move more and get outside, rather than sitting in front of devices all day. Project Noah and iNaturalist are two great apps that you can use to record the plants and wildlife you spot on walks. You can also add a pedometer app to your smart phone and try to walk more steps each time you go out. Exercising as a family helps you stay fit and connect with each other."

SAY YES TO TREATS. "I don't believe in banning foods. There is room in our lives for every food if our lives are filled with exercise, activities we love, and time for ourselves."

EXPLORE YOUR CREATIVE SIDE. "It's important to nurture your mind along with your body. For me, cake decorating is a great way to unwind. (Remember how I said that I don't believe in banning any food? This is the proof!) I have a stand-up panda pan that I use to make the cake, but then I challenge myself to turn the panda into something else. Another of my favorite creative outlets is room redecorating. There's something about moving furniture and seeing the room transform into something new that busts my stress."

SKIP ADDITIVES. "My family and I feel best when we eat foods that don't contain additives or preservatives. I go organic as much as possible and buy produce from local farms when I can."

COOK IN BATCHES. "Healthy eating is much easier if you don't have to cook a new healthy meal each day. To save time, just double up on a recipe you make on the weekend so you have something you can just reheat during the week. We love pasta and we love to grill, so we always make extra of whatever we're cooking and pair our leftovers with a different salad or vegetable to mix things up."

> "IF EVERYONE MOVED A BIT MORE AND ATE A BIT LESS, WE'D HAVE A MUCH HEALTHIER COUNTRY OF PARENTS AND KIDS."

# DR. GWENN'S CHICKEN TACO SALAD

"WITH A FAMILY ON THE GO THAT INCLUDES TWO WORKING PARENTS AND TWO VERY
BUSY TEENS, THIS SALAD IS TRULY A FAVORITE MEAL. IT'S QUICK TO PREPARE, AND WE
CAN ALL EAT THE SAME BASIC MEAL, BUT EACH PERSON CAN TAILOR IT TO HIS OR HER
OWN INDIVIDUAL TASTES BY PICKING AND CHOOSING THE TOPPINGS."

—GWENN S. O'KEEFFE, MD

**Serves 4**

 1 rotisserie chicken breast

 4 cups chopped romaine lettuce

 3 tomatoes, diced

 $\frac{1}{2}$ cup chopped celery

 $\frac{1}{2}$ cup chopped carrots

 1 cup shredded Mexican blend or Monterey Jack cheese

 $\frac{1}{2}$ cup ranch dressing

 16 tortilla chips, crushed

1 Shred the chicken. You should have about 2 cups.

2 Combine the lettuce, tomatoes, celery, carrots, cheese, and shredded chicken in
a large bowl. Toss to combine. Add the dressing to the salad, and toss to coat.

3 Divide the salad among 4 plates, sprinkle each salad with $\frac{1}{4}$ of the crushed chips,
and serve.

NUTRITION PER SERVING: 414 CALORIES • 25 G PROTEIN • 15 G CARBS • 3 G FIBER • 29 G FAT •
9 G SATURATED FAT • 783 MG SODIUM

# ROMINA WANCIER, MD

*Pediatrician at Children's and Women's Physicians in Westchester in New York, attending pediatrician at Maria Fareri Children's Hospital, and assistant professor of pediatrics at New York Medical College.*

HOW DOES A BUSY DOCTOR WITH THREE CHILDREN HAVE TIME TO eat right and exercise? "I remind myself every day that it is my choice to be healthy or not," says Dr. Wancier. "Eating well, challenging my body, breaking a sweat, and being physically active help me stay happy, strong, and energized." That doesn't mean that she's rigid about it. "I believe in conscious moderation. If you eat healthy meals most of the time, you can allow yourself a guiltless treat here and there. If you are physically active more days than not, you can allow yourself to be a couch potato once in a while. Staying healthy does not demand 21 perfect meals and 7 workouts each week."

**LAUGH OFF YOUR WORRIES.** "When I am feeling nervous or anxious, I turn on the television and watch stand-up comedy shows. Scientific research has shown that laughing reduces stress hormones and triggers the release of happy-mood endorphins. It sounds silly, but it works!"

**FRONT-LOAD YOUR CALORIES.** "People who eat healthy breakfasts are more focused, perform better in school, and maintain healthier weights than those who don't. We are all fasting after a full night's sleep, and I believe that skipping breakfast can push our bodies into a starvation mode that drives us to eat larger portions and to make poor meal choices later in the day."

*(continued on page 330)*

GREEN MOJITO
SMOOTHIE (PAGE 246)

MARK'S AÇAI SMOOTHIE

THE SLEEP DOCTOR'S
SMOOTHIE (PAGE 231)

# MARK'S AÇAI SMOOTHIE

"AÇAI BERRIES ARE RICH IN ANTIOXIDANTS, WHICH HELP PREVENT MOLECULAR CELL DAMAGE AND ARE BELIEVED TO SLOW AGING AND DECREASE THE RISK OF CHRONIC DISEASES. MY HUSBAND CREATED THIS SMOOTHIE. IT'S A DELICIOUS, FUN AND EASY WAY FOR OUR WHOLE FAMILY TO EAT FRUIT."—**ROMINA WANCIER**, MD

Serves 2

6 ounces freshly squeezed orange juice

1 packet (3.5 ounces) of Sambazon frozen açai pulp

1 very ripe banana

1 cup blackberries, blueberries, or strawberries, or a combination

Place the juice, açai pulp, banana, and berries in a blender. Blend until smooth. Pour into 2 glasses and serve.

NUTRITION PER SERVING: 176 CALORIES • 3 G PROTEIN • 37 G CARBS • 6 G FIBER • 3 G FAT • <1 G SATURATED FAT • 6 MG SODIUM

**PLAN TO BE ACTIVE.** "For me, exercise has to be carefully planned for the times when my older kids are in school and the baby is napping, or while someone else is watching the kids. On the days I work, I schedule runs or quick gym visits during my lunch hour. On the days I don't work, I go for a long run; take kickboxing, TRX, or Spinning classes; or lift weights. I keep a gym bag in my car with exercise clothes, a change of street clothes, a towel, and toiletries, in case I have an extra hour to myself and want to sneak in a workout."

**SETTLE FOR LESS.** "I make it a point to be physically active whenever possible. A 20-minute workout is better than none, and choosing to move during everyday activities is a must. I try to take the stairs rather than elevators, park my car a bit farther from the entrance, walk wherever I can, and play active games with my children."

**REMEMBER: YOU EAT WHAT YOU SEE.** "Before I had kids, the food in my home was entirely up to me and my husband. Now, I have to feed much pickier and less health-interested palates. I do buy some junky food, but I opt for limited amounts of the healthiest versions I can find. I also try to make healthy foods an easy choice. I prominently display whole fresh fruits and nuts in the center of the kitchen, and I purposely store that junky food in closed cabinets. That way, when someone wants a snack, healthy choices are staring them in the face."

**EAT WELL, EAT OFTEN.** "Eating something every 4 hours prevents dips in blood sugar and keeps me sharp and ready for work and play. I believe that meals with 40:30:30 proportions—40 percent carbohydrates, 30 percent protein, and 30 percent fat—keep me satisfied and provide the best and longest-lasting energy. I always have a piece of fruit, a few nuts, and either a cheese stick or a Greek yogurt in the midmorning and early afternoon. At work, I keep a box of energy bars in my desk in case I forget to pack snacks or I find myself craving something sweet and chewy in the afternoon."

# CHAPTER 7

# How Doctors
# Exercise

D OCTORS ARE SOME OF THE BUSIEST PEOPLE ON THE PLANET, and they often have totally unpredictable schedules. They never know when an emergency is going to occur or a patient will need extra time. And, of course, just like everyone else, they have families, friends, personal chores, and outside interests that they want and need to give attention to. So exercise has to be extremely convenient and provide maximum results with minimal fuss—and in minimal time.

As I mentioned in Chapter 1, not only did the health pros we interviewed have similar diet outlooks, they also all had the same workout strategies. While everyone's particular exercise preference is different—some love the gym, while others prefer the outdoors; some are swimmers, while others are runners—you can distill their workout approaches to these five elements.

- Short, intense cardio bursts. We call these Super Slimmers, and you'll do two a week.

- Strength training. On this plan, you'll do three short workouts each week. Just five exercises firm and strengthen your entire body!

- A few longer, more moderate cardio sessions. There are three Free Cardio sessions each week.

- Stretching. Following each Super Slimmer workout, you'll do a quick but effective yoga-based stretching routine. If you have time, though, you can do this after every workout, or even throughout the day whenever it's convenient.

- Finding ways to move your body at least a little on even the busiest of days. This is called non-exercise activity thermogenesis, or NEAT. You'll read more about NEAT on page 340, but for now, know this: It accounts for a significant number of the calories you burn during the day.

Does fitting all of this in sound like a tall order? Don't worry. If doctors can cover all

---

## RESEARCH REPORT

**FROM THE LAB OF:** Kathleen Martin Ginis, **PhD**, of McMaster University

**GET A JUMP ON EXERCISE** You know how it goes: You plan a workout for the end of the day, but things get crazy and you decide you're too tired. But that's not the only reason. But it's not just because you're tired. This study found that it may be an issue of willpower—putting your energy into one task leaves you with little in reserve to complete another. The researchers had 61 participants work out on exercise machines in the lab. Then half of them were given a test where they were shown names of colors (like "green") printed in a different color ink (like blue) and told to say the color on the screen, not the word (this requires a surprising amount of self-discipline). All of the study participants then did a second workout. Those who had their willpower taxed by the test didn't exercise as hard during the second round as those who did not perform the test. Expecting a hectic day? Wake up early and workout in the morning. You'll be happy you got it over with, *and* you'll find you have more oomph all day long.

---

of these bases during their hectic lives, you can, too. To help you, the fitness editors at *Prevention* (also very busy people!) have condensed the health pros' approaches into one simple-to-implement yet supereffective workout plan. They even incorporated a sixth element that our health pros prioritize: Enjoyment. There's a lot of room in this routine for you to do the activities that are the most convenient for you and that you love the best. This plan is as flexible as possible, so it will fit into anyone's daily sched- ule. Oh, and one more thing: This is truly the best workout strategy for your weight as well as your physical and mental health. And that's just what the doctor ordered.

## HOW THE DOCTORS' WORKOUT HELPS YOUR HEALTH

This routine is designed to maximize your fat burn (with a special emphasis on targeting belly fat), strengthen your heart, and firm and stretch your muscles. It sounds pretty basic, but when it comes to your weight and your health, this workout is literally amazing. The chart starting on page 342 outlines the day-by-day schedule. Here's a breakdown of the components of the plan and their benefits.

### Super Slimmers

Known as high-intensity interval training, or just intervals, our Super Slimmers are short blasts of cardio that make every minute count. You push your body to its limits—in a good way—by alternating high-intensity activity (HIA) with low- intensity activity (LIA) throughout your workout. (The chart on page 336 shows you how this breaks down.) The advantage: You cut your exercise time and speed your weight loss. You can also do whatever activity you like—walking or running outdoors or on a treadmill; using a stairclimber or elliptical trainer; riding a stationary or regular bike; doing calisthenics, like jumping jacks, or even aerobics. You also seriously boost your fat-blasting results. Intervals stoke your metabolism, increasing the number of calories you burn during and after exercise. Some evidence suggests that intervals reduce your body's production of lactate, a compound that helps your body use carbs for energy but inhibits fat burning. And high-intensity cardio also prompts your muscles to develop more mitochondria, tiny energy-making units within cells that use sugar and fat for fuel, and to pump out more adrenaline, a hormone that helps burn belly fat.

## SUPER SLIMMERS

| MINUTES | ACTIVITY | INTENSITY LEVEL* |
|---|---|---|
| 0:00 | Warm up, walking or marching in place | 2 or 3 |
| 2:00 | Speed up to an easy pace | 4 or 5 |
| 4:00 | Push, going very fast | 7 or 8 |
| 4:12 | Back off to an easy pace | 4 or 5 |
| 4:30 | Push, going as fast as you can | 9** |
| 4:42 | Easy pace | 4 or 5 |
| 5:00 | Push, going as fast as you can | 9** |
| 5:12 | Easy pace | 4 or 5 |
| 5:30 | Push, going very fast | 7 or 8 |
| 5:42 | Easy pace | 4 or 5 |
| 6:00 | Repeat minutes 4:00–6:00 six more times in the order listed | 6 |
| 18:00 | Cool down, walking or marching in place | 2 or 3 |
| 20:00 | Finish | |

*For descriptions of the intensity levels, see "Am I Doing This Right?" on the next page.
**If working out at this level seems too difficult at first, do these intervals at a level 7 or 8 and work up to a 9.

The HIA parts of your routine should not feel comfortable. You should be thinking the whole time: "When do I get to slow down again?" Now, "hard" is subjective. It might mean a brisk walk for one person and a fast jog for another. Gauge your intensity based on your own fitness level. See "Am I Doing This Right?" on the next page for guidance. It's equally important to make the LIA recovery period a

# AM I DOING THIS RIGHT?

Understanding and adjusting the intensity of your workouts is the key to getting the most out of this routine. Pay attention to how you feel, then rank the effort you're expending on a scale from 1 to 10. (Exercise physiologists call this the Rate of Perceived Exertion.) During the Super Slimmer workouts, your intensity will vary; follow the guidelines in the chart on page 342. On Free Cardio Days, after a warmup, you want to work up to a brisk pace (level 6) and stay there throughout your workout until it's time to cool down.

|  | HOW IT FEELS | INTENSITY LEVEL |
| --- | --- | --- |
| Everyday movement | You're moving slowly, as if you are window shopping. | 1 |
| Warmup/cooldown | You're walking, not strolling, but you're comfortable. | 2 or 3 |
| Easy pace | You're walking faster. Breathing is easy, and you could sing. | 4 or 5 |
| Brisk pace | Your breathing rate increases. You can talk, but you can't sing. | 6 |
| Very fast | You're breathing hard. You can barely get a few words out. | 7 or 8 |
| Maximum effort | This is the fastest you can go. You can't even think about talking. You should not be able to sustain this pace for more than a few seconds. | 9 or 10 |

true recovery. When you move at a slower pace, you help your body remove the lactic acid that builds up during intense activity so your muscles don't get as tired or sore. And you give your heart and muscles the rest they need so you can maximize your effort during the next HIA segment of the workout.

Doctors and other health pros love intervals because they're perfect for the time-pressed. But that's not the only reason they're popular. In addition to delivering the health perks of weight loss, intervals strengthen your cardiovascular system—your heart, lungs, and arteries. In a McMaster University study, interval exercisers doubled their fitness capacity (which means they were able to use oxygen more efficiently, a by-product of a stronger cardiovascular system) and felt stronger and more energetic in just 2 weeks. The increase in mitochondria improves your muscles' ability to use carbohydrates, increasing insulin sensitivity. The result: Less sugar floats around in your bloodstream, and this lowers your risk of type 2 diabetes, a major precursor to heart disease.

## Free Cardio

If intervals are so great, why not make them your go-to cardio workout every time? Your body is built to be active so moving it daily is key to good health. But pushing it to its limits every day can lead to injury and fatigue. Combining intervals with more moderate cardio sessions helps build a balanced body. All muscles are made up of two kinds of fibers, slow-twitch and fast-twitch, and they are called into action during different activities. Slow twitch fibers have high endurance capabilities. Fast-twitch fibers are activated during sprints and strength training. If you only do activities that call on one form of fiber it's like only doing bicep curls with one arm—you're unevenly fit.

On Free Cardio days, you can do what you do for Super Slimmers, but other activities count as well. Those could be the days you take a hike with a friend, play a game of volleyball, or go dancing. Just be sure that whatever you choose, you're working at around an intensity level 6, where you could carry on a conversation but not sing a song.

Here's another great thing about Free Cardio workouts: They don't need to be completed in one block of time. Studies show that you can break up moderate-intensity exercise into segments throughout the day and still get the same benefits. That means a 15-minute brisk walk in the morning and a 30-minute bike ride in

---

## RESEARCH REPORT

FROM THE LAB OF: **James LeCheminant**, department of exercise sciences at Brigham Young University

**CRAVING CONTROL** Everybody knows that the more you exercise, the hungrier you are, right? Maybe not.

In this study, researchers measured brain activity in women as they looked at pictures of either food or flowers after a 45-minute treadmill walk and then again on a no exercise day. Moderately vigorous activity, it turns out, blunted the women's neurological responses to food. They didn't eat any more calories on the days they worked out than on the days they didn't. And exercising actually led them to increase their physical activity throughout the day separate from the treadmill walk.

the evening satisfies your Day 2 goal. So does taking four 10-minute brisk walks throughout the day.

## NEAT

NEAT stands for nonexercise activity thermogenesis, and it's basically any movement we make when we're not sleeping or performing structured exercise. Painting your bathroom, typing, standing up when you talk on the phone, buying and unpacking groceries, scrubbing the sink, taking a leisurely walk with your dog, fidgeting—these activities and many more count. What's really neat about NEAT is how quickly the calories burned add up. On this plan, we ask that you perform at least 10 minutes of NEAT on strength-training days. But feel free to give it more time or to incorporate NEAT into every day. The more you do, the better it is for your body and your weight.

## Short Sculptor

Metabolism slows by 1 percent a year after age 30. Adding extra muscle can help compensate for that natural slowdown. Muscle, as we all know, burns more calories at rest than fat does. Every pound of muscle on your body burns between 30 and 50 calories a day—even while you're sleeping. A pound of fat burns only 2 to 5 calories. So when you sizzle off the fat and pack on the muscle, you burn more calories just by being you!

This routine works your entire body in five moves. It takes only 15 minutes, but it is as effective as spending 45 minutes in the weight room. How is that possible? When you use more than one muscle group in every move, it raises your metabolism more than doing the same number of isolated moves would. It can also be defined as "functional fitness." Those isolated workout moves are for bodybuilders, who want to achieve a certain look. Multimuscle moves work your body in a way that mimics activities you do in real life, such as picking up a

## RESEARCH REPORT

**FROM THE LAB OF: Emma Varkey,** physiotherapist at the Sahlgrenska Academy at the University of Gothenburg, Sweden

**HURTS SO GOOD** Exercise isn't always comfortable, but it can help control pain, at least when it comes to migraines.

In this study women who suffered from these debilitating headaches either took topiramate (a prescription drug used to reduce the odds of migraines), followed a relaxation program, or exercised three times a week for 40 minutes. They kept records of their headache frequency before, during, and after the 3 months of treatment. All of the women experienced fewer headaches. The researchers concluded that exercise is a good alternative to medication for migraine prevention, especially for people who can't or don't want to pop a pill.

child, carrying groceries, and lifting your suitcase into an airplane's overhead compartment. Think about it: You don't pick up a gallon of orange juice and curl it 15 times. You squat down, pick it up off the shelf, and lift it into your cart. That's functional strength, and you need to work on it to get it. But that doesn't mean that you won't get lean, toned, and firm following this workout—you absolutely will!

To improve your results even more, the Super Sculptor we've designed is a circuit workout. Unlike in traditional weight lifting, where you do a set, rest, and then do another set of the same exercise, in circuit training you move quickly from one set of an exercise to the next exercise, and then you repeat the circuit once or twice. A 15-minute circuit weight routine burns 144 calories, compared to the 54 calories you'd burn during a traditional weight-lifting session (based on a 150-pound person). Some research shows that doing moves in a circuit format also boosts the "afterburn"—the calories you burn after you finish exercising.

## Yoga Stretch

After you complete a Super Slimmer session, you deserve to chill out for a few minutes, and there is no better way to do that than to stretch those muscles that you just worked so hard. Flexibility is an important and often neglected aspect of fitness. You don't have to devote a lot of time to it in order to reap the benefits, which include injury protection, decreased soreness, enhanced movement, and stress relief. If you clear your mind and focus on your breath and movements during a stretching routine, you're doing what's called a moving meditation. That helps lower blood pressure, keeps stress hormones in check, and even fights inflammation in your body.

## Your Workout Plan

Here's what your workouts will look like for the next 4 weeks—and beyond. On Free Cardio days, remember that you can split your workout into 10- to 15-minute chunks throughout the day if you need or want to. If you like, you can do NEAT activities every day, but be sure to do them at least twice a week where indicated.

DAY **1:** Super Slimmer and Yoga Stretch
TIME: 25 minutes

DAY **2:** Free Cardio
TIME: 40 to 50 minutes

DAY **3:** Short Sculptor and NEAT Activity
TIME: 15 minutes for the Short Sculptor and a total of at least 10 minutes of NEAT total throughout the day

DAY **4:** Super Slimmer and Yoga Stretch
TIME: 25 minutes

DAY **5:** Short Sculptor and NEAT Activity
TIME: 15 minutes for the Short Sculptor and a total of at least 10 minutes of NEAT total throughout the day

DAY **6:** Free Cardio
TIME: At least 30 minutes

DAY **7:** Short Sculptor and Free Cardio
TIME: 15 minutes for the Short Sculptor and at least 15 minutes of cardio

You'll barely need any equipment to follow this workout program, but a good pair of sneakers is key. Many of the strength moves can be done without any equipment, but some require 5- to 12-pound dumbbells. A mat is nice, but not necessary. That's it. We kept it simple because we didn't want to decrease your chances of following this plan. In addition to the healthiest workout you've ever tried, this one is probably the most convenient, too.

# YOGA STRETCH

Do the following five poses in order. Hold each pose for 10 to 20 breaths. Then do the series again once or twice.

## WARRIOR I

Stand tall with your feet together, arms at your sides. Step forward with your left foot about 4 feet, keeping your right foot firmly on the floor. Turn your right foot 90° to the left. Raise your arms overhead and look up at your hands. Slightly lean into your left leg while you simultaneously push your right foot into the floor. Hold and step back to starting position. Repeat on the right side.

## DOWN DOG

From standing, bend over at the waist and place your hands on the floor in front of you. Lift your hips so your body forms a triangle. Keep your legs straight and press your heels into the floor.

## CHILD'S POSE WITH A TWIST

Kneel on the floor. Sit back on your heels and bend forward, reaching your arms forward. Slide your left arm across your body under your right arm and turn your head to the right. Hold and repeat on the other side.

## SEATED CHEST OPENER

Sit cross-legged on the floor. Place the fingertips of both hands on the floor behind you. Press down with your fingertips and lift your chest up.

## SEATED FORWARD BEND

Extend your legs out in front of you, feet flexed. Reach your arms up, then lengthen your torso down over your legs. Grab both of your feet with your hands. If you can't reach your feet, place your hands on your shins.

# SHORT SCULPTOR

Warm up for 5 minutes, walking or marching in place. Then do the following five moves as directed, in order, without resting. That's one circuit. Rest for 1 minute between circuits. Do two or three circuits. Use 5- to 12-pound dumbbells. The weight should be heavy enough so that the last rep of each move feels difficult.

## BICEPS LEG EXTENSION

WORKS BICEPS AND OUTER THIGHS
REPS: 8 TO 10

Stand with your feet hip-width apart, holding a dumbbell in each hand, palms facing forward. Contract your abs and curl the dumbbells while you simultaneously extend your right leg to the right side. Return to the starting position and repeat, this time raising your left leg. That's 1 rep.

A

B

## SQUAT TO V RAISE

WORKS QUADS, GLUTES, HAMSTRINGS, AND SHOULDERS
REPS: 8 TO 10

A) Grab a dumbbell in each hand and stand with your feet hip- to shoulder-width apart with your arms at your sides, palms in. Bend your knees and drop your butt back as though you're sitting in a chair.

B) Push back up to standing and at the same time, with your arms straight but not locked, raise the weights in a V shape (up and out so they're slightly more than shoulder-width apart) until your arms are parallel to the floor. Hold for 1 second, then return to the starting position. That's 1 rep.

A

B

## TRIANGLE PUSHUP

WORKS CHEST, TRICEPS, AND CORE
REPS: 8 TO 10

A) Kneel on all fours. Center your hands on the floor or mat in front of you, hands angled toward each other, index fingers and thumbs touching to form a triangle.

B) Lower yourself until you're a few inches above your hands, and pause for 2 seconds. Return to the starting position and repeat.

A

B

## RENEGADE ROW

WORKS CORE, BACK, AND BICEPS
REPS: 8 TO 10

**A)** Kneel on all fours with a dumbbell in each hand. Place your hands shoulder-width apart. Step feet back, balancing on hands and toes with your body straight head to heels. Move your hands to slightly wider than shoulder-width apart and your feet to slightly wider than hip-width apart.

**B)** Keeping your hips parallel to the floor, bend your right elbow to pull the weight up toward the side of your torso. Pause, then slowly return the weight to the floor and repeat with your left arm. That's 1 rep.

A

B

# BICYCLE CRUNCH

WORKS CORE
REPS: 8 TO 10

**A)** Lie faceup on the floor with your feet raised, knees bent, and calves parallel to the floor. Place your hands loosely behind your head. Pull your navel to your spine and contract your abs to bring your head and shoulders off the floor.

**B)** Twist your right shoulder toward your left knee as you straighten your right leg. (Extend your right arm to the outside of your right knee for a bonus challenge.) Return to the starting position and repeat on the opposite side. That's 1 rep.

# Photo Credits

Arthur Agatston: Andrew Duany Photography; Tina Alster: Monica True; Liz Applegate: Blanch Mackey; Christine Avanti: Jonathon Fischer; Tas Bhatia: Landria Voight; Susan Bowerman: Herbalife 2012; Eric Braverman: David Vaughan; Michael Breus: Dr. Michael Breus; Lori Buckley: Kenneth Dolin; Margaret I. Cuomo: Richard Marchisotto Sherwood/Sherwood-Triart Photography; P. Murali Doraiswamy: Duke Photography; Ted Epperly: Courtesy of AAFP; Suzanne Gilberg-Lenz: Claire Brueckner; Keri Glassman: Laura Rose; Melina B. Jampolis: Michael Roud; Lynne Kenney: Mary Henebry; Sally Kuzemchak: Michelle Daniel; Johnathan M. Lancaster: Moffitt Cancer Center; Maryanne Legato: Courtesy of the Foundation for Gender-Specific Medicine; Frank Lipman: Timothy White; Jordan D. Metzl: Nino Muñoz; Judd W. Moul: Duke Photography; Lisa Muncy-Pietrzak: Audrey Chalberg; Gwenn S. O'Keeffe: David Fox; David Pearson: Ball State University; Pamela Peeke: Thomas MacDonald/Rodale Images; Nicholas Perricone: Mauricio Velez; Barbara Quinn: Rachael Short; Alfredo Quiñones-Hinojosa: Keith Weller; Travis Stork: Glenn Glasser; Eric J. Topol: John Arispizabal; Andrew Weil: Weil Lifestyle; W. Christopher Winter: Jen Fariello; Vonda Wright: Duane Rieder Photography; Jessica Wu: Bill Miles Photography; Pamela Yee: Charlie Paolino; Kenneth M. Young: Stephane Colbert

# General Index

Underscored page references indicate boxed text. **Boldface** indicates illustrations.

Diets, <u>10</u>, 11–12, 17–20, 64–65, 273, 308–9.
  *See also* Healthy eating
Dining out
  pitfalls of, <u>4</u>, <u>9</u>, 66–67, 264
  suggestions for, 83–84, 145, 150, 298, 302
Dinners, in 30-Day Plan
  overview, <u>78–82</u>
  menu planner, 88–117
Dinubile, Nicholas, 180–81
Doctors' Diet. *See* 30-Day Plan
Dogs, walking of, <u>338</u>
Doraiswamy, P. Murali, 153–54

Eating. *See also* 30-Day Plan
  frequency of, <u>4</u>, 60–62, <u>84</u>, 301, 330
  healthy strategies for, 20–26, 60–70, <u>87</u>
EGCG, in green tea, 53–54
Eggs, 42–43
Elefteriades, John A., 212
Epperly, Ted, 291, 294
Exercise
  benefits, <u>7</u>, 70, 148, 153, 236, 294, 304, <u>343</u>
  eating and, 185, 192, 268, <u>339</u>
  in patient histories, 305
  suggestions for, 180–81, 198–99, 242, 286,
    299, 330
  timing of, 165, 195
  walking as, 136–37, 139, 315–16
  warming up, 181
  for weight loss, 270

Family relationships, 167, 220, 232–33,
    295
Fasting, <u>84</u>
Fat. *See* Body fat; Dietary fat
Fiber, 30, 34, 46, 285, 315
Fish, 51–52, 68, 85–86, 127, 150, 253
Fitness capacity, 338. *See also* Exercise
Folate, 33, 46
Food
  as medicine, 7–9
  psychology and, <u>8</u>, 69–70, <u>77</u>, <u>87</u>, <u>339</u>
    (*see also* Mindful eating)
  vs. supplements, <u>19</u>, 26, 281, 308
Food journals/diaries, <u>4</u>, 286
Fructose, 208

Fruit, <u>21</u>, 67, 76–77, 194, 214, 298
Functional fitness, 340–41
Fusco, Francesca J., 131

Genetically modified foods, 261
Genetics, 139, 245
Ghrelin, <u>8</u>, 43
Gilberg-Lenz, Suzanne, 241–42
Glassman, Keri, 267–68
Glucose, 18–19, 22–24, <u>24</u>, 61, 62–63
Gluten-free diets, 85, 204, 208, 245
Glycemic index, 22–24, <u>23</u>, 64, 222–23
Goal-setting, 184, 187, 239, 294
Greens, dark leafy, 40–42, 251–52, 261, 289
Gullo, Stephen, 270–71
Gut bacteria, 55–56, 176

Harris, Shelby Freedman, 239
Healthy eating. *See also* 30-Day Plan
  models for, 20–26
  12 prescriptions for, 60–70
Hunger, 70, 84–85, 257, 265, 281. *See also*
    Appetite

Immune support, 252, 253, 260, 309, 321
Inactivity, effects of, <u>16</u>
Indulgences, 86, 296, 302, 325
Inflammation, 19–20, 139, 247, 250
Insulin, 18–19, 61, 338

Jampolis, Melina B., 273, 276

Kale, 41, 251–52
Kasha, 299
Katz, David, 277, 280
Kenney, Lynne, 321–22
Kuzemchak, Sally, 295–96

Lamm, Steven, 298–99
Lancaster, Johnathan M., 167–68
Legato, Maryanne, 301–2
Leptin, 32, 151
Life expectancy, 15–16
Lifestyle habits, 20–26, 60–70, 308
Lipman, Frank, 244–45
Lipshultz, Larry, 170–71

# Recipe Index

Boldface references indicate illustrations.